ESQUIRE ETIQUETTE

a guide to

business

sports

and

social

conduct

by the editors of

esquire magazine

NEW YORK

esquire

etiquette

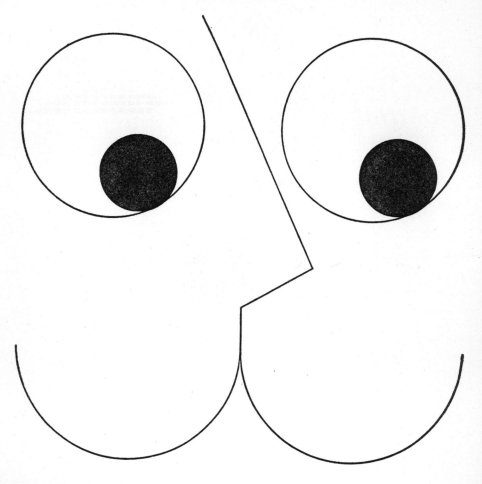

PHILADELPHIA • J. B. LIPPINCOTT COMPANY

ADVISORY EDITORS

OUR THANKS, too, to all those other people and organizations who helped us with technical problems in their domains, including: Cartier's, jewelers and stationers . . . Golf House . . . the American Automobile Association . . . the Sporting Arms and Ammunition Manufacturers' Institute . . . and Constance Spry, Inc., florists.

contents

memo

BUSINESS ETIQUETTE

courte$y pay$

SPORTS ETIQUETTE

introduction and primer for good sportsmen

SOCIAL ETIQUETTE

shall we join the ladies?

tipping

manners for the traveller

memo

TO: *men who can't be bothered with "all that etiquette nonsense"*

FROM: *the editors*

We solemnly swear that this book will not *tell you:*

1. how things should be done to please delicate ladies tsk-tsking over the teacups in their Victorian bowers

   (Instead, it tells you how things are *done, by practical men who know their way around in these high-pressure days.)*

2. how to set a table, manage a wedding, furnish a house or christen a baby

   (But it tells you how to handle women who care about such matters—and it might help you sign up a Lady who has an etiquette book of her own.)

3. how to make a million dollars, break 70 on the golf course or marry a beautiful heiress

   (But it may keep you from making a fool of yourself while you're trying!)

With the help of experts in every field—experts who form our board of advisory editors—we have ruthlessly cast aside all forms which no longer make sense in the world of today. We've been especially rough on those lady-like rules which are not comfortable and natural for a man to follow. In their place, you will find new and current guides on everything from tippling to tipping, from courting to sporting.

We think this book will save you a lot of trouble—and not a few embarrassing moments.

We think it will help put you at ease in whatever strange situation you come up against.

We know it will work . . . so we hope you'll put Esquire Etiquette *to work for* you.

BUSINESS

ETIQUETTE

courte$y
pay$

No one ever got to be chairman of the board on good manners alone, but the rude, crude joe can't always blame his business standstill on a poor choice of fathers-in-law, either. Knowing how to keep people happy is getting to be almost as important to success as work and talent (or their weight in well-placed relatives).

Cynics like to believe that there is a basic conflict between "being a nice guy" and "getting ahead." If so, the conflict is buried deep down under layers of courtesy and apparent consideration. Thus, even if you want them only as a cover, you need smooth business manners.

This is what they're made of:

ON THE JOB

You'll seldom be dead wrong if you apply what you know about social etiquette to a business situation. Both sets of manners have in common a consideration for others, the art of being agreeable, tact—a grease-job on the mechanics of living.

But there *is* a basic difference. Social forms presume social equality. Business is a hierarchy.

Your place in the stratified world of business is determined by your job rather than, as in the social world, by your age or sex. And the governing factor in all business relationships is the job to be done. That is, where a nicety of etiquette serves only to slow down the work, it is usually elided, if not abandoned; where a little politeness smooths the job by keeping people happy, it becomes important.

If you buy that general theory, you'll be able to make a little sense out of the inconsistencies of social versus business etiquette. It explains why a man stands to receive women visitors from the outside to his office, and stands for most male outsiders, too, when he can do it naturally, but does not stand for the comings and goings of his secretary or other junior employees. It explains why the boss calls his assistant "John," but John goes on calling his boss "Mr." until clearly invited to do otherwise. It explains why sellers defer to buyers, ins to outs, employees to employers, seekers to sought-afters. And it may even help to explain the odd fact that in business you do not use the same manners toward everyone, nor even the same manners toward the same person in all circumstances.

If you would fall in with the "system" and use it to your own best advantage, the first thing you should get straight is your place on the organization chart you work under. (And the most democratic, "shirtsleeves" business entity operates under an organization chart, even if it is only a sometimes thing, unwritten and undeclared.)

Next, with your own intra-mural status clear in your mind, try to expand it to include your company's and your own place in your field.

Beyond that, it will always pay you to be clear, in advance, about your purpose in any given business meeting—are you high man or low, buyer or seller?

With those three determinants of "status" tucked snugly into your subconscious mind, you'll be able to apply the general principles of business etiquette in a fashion calculated to "take care of number one."

TWO INVIOLABLE RULES

A lot of business is free-hand, but there are two inviolable rules. They read more like embroiderings on a sampler than entries in a business ledger—but woe to you if you do not at least *appear* to live up to them. They are:

1. *Maintain an impersonal attitude.* To be "business-like" is not necessarily to be cold and formal, but even in the friendliest, most informal office there is little welcome for your private life. You don't ask for a raise just because you have a new baby; you don't miss a deadline just because you have a hangover; you don't pinch fannies on company time; you don't trade on off-hours friendships or make business use of private information. Or, perhaps more exactly, if you do those things you don't seem to.

Inside your office, this means only that you should never let your personal life interfere with the work to be done. You are friendly, in greater or lesser degree depending on the atmosphere in your particular organization, but you don't burden your fellow-workers with your troubles, your prejudices or the enviable aspects of your social life. You know that you can't choose and discard working-associates as you do friends, so you finally figure out that the safest road is to be pleasant but faintly reserved with everybody during office hours. Your relationship with your fellow-workers outside the office is something else again, but at least while you are working the job is the thing.

When outsiders are present, the touch of businesslike formality is even more important. You may call your secretary "Mary" and your partner "Joe" all day, but when a stranger comes into your office you should refer to your associates as you would expect the stranger to address them: Miss or Mr. You may have a running joke with the switchboard operator, but you let it ride when you are placing a call in an outsider's hearing. You may work in your shirtsleeves, but you replace your coat when you are expecting a caller, or when you are walking around the office where there might be outside visitors.

Such "ceremonies" apply on a full-time basis in many firms —notably those which deal directly with the public and those which cultivate an air of respectable solidity to induce confidence. They are expected of employees in almost all companies when outsiders are present—if only so the office will seem to be a place of business rather than a family kitchen.

2. *Be loyal.* This high-sounding maxim means three down-to-earth things: keep your mouth shut about company secrets . . . work with instead of against your boss . . . and stay out in the open area of office politics. There are some small subtleties in each category.

quiet, please

A "company secret" is not necessarily important or even interesting information; it's just nobody's business outside the company, or sometimes outside a single office in the company. The formula for keeping such "secrets" is to give non-specific replies to questions, and never to volunteer any tidbit which your listener couldn't have read in the papers. Most of those who ignore the formula do it without meaning any harm, but if they don't actually cause business trouble by their blabbing they earn the reputation of being careless—or not quite bright.

Here are some routine methods of minding your company's business. If they don't apply to your particular job, they may be worth passing on to people who work for you:

. . . Guard your end of a phone conversation if an outsider is within earshot. If you are taking a message from someone else, and you want to be sure you've got it straight, don't repeat the message in the usual fashion; instead, ask the caller to repeat it, so your clarion tones won't announce a possibly private message to all bystanders.

. . . Cover your papers before an outside caller arrives, or make a habit of keeping them in folders or under a covering blank sheet.

. . . If you must speak to someone else in your organization when he is with an outsider, or with anyone who is not concerned with your message, do it in such a way that the third person doesn't pick up any information. You might use the interoffice telephone rather than the intercom, say, or write your message on a note you can hand over instead of speaking your piece in public.

. . . Give only the necessary, relevant information in answer to questions. When a secretary answers the phone for her boss, the only relevant information is whether he is or is not available for the call; it's a mistake for her to say, "He hasn't come in yet," instead of "He's not in just now," or "He's gone to Chicago" instead of "He won't be in today." When a buyer tells a salesman why he is turning down the offered merchandise, he should confine his reasons to the merchandise itself, not give a report on what he's buying instead. When an account executive tells the client that his copy will be delayed, he shouldn't also tell him it's because the copy chief was up all night working on another account.

. . . Outside the office, confine your shop talk to generalities or things which have been publicly announced. And keep your gripes within the family. You don't have to be a public cheerleader if you don't feel that way, but whenever you cast even the slightest aspersion on your firm the outsider is bound to think you know more and worse things you're not telling. Beyond that, of course, the outsider will wonder why you don't take it up with the boss—or quit—instead of complaining over cocktails.

working with your boss

The fine art of working *with* your immediate superior, not against him, means keeping him informed and backing him up.

To keep him informed, you send him carbon copies of all letters and reports he should know about (if, indeed, you aren't expected to get his approval as you go) . You tell him about your mistakes, or about any deviations from what he has been led to expect in your production, so he won't get into an untenable position out of simple ignorance.

You are constantly aware that your job is a part of his job, so you also give him whatever information he needs to do his job well. In some relationships this includes gossip, but you have to have a real liaison with your boss, and a nice sense of discrimination between conflicting loyalties, in order to get away with tale-bearing.

Backing him up doesn't mean being a "yes man"—not by a long shot. It means only that you spare him from surprise attacks. You voice your objections to his plan to him, not in open meeting with him and his boss. You make a point of being on his team whenever he is up against opposition. Even when you have reservations about throwing your lot in with his . . . even when there's a conflict between your interests and his . . . you keep your stiletto well hidden. If it appears that your own boss can't trust you, no one else will.

office politics

If you can't stay out of office politics (and that's always your best pose, even when you're embroiled!) the least you can do is stay out in the open. Never mind about the guys who seem to get away with playing both ends against the middle—their victories are temporary, and uneasy. They never know but what a victim of a squeeze play will be able to do them real damage in the future. They may choose to ignore the possibility that today's office boy may be tomorrow's president, but they can scarcely fail to appreciate that the business world is a small one.

When you are in the open, in office politics, everybody knows where you stand. That very fact alone should tell you to take it slow and easy, to be a see-no-evil-hear-no-evil-do-no-evil boy, at least until you have a complete grasp of the facts and the odds.

Whether you are an "open" politician or his model—the nice guy with no ulterior motives—you should always live up to these two principles:

Respect the chain of command: It works both ways—up through your immediate superior to his superior to the top, and down through your immediate assistants to their subordinates. You should never run around end; you must *always* "go through channels."

When you have to break the rule—that is, when you can't get satisfaction from your boss and consider the matter worth taking over his head—do it in the open. There are two prescribed methods: a) ask your boss for permission to take your case up farther (and when he agrees, as he almost has to if he is not going to fire you, be sure that those above him understand that you have come up with his permission) . . . and b) put your problem in writing as a joint recommendation to your boss and the higher-up you want to reach.

The second method is too transparent as a first approach unless you have submitted the memorandum to your boss *before* dispatching the carbon to the big guy. So you always try to do the thing through your boss before resorting to carbon paper.

Good executive practice follows the same method on the trip down the line. You should never ask a junior to do something for you without first having asked the junior's boss if it will be all right. If the junior is on his toes he will also tell his boss that you have spoken to him direct, so you might as well keep everybody happy by doing it right in the first place.

Never pass the buck: Again, this applies up and down and all around. Excuses in general are disagreeable and ineffective; they usually reflect on your personality more than the thing they are meant to excuse reflects on your ability. When your excuse is a company policy not of your own making, or something equally impersonal, you weaken your authority and hurt morale by crawling behind it in a carping fashion.

When your excuse is a defection on the part of some other person, it is probably your defection as well: if the other person is below you, his fault is your fault and blame-shifting is taken as a sign that you can't stand responsibility.

If the other is above you, coping with his foibles (or covering up his mistakes) is part of your job, and a buck passed can be a job lost.

If the other is an equal, a competing associate, all you can do is play dumb and leave it to the higher-ups to find out for themselves that he is muffing his job. You can't complain about him behind his back without appearing to be a bigger jerk than you make him out to be—and if you complain about him in his presence you'll only be asking for trouble from another quarter.

Therefore, it comes down to "no excuses."

The best you can do to cover yourself, whether the mistake has been your own or another's, is to think it out ahead of time so you can propose a solution at the same time that you admit the error. The best you can do to remove a continuing handicap in your work is to take it up through the chain of command as an impersonal business problem: no names, please.

To be more specific about the little things encompassed by the above "theories," here are some pointers on everyday office manners.

THE NEW EMPLOYEE

The company's role is to give the new man adequate information or training on what he is expected to do, and to introduce him to his associates and to the company's facilities as pleasantly as possible.

Where there is no published guidebook and no orientation program as such, the responsibility for a smooth start is at least half on the shoulders of the new man himself. When he doesn't know the rules, he should ask; when he can't ask he should watch; and when he's in doubt he should follow the rulebook instead of the example of those who have been there long enough to assume a few privileges. In no case should he seem to "buck the system" or compare his new company's ways of doing things with the way he learned on his last job.

In addition to the business of setting the new man straight on policies and procedures, his immediate superior should see that he is introduced around on his first day and looked out for until he is enough at home to look out for himself.

The introductions, usually performed by his boss or the

11

boss' assistant or secretary, are in the formal business pattern. "This is Mr. Jones, who is joining us in the billing department. Mr. Smith, head of our purchasing department." . . . "How do you do, Mr. Smith." . . . "How do you do, Mr. Jones. Glad to have you with us. If there's anything I can do to help you get squared away, please come back to see me or Miss Evans." . . . "Thank you."

And so on, with each introduction making the oldtimer's job clear, and each oldtimer making an effort to be helpful.

Unless the politeness is obviously impossible under the work-circumstances, men stand and shake hands with other men during such introductions. They stand for introductions to women but leave the handshaking initiative to the woman. Women may sit while acknowledging introductions to new people, but if the new guy is a senior they usually stand.

The new man's first lunch hour is apt to be a dispiriting thing if no one takes him in hand. If the company has no definite policy on this point, or even if there *is* a particular sponsor assigned to the new man, considerate cohorts ask the new employee to join them at lunch. Like all other office lunches, this is Dutch treat—but even so the new employee can't invite himself into a lunch-hour clique. The first move is up to the regulars, and they have forgotten their own first feelings of strangeness if they don't make an effort to welcome the new employee.

On form of address, the first move again falls to the regulars. The new man should not presume to use first names, even if everyone else does, right off the bat. In an informal, first-name kind of office, the transition will be a natural one. Probably those of equal rank will first drop the "Mr." and thus invite him to do the same. But until he is well established, he is wise to continue to use the formal address to his juniors unless he is willing to risk their using his first name as well.

New and Old Employees Please Note: It is NEVER correct to call anyone in business "dearie," "darling," "honey," "baby," "toots"—or "pal," "podunuh," "butch," "bud" or "Mac," either. At best the pet name or palsy-walsy reference is cheap and corny; more often, it is presumptuous and insulting.

YOUR SECRETARY

Your secretary's manners to others presumably reflect your wishes. Your manners to her indubitably affect her work. On both points it is possible to come a complete cropper from mere inattention. Let's take the last point first.

WHAT SHE EXPECTS OF YOU

1. *Clarity* . . . on what you expect of her, on what the job does and does not include, on how you want things done. She doesn't want to be watched over constantly, but she does want adequate information and complete instructions *before* she begins a job for you. She doesn't expect to be able to interrupt you with constant questions, but she does expect you to give her clear answers to those questions she finds necessary to ask.

But her biggest legitimate gripe is being used as a nursemaid, shopper, personal bookkeeper, errand-girl, maid and social secretary *if you didn't make those duties clear when you hired her.* If she's supposed to work for your wife and children as well as for your company, she wants to know about it while she still has a chance to say "No, thanks."

The reason most men don't give their secretaries advance warning of these "extra duties"—and thereby create friction ever after—is that the duties are strictly sub rosa. Some companies give their top executives truly personal secretaries as a part of their salary; like the expense account and the company car, the secretary-of-all-work is an extra inducement, a hedge against the income tax. But in most companies a secretary is hired strictly for business; if you have so little office work for her that she has time to manage your personal affairs, you don't need a secretary.

Thus, if you ask her to do something which is beyond the scope of her regular office work, realize that you ask a *favor*. And realize that "one good turn deserves another"; you'll have to match the illegitimate service with some illegitimate time off, an occasional thank-you present, a less demanding attitude toward her real work. Also, her doing you personal favors puts your relationship on a more personal basis, with its own set of obligations.

Even if you can rationalize asking her to do a few personal things for you, never ask her to do anything which is inherently demeaning. It costs her money to wear that white collar; it shouldn't cost her pride as well. She probably expects to dust your desk and fill your carafe; she may take it on herself to hang up your hat and coat and trot out for your coffee—but she'll hate you if you take these services for granted. You had better share the "dirty jobs," to protect her self-respect and your own.

Above all, protect her from your wife. Maybe your secretary will gladly do a chore she knows your wife should do if *you* ask her—but if your wife calls her direct she can only begin to brood about women's relative rights. And she'll have a real case.

2. *A little consideration for her as a person.* Drawing room manners are out of place in an office, and you are not expected to hop to your feet and hold a chair for your secretary every time she comes in for dictation. But take care not to treat her as if she were a machine.

Say a pleasant "good morning" when you come in; say

"please" and "thank you" at every opportunity; give her a hand when you see her trying to carry too heavy a load—don't expect *her* to carry in the chairs for your meeting; show a little interest in her health and state of mind.

Accord her the respect due her as an individual. She does not want to be referred to as "my girl." She wants to be asked before you give her services to someone else for the afternoon, even if she knows that she has little choice in the matter. She wants to be called Miss or Mrs. in front of strangers; at least, she won't be flattered if your "Mary" provokes everyone else into addressing her with familiarity. She wants to be introduced to people she is going to work with. She doesn't expect you to present men to her, as you would in a social situation; she would be embarrassed if you introduced her when there was no purpose to be served; but she feels menial and inhuman if you fail to say at least, "This is my secretary, Miss Jones," before asking her to take dictation from a stranger.

And give her credit for having a life of her own. The number one gripe of all secretaries is being asked to work overtime without advance notice; overtime pay is quite beside the point, which is infringement of the secretary's right to have made previous plans for the evening. Invasion of her lunch hour is another peeve. If you ask her to run an errand on her way to lunch, you should allow her extra time away from her desk.

She also has a little pride—and a temper. You'll provoke them both if you continually use her as an excuse. Don't blame things on your secretary; it's too easy. If she really failed to give you a message or really forgot to mail something—that is, if she really deserves the blame—don't advertise it. Tell *her* about it, in private, or get rid of her if she's as bad as you keep saying.

3. *A faint understanding of her work.* Her time is probably yours to waste, if you want to be technical about it, but

you can't both waste her time and berate her for falling behind in her work.

The usual ways of alienating secretaries by underrating their work-load are simple:

mark every letter "Rush"

insist that something must go out tonight (especially something which you've stalled on all week), then leave before it's finished so it has to wait until morning for your okay, after all.

make minor corrections on typed material in ink, so it has to be typed over again *in toto*. Penciled corrections can be erased and often the small changes made on the typewriter.

keep your secretary sitting at your elbow while you make phone calls, rustle around for papers you should have had on hand before you called her in, figure out what you're going to say or otherwise expose the fact that you aren't prepared to dictate.

interrupt her "Rush" work with unimportant little items, explaining, "This won't take long."

keep papers on your desk instead of letting her file them, then holler at her if she can't find them or doesn't follow-through on them.

The counter-measures are just as simple: assume that she knows her job better than you do and that she'll do her job better if you give her a chance to *plan* a little.

4. *A little confidence in her ability and judgment.* You only make it tough for yourself, and impossible for her, if you keep secrets from your secretary. The biggest secretarial complaint in this department is making a secret out of your whereabouts. When you go out, let her know where you're going, how you can be reached and when you expect to return. She'll know better than to pass the information on to everyone else—but she needs it in order to cover for you, or fill in for you in your absence.

WHAT YOU EXPECT OF HER

On the other side, this is what you have a right to expect of
your secretary. She can't very well correct your manners toward her, but you can and should correct her if she is not living up to these standards when she represents you:

1. *Polite handling of your telephone calls.* The biggest
and the smallest shots answer their own telephones—the biggest because their concern is with policy and public relations
rather than daily output of work, the smallest because they
have no alternative. But most men in between like to save
time by having their secretaries place their outgoing and
screen their incoming calls.

There is definitely a right way to do each. Since you have
doubtless encountered the *wrong* way more often, we'll go
into the proper technique in some detail. Your job is not
only to school your secretary in these procedures but to check
up on her from time to time.

Placing calls: You ask Miss Smith to "get Joe Evans" for
you. You also tell her, then and there, whether you will
speak to anyone else in Joe's absence or whether you'd like
Joe to call you back. In the latter instance, if Miss Smith
doesn't already know your schedule, you point out that you
will not be there to receive calls from 12 to 2 or after 4 or
whatever.

Miss Smith dials the number, goes through the switchboard at Evans' firm and arrives at Mr. Evans' secretary. She
then says, "Mr. Blow of the X Company is calling. May he
speak to Mr. Evans, please?" If Mr. Evans' secretary then explains that Mr. Evans is not available, your secretary follows the instructions you have given her for this eventuality.
(If she had to interrupt you and keep the girl at the other
end dangling while finding out what to say next, you might
better have placed the call yourself.)

If, on the other hand, Mr. Evans' secretary says, "Yes, he's

17

here. One moment, please. . . ." Miss Smith then signals you and you pick up the phone, ready to talk, *immediately*. You are not down the hall or talking on another wire. Your secretary does not jockey with Evans' secretary for the dubious honor of putting her man on the wire last. Even if Mr. Evans' secretary is one of those protocol kids and goes to great pains to get you on the line *before* ringing her boss, the proper thing is for you to be there waiting when Evans picks up the phone. Nothing will irritate him more than to be greeted by your buffer, saying "Mr. Blow calling; one moment, please." That maneuver, however common, is foolish, pompous and revealing. More than that, common sense should tell you that since *you* are making the call, the burden is on you to *be* there to talk when the connection is made.

The time you save in calling through switchboards and other secretaries is in the dialing, the message-leaving, the waiting if Mr. Evans is on another wire—*not* in the few seconds during which one secretary triumphs over another.

When placing calls to a junior within your own organization, it's permissible (if not exactly friendly) to keep him waiting at the other end, or even to have your secretary speak to him in your place. When calling equals or seniors, however, unless it's a matter which the secretaries can handle between themselves, it's best to make the calls yourself.

Screening calls: The degree of screening practiced in your office will depend on your own particular telephone problem and the responsibility you think you can safely entrust to your secretary. Given a clever girl, whom you take pains to keep informed on your projects-in-work, you may be able to avoid all nuisance calls. If your secretary is a dunce, or not close enough to your work to use her own judgment, you'd better tell her that you'd rather speak to all the insurance salesmen in town than risk annoying one customer.

In any case, there will be certain people or representatives of certain companies whom you will want to speak to without delay, regardless of your own convenience. Be sure your secretary knows the names and affiliations of such people. And then be sure that she treats all other callers with the same courtesy, even though with different results.

The caller who is turned away by your secretary must be convinced that you are not in—to *anybody*. She cannot appear to be making up her mind whether the caller is or is not important enough to talk to you. It is imperative, therefore, that she say you are not available *before* she asks, if she must, who is calling. Once she asks who is calling, she must put him through to you—*unless* she has already explained that she will not be able to, or *unless* she can appear to save *his* time by filling in for you.

Admittedly, this fine point of good manners is ignored more than it is observed in the everyday rush of business. The whole problem would be academic, of course, if every caller were sensible enough to volunteer his name and/or the purpose of his call *before* asking to be put through to Mr. Executive. But—let's face it—a lot of callers neglect this simple duty, and not all of them are creditors! Unless you really believe that their rudeness of omission deserves your rudeness of commission, you cannot excuse the practice of saying, "Who's calling?" *before* saying, "He's not in just now." If you can't risk talking to a single unannounced caller, your only recourse is to have your secretary say you're out—to everyone who fails to identify himself.

The "screened" caller should feel either that you will act on his message as soon as you are free, or that your secretary has helped him as much as or more than you would have. The good-will engendered by this "turn-'em-away-with-a-service" technique is cumulative. As they learn that your secretary knows your business and can be relied on to follow through with or for you, your callers will come more and more to give their messages to her instead of insisting on speaking to you.

Here are some sample conversations to illustrate the technique:

YOUR SECRETARY: "Mr. Blow's office.
(She may add, "Miss Smith speaking," if she thinks it helps build up the personal-confidence touch.)
CALLER: "Is Mr. Blow there, please?"
(If the caller were polite, himself, he'd give his own name— but then we'd have no problem in secretarial technique!)

When you have told her you do not want to be disturbed:

YOUR SECRETARY: "I'm sorry, but he's not available just now. This is his secretary. May I help you, or is there anyone else you'd care to speak to?"
(NOT— please note— "What did you want to speak to him about?")
CALLER: "No—when could I reach him?"
(This caller is a particularly dull-witted type, or maybe a bill-collector deliberately hiding his name. A real problem!)
SECRETARY: "I expect to hear from him in about an hour" . . . or . . . "He's in a meeting which will probably last until lunch time" . . . or . . . "He has someone with him just now; I'm not sure how soon he'll be free . . . May I tell him who called?"
(The purpose of the explanation, which may be a big lie or the unrevealing truth, is merely to soften the pry. Bad forms include: "He's busy" (so is the caller) . . . "He's tied up" (bound and gagged?).
CALLER: "Well, I'll call again this afternoon."
(A hopeless case, but the secretary can do nothing but go through the whole routine again when he calls back —or put him through when you are no longer incommunicado.)

To a more polite caller, your secretary might have read your "Do Not Disturb" sign like this:

CALLER: "This is George Bigshot. Do you know if he's had any word on that Niles deal yet?"

SECRETARY: "No, I don't—but I know he'd want to speak to you about it. He's in a meeting, but it ought to break up soon" (or whatever is true). "Could he call you back, or do you think I should call him out of the meeting now?"

(And then she does whichever Bigshot's sense of urgency dictates.)

When you are in but can't answer the phone for a few minutes:

SECRETARY: "Yes, but he's on another wire. Would you care to wait, or could he call you back?"

("I'll wait" ends that. Your secretary's remaining obligation is to get back on the phone every minute or so, if the wait is a long one, so the caller can't think he is abandoned. If the wait-er gives his name and it is someone you would not want to keep waiting, she may stick a note under your nose as you talk on that other wire or whatever it is that you're doing. When you are finally free, she says, "Thank you for waiting. I can connect you with Mr. Blow, now"—and does so.) However, if the caller's original reply is:

CALLER: "Would you have him call John Evans, please?"

SECRETARY: "Will you give me the number please, in case Mr. Blow hasn't it handy?"

(This, unless *she* knows the number.)

CALLER: gives his number

SECRETARY: "Thank you. I'll ask him to call as soon as he's free."

(Her obligation now is to see that you return the call whenever she said you would or to call Evans herself

21

and explain why you were unable to call back. In the latter case, her purpose will be to find out what it's all about, and this she usually does by asking how she may help or, as a last resort, by saying that you might not get back until after office hours and wondered if she could take a more complete message for you.)

2. *Courteous handling of your visitors.* When someone has a definite appointment with you, he should not be kept waiting but should be shown to your office at precisely the time agreed upon. But things do go wrong with the best of schedules, even when guarded by the best of secretaries. If you simply cannot help being late, the best thing you can do is go out to the reception room yourself and give your apologetic explanation in person. But if you are really stuck—off in the Siberia of the boss' carpet, say—then your secretary is your substitute. She should go out to your visitor in person, explain your absence, convey your apologies and then give as definite an idea as she can of how much delay is inevitable.

If the visitor chooses to wait, she should then make sure that he is comfortable. If it is feasible, it's nicer to have him wait in your office than in the reception room; your secretary leads him there. In either place, he will want something to read and perhaps the opportunity to use the telephone or otherwise put the waiting time to good use. But it is by no means necessary for your secretary to "entertain" him; even if she seats him next to her own desk, she should go on with her work as soon as she has seen that he is comfortable.

A visitor who is expected should be announced immediately. If you are closeted with another person, your secretary interrupts you to say something like, "Your three o'clock appointment is here. I thought you'd like to know." (She doesn't mention the visitor's name in the hearing of an outsider. If you are not likely to remember who your "three o'clock appointment" is, she writes the name on a slip of paper and hands it to you, or uses your private phone instead of the loudspeaker system.)

A visitor who has no appointment may be handled less ceremoniously—at least in a town where appointments are the norm and in an office where the executives are not purposefully available to see everyone who drops in. The problem is somewhat the same as that posed by the anonymous phone-caller, but since most big city business people are apologetic about dropping in, and understanding if they are asked to make an appointment for a later time, the turn-away may be done by telephone from your secretary's desk, or even by relay through the receptionist, without undue affront. When you would really like to see a drop-in visitor but can't break your schedule for a visit in your office, you may want to go out for a fast hello in the reception room. In such case, you or your secretary always explain why you are not free—and you take the initiative in suggesting another, specific time when you *will* be free.

Getting rid of visitors who have overstayed their leave can also be done gracefully, and in this case the impersonal secretary runs less risk of offending the visitor than does her boss. This is the routine: You tell your secretary, before the visitor arrives, how much time you want to give him. A few minutes before that time is up, she comes in to say something like, "Excuse me, Mr. Blow, but it's time for the plans board meeting." The appointment she reminds you about may be real or fabricated. If you really want to continue your conversation, you may ask her to let the real or phony plans board know you'll be a little late. But in any case, since you *too* had to be reminded that the time had flown, the visitor will begin to wind up his business without feeling that you wanted to be rid of him.

3. *Confidential treatment of your business and private affairs.* As indicated on page 7, your secretary should not

volunteer too much information about where you are or what you are doing. When you leave her a number where you can be reached, let her know if she may give the number to any- one who calls you or if you prefer that she relay messages by calling you herself. If there are things you don't want even your boss to know, you had better tell her specifically; other- wise, a blanket instruction to be general in her replies to questions will be enough.

If you share your office with your secretary, you will do well to arrange a signal which means you'd like her to get out while you talk to a visitor in private. "Will you leave us alone for a while, Miss Smith?" embarrasses everybody; it's easier all around if you can convey the same idea, by prearrange- ment, with something like, "Will you see if you can settle that business with the merchandising department, Miss Smith?"

A polite secretary will get up to leave whenever she realizes that a telephone call which has interrupted your dictation is a personal one. It's up to you to wave her back into her chair if it is not so personal as all that.

A trained secretary will keep your papers in folders, hid- den from the eyes of passersby.

In general, she'll keep secrets. But sometimes she'll have to be told what is a secret.

4. *A business-like air.* The business-like air means calling you Mr. in front of outsiders, who might think the first-name routine a bit cozy . . . wearing clothes suitable for the of- fice . . . smoking at her desk, if at all, only when there are no outsiders present . . . confining her personal phone calls to the short and minimum . . . asking if you will need her any longer *before* she covers her typewriter and puts on her hat . . . waiting to be recognized, when she has stepped in to speak to you, before interrupting whatever you are doing . . . maintaining a certain office decorum in spite of years of close association with you.

Your secretary's job is just as interesting as you make it. You can build allegiance, inspire her interest in your business, only if you treat her as a human being whose allegiance and interest are worth having. Congratulations on jobs well done, sharing of the credit when a project she has worked on comes out well, inspiring her to take more and more detail off your neck by showing your appreciation when she does— all are bound to pay off.

Still, they can pay off too well. A secretary's reward as often as not comes in the form of reflected glory. Because she thinks it adds to her own importance, even the best trained secretary may begin to plump you up out of all proportion to your actual importance (or in contradiction of your canny knowledge that really important men seldom *act* important). Watch out lest she put on airs that will reflect on *your* manners and good taste.

Watch out, too, if your secretary's "identification" with you begins to resemble a large, fat crush on you. You may have asked for it, but you can't afford to encourage it. Stick to (or return to) a business-like attitude; try to keep your personal life out of the office. Act in general like the poor dumb male she thinks you are—as if nothing could surprise you more than to be told that your secretary is secretly in love with you. Don't, whatever you do, tease her or talk to her about it—at least not unless you're prepared to do something about it!

TRAVELING WITH YOUR SECRETARY

Mrs. Grundy no longer requires you and your female secretary to travel in separate railroad cars, sleep in separate hotels or handle your private dictation in public places.

These days, you take traveling and hotel space to suit the convenience of your business more than to quell the tongues of old-fashioned gossips. You take separate rooms, of course, but they may be in the same Pullman car or in the same hotel so long as they are not adjoining. The usual hotel practice is to put unmarried people on separate floors, and if your office has wired for reservations for you and your secretary that will be done automatically. But if you find yourselves on the same floor it is better to ignore the circumstance than to make a big fuss about it.

Any business done in the hotel room is better done in your room, not hers—in the living room, if you have a suite, or in your made-up bedroom if not. Etiquette does not require you to keep the door open, but neither does business-privacy require you to lock and bolt it, or barricade it with furniture. If you can confine this business to normal working hours, fine, but if the work demands breakfast and midnight sessions the only requirement of etiquette is that you work. In any case, you and she are the best judges of the proprieties.

It is still advisable to be a little more conventional with your secretary than you need be when traveling with a woman of business-rank equal to yours. An associate is responsible for herself, but a junior employee is presumably at your bidding. So the burden of after-hours decorum is on you. You don't have to take her to dinner or a movie, but if neither of you has anything better to do you may. The hotel dining room is a better place for dinner than the ex-speak down on the waterfront, though, and pub-crawls are out of bounds.

Expenses are presumably on the company, so it doesn't matter which of you handles the money. She'll doubtless be the one who makes out the expense accounts on your return, so there is something to be said for her keeping the records. This little chore in itself emphasizes the business-like, unromantic nature of your association, so by all means push it off on any young innocent who might develop fears (or ideas) as a result of your trip together.

OTHER EMPLOYEES WHO
REPRESENT YOUR OFFICE

The company will instruct its receptionists to dress conservatively, sit quietly and attentively, speak softly, address and refer to employees formally, stay off the telephone except on matters of business, abandon chewing gum. It will establish its own policy as to whether or not receptionists may read, knit, do office work—depending on the traffic and degree of efficient formality it wants to maintain in its reception room.

If those things are beyond your interest or control, there is nevertheless one point of good reception-room conduct which concerns you directly. When the receptionist calls you to say that someone is there to see you, she should always speak in the third person; "Mr. Jones to see Mr. Smith"—*never* "Mr. Smith? There's a Mr. Jones out here to see you."

If your company is lax about stopping all visitors at the reception desk—and if the laxness is not a part of a studied Open Door policy meant to govern everyone in the office—you may make your own private arrangements with the receptionist. Suggest a technique similar to your secretary's in screening calls: "May I help you?" instead of "Waitaminute! Whodya wanna see?" . . . "Let me ring his office to see if he's in. Is he expecting you?" instead of "Who are you?" or "What did you want to see him about?" . . . "Miss Jones, Mr. Smith's secretary, will be right out. Won't you sit down for a minute, please?", instead of "He's busy."

Mail boys should be asked to move around the office quietly and to avoid interrupting others with chitchat as they make their appointed rounds. They should *lay* the mail on desks or in file boxes, not dump or throw it.

Payroll clerks should be instructed never to leave a check with anyone but the person to whom it is addressed. It should be, but is not, needless to say that the amount should not be visible on the outside of the envelope. A man's salary should be the most closely guarded secret in the office.

Switchboard operators should be told not to indulge in long, hard rings of telephone bells. Anyone in a position to answer an office telephone can hear a single, soft buzz; if he doesn't pick up the phone immediately there's a reason—and the reason remains even after his eardrums have burst.

THE BUSINESS OFFICE

In every office, there is some poor guy whose job it is to watch the nickels and dimes which the staff is fiendishly dedicated to throwing out the window. This character, it is true, often seems ideally suited to his work; he appears to take a genuine delight in pinning terse warnings onto desk lamps left burning during the lunch hour or in issuing memoranda on the recent alarming increase in the consumption of scratch pads.

Some of these cost-accounting machines, however, might show themselves to be real human beings, with blood and feelings and maybe even a few brain cells deep inside, if they were treated with less ridicule, less open hostility and more appreciation of the fact that they are just doing a *job*.

Just for fun, *try* a little consideration and courtesy in your dealings with the business office. Who knows—you just might establish a workable truce, or even eliminate this one source of annoyance from your day-to-day office life.

To live up to our feeble hope of reform in this department, we might also suggest a radical notion or two to the penny-hawks themselves. To wit: try concealing your conviction that all your company's employees are either criminals or delinquents. Try using a positive approach instead of the usual corrective one. Try pretending that some of your fellow-executives understand their jobs and requirements as well as you understand yours. And consider that some of them may not understand *why* you harp on things they call "petty."

Perhaps your memo about turning out lights could explain the problem in terms of stock dividends or salary increases. You may not be free to split the savings among the employees, as did one advertising agency head, but if you lift the "annoyance" into the realm of big money you may win both cooperation and increased respect for your job.

The office-manager problem, a universal one, might be a telling example of the importance of tact and the "you" approach. It's hard to say, for, so far as we know, neither side in this endless war has ever given good manners a fair trial.

THE TELEPHONE

For the worst business-sins against good telephone manners, please see page 17. The warning there applies to you as well as to your secretary.

In addition, here are the rules for efficient and pleasant conversations. With their help, you might transform the telephone from torture rack to effective tool.

Save time, at both ends: The business phone is no place for idle chatter. If the business involved cannot be disposed of in a few minutes' telephone conversation, write a letter or make an appointment instead of tying up lines and offices with long calls.

When answering the phone, dispense with the meaningless "hello" in favor of an identifying greeting:

The switchboard operator says, "Jones and Company"—in a pleasant tone which also says, "at your service." Whoever next answers the phone says, "Production department" or "Mr. Smith's office" or whatever is necessary to "place" the extension. If that person is prepared to handle the call, rather than act as a secondary switchboard, he should also give his own name: "Production department, Jones speaking." or "Production department, Mr. Jones." (The self-applied "Mr." is acceptable in business, never in social usage, but if Mr. Jones is sensitive to airs of self-importance, he will say "Joseph Jones" or simply "Jones" rather than "Mr. Jones.")

By the time the next person answers, all the necessary identifications have probably been dispensed with. Say that the next person is Mr. Smith, whose secretary has answered the call before him. She buzzes him and says, "Mr. Haynes of Consolidated on line 4"—then rings line 4. Mr. Smith can then advance the conversation one step further by saying, when he picks up "line 4," "Good morning (or Hello) Mr. Haynes." This spares Haynes the necessity of repeating his identity, lets him know he's finally got Mr. Smith at the other end and encourages him to plunge directly into the business without further delay.

If Mr. Smith and his secretary have no such announcement routine, the secretary will at least have said she is ringing Mr. Smith, so there's no need for Smith to bark his name into the telephone. "Hello" is a suitable greeting, here, but only because there is no mystery about who is speaking.

When making a call, get on with it.

To the switchboard operator, give the name of the person you are calling, or, if you don't know who might be in charge of the business you're calling about, give her a general idea of your mission so she can connect you with the proper office.

In places where she is receptionist and call-screener as well as switchboard operator, she will indicate that she'd like to have your name, but in most instances your name is beside the point.

To the next person who answers, give your name in the same breath with your request to speak to a specific person. If your name alone is not sufficient identification, add your affiliation: "May I speak to Mr. Smith, please? This is John Haynes of Consolidated." Do this even if you suspect that it is Mr. Smith himself who has answered. To start out with "Mr. Smith?" puts Smith on the defensive; to ask his secretary the bare "May I speak to Mr. Smith?" makes it necessary for her to spar with you for your name.

If you are then connected with Mr. Smith, launch immediately into the purpose of your call, repeating your name only if his greeting indicates that you have not been announced (see above). If Mr. Smith is polite he will not feel comfortable asking you what's on your mind, so he is doomed to sit and listen until you get to the point. Please remember this when you are tempted to "warm him up" with inquiries about his health and his family. Nine times out of ten it is more flattering to him to show that you consider his time valuable than to show that you remember the names of his children.

If you are not put on Mr. Smith's wire immediately, you may be sure that his stumbling-block secretary is acting under Smith's instructions, so nothing is to be gained by maintaining an air of mystery about the purpose of your call. If it is a personal matter (and no fooling!), if it is confidential (even from a private secretary?), or if it is too complicated to explain in the general terms the secretary wants to hear, you may say so. But say it apologetically, so the secretary will know you are not being uppity about what you must know is a routine part of her job.

But if your business is not personal or confidential or complicated, your failure to tell the secretary about it will be ascribed by her to ignorance or ulterior motive on your part. Neither helps you get through to Mr. Smith, so volunteer your reason for calling. This will not only speed your path to Mr. Smith if he is available; it will also save your time if your next step is to leave a message.

During the conversation, remember that the person at the other end can't *see* you. He can't read your lips, so speak clearly and distinctly. He can't read your facial expressions, so watch out for sarcasm and other forms of humor which say one thing but mean another. He can't tell what you are doing if your attention is diverted or if you leave the phone, so explain and excuse all interruptions.

That last is responsible for most annoyances. You can avoid them if you will always make an explanatory remark before putting the phone down, always say something like "Thanks for waiting" or "Sorry it took so long" before resuming the conversation, and never keep anyone waiting at the other end of a dead phone for more than a minute. If you must look something up, say so, and if you have not completed the sortie in a minute, return to the phone to explain and to offer to call back if the other prefers not to wait longer.

Incidentally, if you're the one who has placed the call, it should never be necessary for you to "look something up." You're the expert on what you called to discuss, and the least you can do is have all the pertinent information before you when you reach for the phone.

When ending a call, bring it to a definite close. Here the courteous "Goodbye" is not mere window-dressing; it serves notice that you are about to hang up. Wait for the answering "Goodbye" before you replace the receiver.

Generally speaking, the person who makes the call is responsible for ending it; he is the one who knows when his mission has been completed. But the man at the receiving end can lay the groundwork for the other's goodbye with a few closing phrases indicating that he has "got the message." Callers should be alert to these signals that their time is running out. Otherwise, the callee may abandon politeness in favor of a fast "goodbye."

When a call is cut off before its conclusion, the blame cannot usually be fixed. Unless the callee himself has accidentally interrupted the connection, he waits for the caller to place the call again.

When leaving messages, always give your name, your number and, if this will not be clearly understood by the person who receives your message, your firm and the reason for your call. Also, *be there* when the return call comes for you. Few things are more annoying to a busy man than a message which says only "Call OR 9-2566"—but one of them is making the requested call in vain. The New York and Hollywood jokes about people who spend whole days calling each other's secretaries back and forth are not funny to the people involved. If you would avoid this foolish fate, stand by for return calls, and/or incorporate into your message the fact that you will not be available at certain hours.

In general, it's best not to put the other to the trouble of returning your call unless he can be expected to have a faint interest in what you have to say. If you are 100% the seeker and just talking to you will be favor enough, volunteer to call back yourself instead of asking that your quarry call you—but then leave it up to the secretary. She may prefer to call you at her boss' convenience rather than have you calling again and again.

Once your message has been accepted and you have been given the assurance, direct or indirect, that your call will be returned, you may reasonably assume that a failure to return your call has a reason. Don't call back, yourself, until you have allowed a reasonable time for the return call—unless, that is, you can afford to have your quarry think you are hounding him. If you *must* call again, give a reason which takes the edge off your prod: "My line has been busy for the past hour and I was afraid you might have been trying to get me" . . . or . . . "I find I'll have to be out of the office for the rest of the day, so I wondered if I might speak to Mr. Smith now, or call him back in the morning?"

When taking messages for others, make them as complete as possible: name, number, subject (if it can be politely extracted) and the date and time the call came in. By all means write messages down; you should not rely on memory or on the chance of speaking to the messagee in person. Put messages in a place where they cannot be missed—on the telephone itself is a good spot if there is no appointed place. And if you have made any promises to the person who gave you the message—the promise is implicit if you are secretary or assistant—follow through.

When transferring calls, stay on the wire until the new connection has been made or until the switchboard operator understands what is required. (And let the caller know what you're doing! There must be a special place in Bell-hell for people who flash their operators without first warning the caller of clicks to come! Don't force the caller to repeat his mission over and over to a chain of middlemen. And if you don't know who should handle the call, find out before sending the caller on a telephone chase around the office. Like the waiter who growls, "Not my table," the indifferent telephone answerer who says, "You have the wrong department" and then makes no effort to be helpful is the curse of the courteous—and a business liability as well.

When bothered by a "wrong number," either a mistaken direction inside the office or a real mis-dial, don't take your bother out on the caller. The mistake is impersonal, at worst. Initial identification at the answering end shortens the hassle, and an exchange like this makes it as painless as possible: "I'm sorry, but there's no Mr. Cartwright here. Were you calling MU 8-7796?" . . . "Nine-*six?* Oh, I have the wrong number. I'm sorry to have disturbed you." On the other hand, it only complicates and prolongs the agony if either end shows annoyance, hangs up abruptly or goes into irrelevancies like, "What number were you calling?" or "Who *is* this?"

Although it is of course desirable to have everyone who telephones you think of you as polite, pleasant and accommodating, there are times when it is the height of rudeness to be receptive to telephone calls. You should not receive calls when they interrupt someone who has a prior claim to your time.

The man who makes a visitor sit vacantly while he answers the phone and the one who has his calls transferred to the conference room are real business scourges.

Although it is hard to believe, these pains are topped by one greater offender against everyday manners—the man who *makes* calls while others are in his office to talk to him.

If you are not staffed to have a secretary or the switchboard operator waylay your calls *before* the jangle of the telephone interrupts the planned business at hand, the least you can do is say, "Excuse me" or "I'm sorry," in genuine contrition, before picking up the phone. And then you should by all means ask your caller if you may call him back at another time.

If the person in your office is a subordinate, you might be justified in dispensing with the business of the call in a few sentences, but it is always better not even to start a conversation that may last more than half a minute—and it is never excusable to take up the time of a conference.

"May I call you back?" means, as clearly as if you said it outright, that you can't talk now. Your caller can only say, "Of course." In return, then, you indicate how long it will be before you can return the call. And then you're honor bound to do it.

"Meetings" on the telephone open up another problem. Whenever you are putting a third person on the line, be sure to tell your caller that you are doing so. No eavesdropping, recording or secretarial note-taking should be done without the knowledge (and therefore tacit consent) of the person at the other end of the conversation.

THE CONFERENCE

With this one slogan you can sidestep most of the mantraps which yawn at the conference table: *Don't be "bright"; be useful.*

Whether the conference has been called to formulate a policy or (more often) to formalize one already made higher up, it is not meant to be a stage for show-offs. Most of those who use the conference to advance their own stock are easily recognized as bores or time-wasters or both. So good manners and grand strategy impose a few restrictions on your conference conduct.

Your first duty is to lend your physical and mental presence. You should be on time, and if you would avoid the problem of whether to stand for the leader's entrance, you might well remain standing until the meeting has been called to order. You should then be prepared to stay there, and to stay reasonably awake, until the meeting is over.

The dedicated doodler is forgiven only if he shows in other ways that he is listening with interest and thought. The bustle-boy who takes phone calls, whispered messages and short powders throughout the meeting leaves an impression not of importance but of inefficiency. If you must answer the phone, do it outside the conference room; if you must leave the meeting, get permission from the chairman and later apologize to the group.

The conference leader sets the tone and determines the routine of the meeting. If he has not assigned seats to the participants, he nonetheless expects conferees to show some regard for protocol as they fall into chairs: the seat at the head of the table is for him; the chairs flanking him are usually for appointed assistants or top-flighters who have prescribed roles in the meeting. Wise juniors shift their weight a little, letting the shots have first choice of chairs, before taking their own places.

For similar reasons, a junior is seldom the first to speak, unless directly called upon, when the conference leader has "thrown the subject out for discussion." Once the discussion is under way, anyone may register his views whenever they fit into the logical flow of talk. But everyone should guard against interrupting another speaker in mid-argument and, junior or senior, a conferee should always speak to the chair or to the group at large. Whether he is officially recognized by the chairman, as in a formal meeting, or merely given an opening and the group's attention, he should avoid private, personal or prolonged argument with any one other member of the group.

FIVE CHARACTERS

Whatever the bent of the conference leader—whether he models the meeting after Roberts' Rules of Order or after a fraternity bull session—he never welcomes these characters:

1. *The Cliché Expert.* This one is forever noodling something or wrapping it up in a ball of wax or fitting it into the overall picture or playing it by ear. He also thinks out loud, puts it on the line, bats it out of the park and goes over the top with it. If he really has something to say, which is not likely, his cringing listeners will fail to notice what he says because of the way he insists on saying it.

True, some clichés are indispensable. No conference could run smoothly without the Dale-Carnegie-isms which protect other egos and soften impending criticism, so you need feel no embarrassment at frequent use of, "Yes, but on the other hand . . ." "That's an interesting point, but . . ." "I hadn't thought of it quite that way, but . . ." "It seems to me . . ." "I don't know as much about the production end as John does, of course, but . . ." "Am I right in assuming . . . ?"—and so on.

But watch out for the clichés which are not excusable on the grounds of salving feelings. They obscure thought, but they do not obscure the *lack* of thought nearly so well as their admirers expect.

2. *The summer-upper.* A certain amount of summing up is necessary to the progression of a conference, but the job belongs to the chairman alone. If he defaults, it's not because he hasn't heard what has gone before but because he gives the conferees credit for having understood as well as he. Congratulate yourself, if you must, for getting the point—but do it in silence, not in delaying speeches which can only annoy the group.

3. *The paraphraser.* In his benign form, this fellow knows very well what he is doing and does not try to conceal the fact. He starts out with a frank, "In other words . . .", thereby putting himself in a class with the Summer-Upper. If he weren't so anxious to say something, anything at all, he'd have sense enough to keep quiet rather than repeat what has been said before.

In his malignant form, however, the Paraphraser is beyond explanation. Whether he is stupid himself or simply takes his listeners to be stupid (no one is ever quite sure), his horrendous habit is the same: he re-phrases an idea someone else has developed, and booms it forth as his original master solution to the problem at hand.

4. *The Watchful Waiter.* This one has come to the meeting with one idea. If he is part Summer-Upper, or part-Paraphraser, his idea has been simply to wait until someone else suggests an idea he can appropriate. In any case, he lies in wait for the chance to make a strong statement. Once he has made it, he no longer pretends to listen to anyone else or consider alternatives to "his" idea. He has accomplished his purpose of registering himself on the meeting, and if the others are as dim-witted as he thinks he may even have scored as the meeting's hero.

5. *The Impassioned Pleader.* Unlike the other four, the Pleader probably has something to contribute to the meeting. His trouble is that he thinks his end justifies any means. He discards all tact, all rules of good behavior, all recognition of the fact that he has to get along with his conferees now and later. He ridicules other points of view, jumps on everyone who happens to misquote a figure or misapply a principle. He interrupts. He resorts to sarcasm and personal remarks.

Finally, he usually comes around to attacking the motives of those who do not enthusiastically agree with him. If the decision of the meeting goes against him, or if the leader is at last required to put him in his place, he sulks. In short, he makes it almost impossible for the others to swallow his ideas even when they want to.

Other types, whose labels alone will remind you of your unhappy exposure to them, include the Raconteur, the Digressor and the Chameleon (or Yes Man).

THE CHAIRMAN

Nothing can be done about those conference scourges, at least not by their fellow-conferees. Several courses are open to the chairman, who is supposed to avoid wasting the group's time insofar as he can without hurting any individual's feelings. He can pull the meeting back to the point by a gentle suggestion that this other "interesting discussion" might be resumed after the initial question is settled. (But then he had better make a note of the question left hanging, so he will be sure to re-introduce it before adjourning the meeting.) He can call on silent members of the group for their opinions, in order to indicate that he thinks one man has been doing too much of the talking. (But this is risky if the silent ones are silent by choice, or if they feel pressured to say things they have not thought out.) He can ask "why" and "how" questions to bring monologists back to facts. He can break up side arguments or private conversations by giving one of the offenders a specific duty.

But perhaps his greatest control comes before the conference is called: must it be? Many a conference is meaningless on its face, doomed to be a time-waster even without the help of our conference-characters. And many a really necessary conference would be shorter, more effective, less vulnerable to the characters if the chairman planned it in advance. Here is the least he can do if he wants to avoid economic waste and uncomfortable incident:

Give advance notice of the purpose of the meeting, including
    a specific or general agenda
Give people a chance to prepare their own arguments, sound
    out their opposition
Speak in advance to individuals of whom he will expect par-
    ticular information
Set a definite time limit on the meeting

And call the meeting for a respectable hour—*not* directly after lunch

VISITING OTHER OFFICES

When you want to see a fellow-worker in your company, it's wise to telephone ahead and ask if you may come around. Simply barging up to his desk, in the expectation that he will be happy to talk to you then and there, shows a lack of consideration for his convenience. Only a superior can get away with it consistently.

You have a perfect right to summon a subordinate to your office. You would naturally expect to go to your boss' office. When your business is with someone of a rank equivalent to yours, you should ask him to come to your office only if there are other people or unwieldy props involved. Most times, you should assume that it's your move; *you* want to see *him,* so you go to him.

For pointers on visiting outside offices, see "At Liberty," page 52. The information about making appointments, announcing yourself to the receptionist, manners in the office and taking your leave apply to everyday office calls as well as to job interviews.

GOING UP

The man on the make in business has to watch out below, lest those he leaves behind have good reason to hope he will fall on his face. If he doesn't really care what the also-rans think of him, he should at least consider the difficulties of making a good show on a new job if his mail is held up or if his routine requisitions keep getting lost. And, who knows, maybe one day one of his abandoned pals will be in a position to cream him.

Few will expect him to continue to have lunch with "the old crowd" in the stockroom after he's moved to the executive floor—and his sense of power politics may tell him that he must "burn his bridges," whether he wants to or not. But he can't afford to seem a thankless opportunist. He had damn well better remember the names that go with those shoulders he climbed on, and make an effort to be as friendly, as unassuming and as accommodating as ever in all his brushes with those he now outranks.

If he honestly can't take his loyal secretary up with him, or see that his hard-working assistant steps into the job he leaves, he owes them both an explanation—and probably a sincere promise for the future, as well.

All this a "nice guy" will know by instinct. If he needs a warning at all, it's only because his sights will naturally be set in the opposite direction. His former associates will forgive him his success if he grows with his job—but he should take pains not to swell with it.

Those above, too, will be watching to see how he adapts to his new and bigger job. He should appreciate that he is in a kind of no-man's-land, for a time, and avoid all moves that look presumptuous, cocky, power-conscious—or obsequious.

LITTLE THINGS THAT COUNT

Here are some little things you should watch out for as you move up. Higher-ups view them dimly:

announcing your promotion yourself

If this is done at all, it must be on the initiative of your own company. If you are asked, of course, you do not blush or paw the ground instead of supplying a picture and biographical material needed for a press release. But the request should come from your bosses or your public relations department. If it comes from a journalist friend, instead, you should ask the company's permission before releasing the information—and ask it as if you were inquiring about an impersonal company policy, not as if you wanted congratulations for getting the company some free publicity.

In the absence of a general and official announcement to your fellow-workers, your best move is to wait for the word to get around. You can't deny it if your office friends ask, but you can cover yourself with a remark like, "Oh, has it been announced? I didn't know if I was supposed to say anything yet."

In leaving certain jobs, you will want to write the news of your replacement, along with your thanks for past cooperation, to the outsiders you have worked with, but here again you should get prior permission from your superiors.

In short, a premature and independent announcement of any kind may be more than unbecoming horn-tooting on your part. Your promotion may be part of a group of company changes, or there may be some other reason why the company prefers to handle the announcement in its own way at its own time.

making immediate changes in your work schedule

Pretend you're a new employee for a while—that is, live up to the rules. For all you know, you were promoted simply because you managed to eat lunch in an hour. There'll be plenty of time to catch up on your morning sleep or impress the charwomen with your late hours after you are "in."

jumping into familiarity

. . . with people you have treated with respect in the past, including yourself in established executives' lunch groups, etc. Again, like the new employee (see page 11), feel your way. Your guideposts may not be as clearly marked on this higher level. No vice president is going to say, "Call me Joe" to you—it would sound patronizing to his own ear—but he won't want you to start Joe-ing him before he has demonstrated his friendly respect, perhaps his dependence, on you. In this, as in all subtleties of "status," take it easy. Save your bold moves for a time when you are secure in your new job.

taking over with a broad axe

Sure, you've known for a long time what you'd do if you had the authority. But before you start sending out those positive memoranda which are supposed to showcase your fresh approach and your big ideas, take a little time to find out why things were being done the way they were before you came to the rescue—and whose large toes you may be stepping on in your reforms. Apart from the practical aspects of selling your ideas (see below), there is a question here of responsibility, if not of humility.

HOW TO SMOOTH THE CLIMB

Adept handling of these two recurring problems will speed and smooth the upward climb. They involve manners as much as they involve business judgment, because they are intimately related to personalities and "feelings":

1. *Getting a raise.* Entirely divorced from the merits of the matter—which may be that no employee is worth what he costs to any employer, and that no raise is large enough to

buy any employee's brains—this is the convention: you are
expected to show appreciation, if not outright gratitude, for
any raise you get. It is bad form to grouse about money,
whether your complaint is made in the front office or in the
"privacy" of your own circle.

This means that you have to appear to be happy with what
you get—if you take it. If you don't like it (or don't want to
pretend that you like it) you have to leave it.

Your effectiveness in salary negotiations is always con-
tingent upon your alternatives; the risk of asking is that you
must always be prepared to leave if you don't get what you
ask. Thus the primary rule is take it or leave it—but with a
smile.

Having digested that basic principle, you'll find the rest
of the raise-business falls into place automatically. First, it's
better not to ask for a raise, but to force one by plain and
simple demonstration of your worth. The only time when
an outright request is your first, best move is when you know
a routine raise is on the way and you're afraid it will be too
small. Other times, everyone is always much happier if the
issue can be dodged rather than faced. Management thinks it
is wise and noble to have recognized your value; you think
you are appreciated; neither nice feeling is dimmed by the
knowledge that an open prod was necessary.

When the indirect approach doesn't work, or doesn't work
fast enough, you make a move. But first you marshal your
forces:

You should be sure that the answer cannot be in the form of
a criticism of your work, for your only valid argument is
that you are doing the work better (or doing more) than
when you took the job at the present price. Doing the
same job in the same way for an impressive number of years
means nothing, of itself, and your personal problems with
finances are embarrassingly beside the point.

You should know exactly what you will and will not settle for.

You should be realistic about your alternatives. If there is not an immediate job you can move to at the better figure, you should be pretty sure that you can find one in whatever time you can afford to spend looking, or that you are willing to give notice anyway.

That last is a most important point. If you are not prepared to leave, don't ask for a raise. Ask a raise for a subordinate, perhaps, by way of suggesting that your *department* deserves more money. Ask advice in handling your job or increasing your value to the company, if you like, in order to register your itchiness. But don't let the session hinge on your salary.

Although you have planned so carefully, you manage the interview in a way to belie that fact. You are neither aggressive nor apologetic—just matter-of-fact, pleasantly confident.

There is a fine, large question of "face" here; you can't let your "or else" attitude show, or you'll be challenging your boss to call you, in defense of his own self-respect. And for your own good you don't want to make him act or decide at the moment of surprise; all you want him to do is think about it. You're in no hurry.

If you can pull it off, you'll avoid a scrap, a show-down and a lot of things you'll both wish hadn't been said. If you get the raise, you'll both feel it's right. If you decide to leave, you'll do it pleasantly. You appreciate his problem; he understands yours. There are regrets, real or merely polite, but there is no anger. Hearts . . . flowers . . . and maybe some money, too!

2. *Selling an idea.* Sour students of mankind say that no one takes kindly to an idea he hasn't thought of himself, and that the originator of an idea is so ego-involved in it that he can't stand criticism of his brain-child. On the other hand,

executives are supposed to have impartial judgment and idea-people are supposed to be able to think 'em up as fast as anyone can turn 'em down.

The following technique makes allowances for both theories, so can probably be relied upon to save feelings—*and* ideas.

Never present a finished plan or idea to your boss. Even if it is really done up brown, present it as if it were "in rough," almost as if you *need* your boss' thinking on it before you take it further. That gives him a chance to add a little something to make it his own, if he must, or at least to identify with it as he cannot with a *fait accompli*.

This doesn't mean you should propose ideas you haven't thought through, only that you should propose them as if it has occurred to you that they are not perfect.

Don't insist on selling the whole idea at once. Be content, when you must, to let the whole "grow" on your boss while you settle for okays on the parts.

Show the need for an idea or plan before outlining your solution, but don't appear to think that yours is the only possible answer to the need. Once you have agreement on the problem, you'll have a reception for your solution, and even if the details of your idea are not approved, the fact of your recognition of and attack on the problem will have registered.

If you're dealing with an idea-stealer, there's very little you can do about it. The usual practice is to put all ideas in writing, keeping a carbon as "evidence" should you one day have to prove that you are the brainpower behind your boss. But this device puts an added burden on the idea at the outset, and it is transparent, besides. If your boss steals ideas on an as-is basis, he'll turn yours down; if he adds something of his own to ideas before making off with them, who's to say that his touch didn't make the difference between your dumb notion and his brilliant plan?

No, your only hope is that he, at least, will realize his dependence on you, and take you with him when he moves up. Whether in hope or despair, you have to see no evil, hear no evil, speak no evil.

GOING OUT

Being fired is seldom the disgrace it seems at the time, and resigning is not always as smart or noble as you pretend, so both exits should be made with as little speechifying as possible.

If you are leaving in a huff, you should be at great pains to conceal the fact from your fellow-workers. If you haven't told the management how you really feel about the whole thing, you should certainly not tell anyone else. Even when you have been perfectly frank with your ex-bosses, nothing but gossip is to be gained from rehashing your problems at the water cooler. Your best exit line—in terms of present pleasantness and future references—goes something like this: "I've enjoyed working with you. I'm sorry it had to come to an end." This should also be the theme of any letter of resignation you write for the accounting department's records. Let your exhaustive reasons come out in the front office, not in the files.

Whatever the background music, your retreat should be an orderly one. Leave your job without loose ends and needless mysteries to plague your successor.

You may think your work will be more appreciated if your absence is noticeably inconvenient to everyone concerned, but on the long haul you'll win more respect *and* appreciation if you leave your affairs in order.

Your desk should be clean, of course; no one likes to take over a lot of cryptic notes and old envelopes. (But clean your desk into a wastebasket, not into your home files. It's bad business to rob the company records, even for so noble a purpose as filling out your work-sample book. And it's bad taste to use a former employer's letterheads, even when they are imprinted with your name and thus are worthless to the company, after your departure.)

Your pending projects should be outlined in a memo, to your department head or to your successor or both, with all the information needed for follow-through included. Your "contact book" or list of whom-to-call-for-what should be up to date and, if it exists only in your head, put into writing for the guidance of your replacement. The "dirty jobs" you have put off for a slow day should be finished before you leave, even if you have to burn your own oil some midnight to do it.

In the upper strata, executives often find and break in their own replacements before they leave; they make a point of deferring the future until the past is under control. At any level, it's good to invite your successor to telephone you if he needs advice.

If you will want to use your former employers' names as references in the future, and if there's any chance that the men you worked with will forget you or move out of reach, it's all right to ask for letters of recommendation as you leave. General letters are seldom so good as those designed to help you get a specific job, but you may want at least a statement on the duration of your employment, the scope of your job and the atmosphere of sweetness and light in which you are departing. Ask for this in your closing interview or—better— offer to write it yourself for your boss' correction and signature.

Later on, when you think your references are about to be checked by a potential employer, write or telephone your ex-boss to alert him—and to hint at the qualities needed for this new job you're after. Unless you have gone out on a black wave, everyone who knew you when will be glad to help; no one will take it amiss if you suggest the most effective way to help.

TIPS FOR THE TOP MAN

You need not go around proving you're the boss if you *are* —a fact worthy of note by tough guys in the middle brackets as well as by those who have reached the top.

So here are some suggestions to tuck into your velvet glove:

Don't order; ask! It amounts to the same thing, but it sounds—and works—better.

Remember that people work *with* you, not *for* you. They know better, but they like to be spoken of as associates, not as slaves.

Listen! Now that you are where you are, the burden is no longer on you to get there fustest with the mostest. You can afford to let others give you the facts and propose the course of action; all you have to do is draw them out, then make them think that your ultimate decision is based on their work rather than on your instinct or natural superiority.

When you talk, remember that your subordinates have to listen. They think they have to laugh at your jokes, show interest in your Angus bulls, hide their conflicting political opinions, swallow your advice, pretend the oldest saw and the weariest maxims are dewy-fresh. Consider that your chatty little visits around the office may be resented—as time-wasters, if not as spying expeditions. And remember particularly that your scale of living is probably out of reach for many of those you talk to: they may secretly register more than admiration for your new Miro, more than interest in your trip to Europe, more than gratitude for your offer to have your chauffeur "drop" them. If you find that a friendly interest in your employees' private lives is welcome, fine, but you can be pretty sure that you'll be the loser in any *exchange* of personal confidences.

Once you realize that you have no way of gauging the real interest of your audience, you may well decide to stick to business. In the long run it may be wiser and safer, if a little bit lonelier, to try to be a good boss, not a pal on the side.

Keep your promises. Like children, employees remember. Unlike children, they can never remind you of a bet or a promise; they can only ascribe all sorts of mean motives to a simple lapse of memory on your part. It's important, therefore, to make a note of every promise—whether it is something important, like reviewing a salary situation within a given period, or something you think inconsequential, like buying the receptionist a box of candy if she can sidetrack a salesman for you.

When you make promises which your staff will have to fulfill (as to clients), remember that there's more to it than your promise. If you are not entirely aware of the difficulties which might be involved on the production level—and it's the rare top guy who is—consult the man who will have to follow through before you give a firm delivery-date or make a binding promise.

Criticize, if you must, only in private—and do it objectively. The established technique is to praise for something general before correcting something specific, to minimize the mistake or share the blame whenever possible, and to approach the solution as a problem you and the culprit have in common. In any event, never chew anyone out in public or in anger. And that goes for the office boy as well as for your assistant vice president.

Respect the chain of command on routine matters, but think hard before you pass down the buck of firing someone.

It's an unpleasant duty at best—probably even for the man who coined the slogan: "Don't fire anyone; find him another job, instead." If the boot is to be administered at *your* insistence, you're the man to do it.

"AT LIBERTY"

The routine "etiquette" of the job hunt is simple, straightforward and, doubtless, familiar. Adherence to the following code helps you create the impression of poise, knowledge of business methods, capable efficiency, stability, sincerity. On the other hand, mis-steps in these little areas of etiquette may undo a lot of your good work in the more important area of technique.

MAKE AN APPOINTMENT

Unless you're going to see a personnel man whose entire day is spent interviewing people as they turn up—and that's a dreary prospect, to begin with—you should never "drop in" on anyone. If your credentials are such that the executive thinks he must drop everything to see you, the resulting interview cannot but start off on a note of annoyance. If you have no such compelling entrée, you will very likely be asked to telephone for an appointment at another time. Either way, your surprise attack sets you off at a definite disadvantage.

Your request for an appointment may be made either by telephone or by letter. If you choose to telephone, you must be prepared to make your request to the executive's secretary, in full expectation that she will have to speak to her boss and give you your answer later. You commit another sin, to your disadvantage, if you try to run the secretary's screen when you don't know her boss, and when you are calling on a matter of so little immediate importance *to him*. If, then, you think you can state your case better than a disinterested secretary can, your best move is to write a letter in the first place.

The exception might be when you are well sponsored: a friend of your quarry's has given you permission to use his name or—better—has paved the way for your call. Or you have a letter of introduction from someone whose name or position will mean something to the executive and to his secretary as well.

But however you do it—and the method deserves careful planning—make a definite appointment.

DRESS WITH CARE

Dress with care to make a good first impression. You've heard that piece of advice a million times, but it's worth reviewing before you step into the interviewer's web. Your clothes should be conservative by business standards (see page 215); your grooming should be flawless, although not blatantly so—heels straight, shoes shined, chin smooth, nails cleaned, hair cut, etc. (On a concentrated job hunt, this often calls for pre-interview sessions with comb and soap, in public washrooms.) And beware of obscuring this neat and knowing front with a pack-horse load of packages: if you have collected a lot of odd magazines and parcels during a day of pavement pounding, check them somewhere before you approach the receptionist's desk. If you are toting samples of your work, take care that they are compactly carried in a single briefcase or portfolio.

BE PUNCTUAL

If you are early, ask the receptionist not to announce you until the appointed hour. If you are going to be late, telephone ahead to explain; if you will be more than a few minutes late, it is polite to ask if it would be more convenient for the executive to see you another day instead. But don't be either early or late if you can possibly help it, and you usually can. Be on time, to the minute.

"PRACTICE" ON THE RECEPTIONIST

Consider that your interview begins the moment you enter the company territory. Try to make as good an impression in the reception room as you hope to do in the inner sanctum. These are the basics:

1. *Remove your hat* as you approach the receptionist.

2. *Announce yourself* to her clearly and precisely. The best announcement is: "I have an appointment at two with Mr. Executive. My name is John Jones." Certain other variations are equally correct—"John Jones to see Mr. Executive. He's expecting me," or the handing-over of your business card with the announcement that you have an appointment to see Mr. Executive. But you'll find that you fare better with the receptionist's attention and her memory if you say "appointment," then the name familiar to her, then your own name.

It is *not* correct to use the title "Mr." in announcing your own name. "Dr." may be necessary if you are a medical doctor, but it sounds self-important if you are a Ph.D.

If you have no appointment, it will doubtless be necessary for you to explain why you want to see Mr. Executive. The receptionist has probably been instructed on how to handle surprise callers in general, or job-seekers in particular, so there is worse than no future in trying to buck the system at her level. While she makes the call to announce you, step away from the desk to avoid the mutual embarrassment which might result if you should hear the other end of the conversation.

3. *Then await the receptionist's instructions on what next.*
If she asks you to "have a seat"—do it. Pick up a magazine and
wait quietly. It is always a mistake to banter with the receptionist, if only because your man may come out into the waiting room while you are in mid-inanity. Unless you have been
told that there will be a long wait, it is sometimes a mistake
to smoke; you don't want to have the added encumbrance of
a cigarette when you are collected by Mr. Executive or his
secretary. Most other time-passers are risky, too: you certainly
don't ask to "make a few calls" from the receptionist's phone,
and almost any side trip which occurs to you will make you
among the missing when your time comes. So just sit quietly
and read.

If you are kept waiting beyond your power to wait—if, that
is, you really must be somewhere else in less time than it will
take to have your interview—you've got a problem. It's not of
your own making, but the consequences are apt to be of your
own taking. You might explain to the receptionist, and ask
her to offer your regrets—but you had better not let her call
in, then and there, lest Mr. Executive think you are prodding
him. If you fear that she will later say simply, "Him? Oh, he
left!", it would be wise to leave a short explanatory note for
her to send in after your departure. Include in the note an
apology for not having allowed enough time, and a promise
to call for another appointment.

4. *Thank the receptionist* for her ministrations whenever
the opportunity arises. The final "thanks" is the one most
often overlooked. This may be when she tells you that you
may go in now—or, if you are summarily called for by someone from inside, it may be as you pass through the reception
room on your way out.

5. *When anyone, man or woman, comes to speak to you* in
the reception room, stand up for the conversation. If Mr.
Exec's secretary comes to lead you to the inner sanctum, hold
doors for her and follow her down the hall without initiating

55

a personal conversation. Thank her when she ushers you into her boss' office.

FOLLOW THE LEADER

Once in the interviewer's office, follow his lead:

on the introduction—perhaps his secretary will make a standard introduction or announce your name, in which case you have only to say a polite and formal "How do you do." But if you have been merely shoved into the office, and if the interviewer does not immediately greet you by name, you say, "How do you do, Mr. Executive; I'm John Jones."

on the handshake—it's well to have your right hand free, just in case, but he's the one to offer his hand first.

on when and where to sit—remain standing until he indicates a chair.

on what to do with that coat and hat you're carrying—if he says nothing, put them on a nearby chair or in a neat pile beside your chair. Never put anything on his desk.

on smoking—wait for him to offer you a cigarette or suggest that you smoke if you want to. It's not good manners to light up in any stranger's office without permission, and when the stranger is a job-interviewer, who might have a reason other than thoughtlessness for not having made the suggestion himself, it is not wise to ask for the necessary permission.

on the direction of the interview—you'll run into all kinds, from the man who never lets you get a word in, to the one who just sits and stares at you. Your job is to roll with the punches.

If he doesn't soon take charge of the interview, or if he asks one of those killer-questions like "What can I do for you?" or "Tell me about yourself," you may start off by referring to your initial letter and asking if you may give him more detail on your background. It is more usual for the interviewer to ask specific questions, to volunteer whatever information he cares to give about his company's needs, to give you circumscribed openings to outline your ambitions and qualifications —in short, to hold the reins. So be sure that whenever you seem to be running the interview it's because *he* wants it that way.

Be careful, in any case, not to interview *him*—an apparently increasing tendency among first-job seekers. They act as if the interviewer should sell the company to them, when of course the purpose of the interview is exactly the opposite. They forget the prime rule of job-hunting technique—the "you" approach, the business of putting their "sell" in terms of the potential employer's needs rather than in terms of their own hopes and dreams.

Clever application of this technique takes a little advance research on the company, in order to understand its needs and fit your pitch to the job. But even the most haphazard job-seeker should know better than to interview the interviewer.

If he gives you a definite opening, if he asks you plainly what you'd like to know about the job or the firm, you should appear to be concerned only about long-range things. You may ask about the opportunity to use a particular bent or skill you want to impress upon your inquisitor. You may ask about the chance for advancement. But make it clear, in the way you phrase such questions, that you realize it will be up to you to prove your skill or earn your advancement. Show that you expect to be on trial, at first, and hide it deep if you also expect that the firm will be on trial with you.

And if things which the interviewer cannot but interpret as petty are important to you—things like lunch hours, overtime payments, desk space, vacations—find out about them some place else. Don't ask! Once you are definitely signed up for the job you may inquire about such things as a matter of information, but during a job-interview all questions except those about the work itself are premature—and fatal.

There is another trap which may open up before you

during a job-interview. When you are asked why you left a previous job or what you thought of a former employer, don't, whatever you do, gossip or complain. Never reflect on other companies or people; never go into exhaustive detail about your private life and its influence on your job moves. Whenever you have a choice between two ways of explaining something, take the impersonal and the positive way rather than the personal and the negative.

on the question of salary—what you will be paid is an academic question until you are offered the job, so you should never be the first to bring the money problem into a job-interview. When the interviewer himself has introduced the money question, your response will be determined more by your alternatives and by psychology than by etiquette—but try not to seem aggressive, arrogant or insulted during the delicate exchange. It's no fair putting the interviewer on the spot he has marked out for you to stand in. Like your own interests, etiquette will be served if you can keep the discussion pleasant and reasonably impersonal.

As a first-job seeker, your role is simple: you just don't care about money, because Opportunity and the Future are so much more important. It never occurs to you that this company will offer you less than a living wage, and you are humbly confident that your ability will tell in time. (Your bargaining power is next to zero, anyway, so you might as well be nice about it.)

Higher up on the scale, you attribute equally worthy character to the company by assuming that they wouldn't think of paying you less than your job resumé shows you were worth to other, lesser firms. When, to your surprise, they offer you less than you and/or the job are worth, you apologize for taking up the interviewer's time, express your regret that you can't afford to pursue the quest for a job which sounds so interesting, and that's that. If you're going to accept the job, regardless, don't be a martyr about it. Save face, if you like, by emphasizing your interest in opportunity over money— but don't make the interviewer feel like a heel for pulling you down the ladder.

All of which is convention's disguise for the truth that money matters, on both sides of the interviewer's desk. But in order to play the game, you have only to follow the leader, know in your own mind what you will and will not settle for, accept without reservation or decline without rancor. Don't hedge, except as a last resort or except when the offer is also hedged.

on when to go—your exit cues are many. They range from clear-cut closing remarks, usually in the form of a "thank you for coming in," to a vacant and preoccupied stare. But in any case they should come from the interviewer. It should not be necessary for him to stand, abruptly; you should have been able to feel the goodbye in the air far enough in advance to gather up your gear, slide forward to the edge of your chair and launch into a thank-you speech of your own. Nor should it be necessary to ask that embarrassing question, "Am I taking too much of your time?"; if that thought crosses your mind, it's time to go.

Again, the interviewer should be the first to offer his hand and suggest what happens next. You have the last word only if it is a promise to send him some additional material he has expressed an interest in, or to refer to a trial assignment he has given you. You should not ask, at that moment, if you may see him again, or call him for a verdict, or otherwise make him feel uncomfortably pressured. Your best closing line is a composite of "thank you" and "goodbye."

FOLLOW UP, POLITELY

The best follow-up is a letter. Its stated purpose is to thank the interviewer for his time, interest, advice or whatever he gave most of. Its hidden purpose is to give him a clincher argument for your cause.

The worst follow-up is a daily phone call to find out if he has "done anything about the job." Regular calls may impress your name upon him—but not favorably. Be content that your eagerness and vitality got through to him in the interview.

THE UNDERCOVER JOB HUNT

In the big leagues, the job-interview is usually disguised as something else—a get-acquainted lunch, perhaps, or a meeting on some foreign subject. Often the job goes gunning for the man, who is presumably quite happy in his present job. Since there is less distinction between the seeker and the sought, there is less need for deference on the part of the job-prospect. But the basic principles still apply and there is usually one additional requirement: secrecy.

It is not good manners to talk about the job offers you turn down—particularly when your blabbing will expose a bit of attempted piracy by a rival firm. (Sometimes it's good strategy, as when you want to let your present employer know that you are "loyal" and perhaps deserving of a reward, but the information should still be treated as confidential.)

It is both good manners and good strategy to accept such offers conditionally. It does no harm to show your employer-to-be that you are "responsible" and will not quit your present job without first providing for a replacement; and it does no harm to give your present employer a chance to counter the new offer.

THE OTHER SIDE OF THE DESK

Some interviewers are committed to a technique which puts the job-hunter on assorted spots. Experience tells them what etiquette would deny: that a prospect who is ill at ease will reveal more of himself than a prospect who is made comfortable.

Yet even the "tough guy" inquisitor can afford to be polite about the little things. It won't spoil his technique to give his applicant a chair, look the prospect in the eye and listen instead of poking around in irrelevant papers or talking on the phone, say a "please" and "thank you" now and then, put his turn-down in terms of the job rather than the person, offer a little encouragement, conceal impatience and avoid abruptness.

His tough approach should tell him, if consideration for others does not, that it's bad business to make false promises or to conceal unpleasant truths about a job-opening.

And maybe, just maybe, if he tried the Golden Rule instead of the Iron Hand in an interview sometime, he'd find that it pays to be "nice."

PAPERWORK: BUSINESS LETTERS AND CARDS

The following rules are not necessarily binding on sales letters, collection letters and other such special types which must rely heavily on winning the attention of the reader. But for everyday business correspondence, here are the guides to "good taste":

LETTER PAPER

Business letter paper should be of a quality good enough to represent the business properly, but there is a wide area of choice as to weight and finish. A sleazy paper with a sloppily

61

printed letterhead cheapens any message, any sender; on the other hand, an extravagantly heavy paper, engraved in letters which stand high as a forest, would be inappropriate for a bargain-sale house.

A happy medium might be a 20-pound paper, with sizeable rag content, engraved for top executive or special use, printed for routine, office use. But it won't cost you anything to consult the top stationer in your city for specific advice in terms of your particular business needs.

Two paper sizes are standard for business: 8½" x 11" and 7¼" x 10½". Most offices stock both sizes and choose between them depending on the length of the letter. The envelopes and plain second sheets must match the letterhead. It is permissible to use a slightly heavier matching stock for the envelope if the letter paper itself is not opaque, but the second sheet should always be exactly the same paper as the first, lacking only the letterhead inscription.

The 8½" x 11" letterhead takes a 9½" x 4⅛" envelope, in which case the letter is folded in horizontal thirds, or a 6½" x 3⅝" envelope, in which case the letter is folded first in half and then in thirds. The 7½" x 10½" paper, called the Monarch size, uses an envelope 7½" x 3⅞" and the letter is folded in horizontal thirds.

Conservative taste, always a governing factor in business dealings with strangers, dictates that the paper be white. A woman's magazine might use a pink paper, say, or a manufacturer of marine supplies might consider blue, but the rare exceptions should have an apparent reason. They have to be handled quietly (and usually expensively) to be successful.

THE LETTERHEAD

Again by conservative stands, the letterhead should be done in a single dark shade—black or blue preferred—and it must run across the top of the paper. It may be identifying, but it should never be overwhelming; if it takes up more than one eighth of the paper it is probably too large, and if it uses pictures, trademarks, second colors and slogans which are not inherent in the company name, it looks more like an ad than a letterhead.

The name of the company, the type of business (if that is not a part of the name itself) and the business address are the only elements necessary to every letterhead. Where the firm has more than one address or a whole string of subsidiary divisions, the vital one is that of the originating office. Here are three ways of handling the branch office (or product division) problem:

The Little Widget Company
488 Sampson Avenue . New York City 11

Chicago office:
13 West Michigan Avenue

The Little Widget Company
New York . Chicago . Hollywood . Miami

13 West Michigan Avenue
Chicago 11, Illinois

The Little Widget Company
13 West Michigan Avenue . Chicago 11, Illinois
(or—Chicago office: 13 West Michigan Avenue)

The last is probably the most direct and least confusing, but all three are acceptable for use by the Chicago office.

Other information may appear on the letterhead if it is pertinent and if it does not clutter the design:

1. *The telephone number.* This is a help to local correspondents but superfluous on out of town letters; and remember that a change in number can transform a lot of expensive

63

paper into scratch pads. If the number is used, the dial abbreviation may be capitalized or set apart, but the whole exchange should be spelled out. The number may stand alone, or it may be preceded by "Telephone" or "Telephone Number." "Tel." and a little drawing of a phone do not contribute to the desired effect of dignity.

2. *The name of the letter-writer, or his name and title, or his department or office.* When used, this information appears to the lower left of the main letterhead. It may be on one line or two:

The Little Widget Company
etc.

A. L. Johnson
Executive Vice President
(This would be used only on correspondence signed by Mr. Johnson. He could dispense with a typed signature even if his writing were illegible. If he used a typed signature, he should not repeat his title.)

The Little Widget Company
etc.

Office of the President
(The president's letters would carry his title with his typed signature: Frederic Jones, President. The letters of his immediate staff would be signed:

Alan Howard
Assistant to Mr. Jones
or: Assistant to the President

The Little Widget Company
etc.

Promotion Department
(This would be used by all members of the department, who could then further identify themselves by title as they chose.)

64

The Little Widget Company

etc.

Promotion Department

Joseph Blow, Director

(This could be used by Blow's staff as well as by Blow himself.)

Long lists down the left side of the paper—lists of officers, sponsors, branch offices—are not good usage except for promotion letters where this added information adds to the "sell." Even then, the lists should be matter of fact, in small, light face, and not overpowering.

Pertinent letterhead information is repeated on the envelope in engraving or printing style to match the letterhead. This may be in the upper left-hand corner of the envelope, as the post office prefers, or on the back flap. Slogans and extraneous tidbits have even less place here than on the letterhead. If the sender's name or office is included (not a usual practice), it usually appears above the firm name and address.

Paper for interoffice correspondence is bound by economics more than by etiquette. Cheap paper, colored paper, mimeographed or printed paper—anything goes when "it's all in the family." Headings usually include company name, originating office if a branch is involved, spaces for typing in names of sender and addressee, date, subject.

Personalized memo paper, usually intended for scribbled notes within the office, can also be practical and uninhibited. One caution: juniors should not order such memo pads, however convenient, on their own. Like a rug on the floor and a name on the door, the personalized memo pad is a status-symbol in some offices.

MECHANICS

All business letters should be typed, of course. Elite versus pica type is a matter of choice, but oddities like italics and small capitals are beyond the pale for normal business-like correspondence.

The typing should not call attention to itself, which means that the copy should be clean, centered, punctuated for smooth reading and correctly spelled.

The typing-style may be either block or indented, but it should be consistent throughout the letter.

Block, the more modern, starts all lines flush with the left margin, uses double spacing to separate single-spaced paragraphs.

The indented style starts the inside address at the left margin, indents each succeeding line three to five spaces. The salutation is flush left. In the body of the letter, paragraphs are indented three to ten spaces, and the use of double-spacing between paragraphs is optional.

Both styles drop the complimentary close and signature to the lower right corner of the letter.

Every letter begins with the date written in full, flush with the right-hand margin. "February 1, 1954" is the best business form. Although "1 February 1954" is used by government agencies and old-fashioned companies, and months are sometimes abbreviated, no business letter should start with "2/1/53" or, simply, "Wednesday."

Next comes the inside address, of two to five lines. It is exactly the address you put on the envelope; it has no punctuation at the end of the lines. Its elements are: individual addressed . . . individual's title . . . company name . . . company street address . . . city, zone and state. Corporation, street, avenue, company and the names of states may be abbreviated, but they are better spelled out. Numbers are written as figures.

When you know the addressee's full name, it's best to put that on the first line. There is, however, an alternate form—a nice dodge if you don't know the addressee's first name:

Mr. A. L. Johnson	The Little Widget Company
Executive Vice President	488 Sampson Avenue
The Little Widget Company	New York 11, New York
488 Sampson Avenue	or
New York City 11	Attention: Mr. Johnson
	(or Attention of Mr. Johnson)

The salutation is "Dear Mr. Johnson:". A comma instead of a colon after the salutation and the use of "My dear . . ." are social rather than business forms. Three dots sometimes replace the colon—"Dear Mr. Johnson . . ."—but a dash looks rude and a semi-colon ain't good English.

When you are addressing a company without the name of a particular person, the salutation is "Dear Sirs." "Dear Friends" is a ridiculous form of address for people you don't know. "Gentlemen" is old hat. So is "Mesdames," but no one has yet thought of a dignified way out of this form of address to a group of women.

If you've been worrying about how to address a married woman in business, don't. Even after you've noticed a wedding ring you can't be sure that she isn't using her maiden name in business. Rather than ask (when your question might embarrass an unwilling spinster) . . . rather than use "Mrs." before a woman's first name . . . stick with "Miss." If she's using her married name and if she cares about this point she will use her proper Mrs. name in her typed signature: "Mrs. John Jones," typed below her signature of "Mary Jones." But in the absence of any such clue, make them all "Miss."

Watch out for your secretary if she is not reliable on first naming. Sometimes it's as bad to salute old Joe with "Dear Mr. Bobbin" as it is to address the prominent and distant William deSnob as "Dear Bill"—but if you can't remember to dictate salutations, you'd better ask her to write "Mr." in the absence of special instructions.

The barest typed signature is your name. Make it your full name,* even if you are going to sign it with your nickname only, for this letter is going to rest in somebody's files. Below your name, your title or your department should be typed out, if that information does not appear on the letterhead; your correspondent has a right to know by what authority you write what you write, so don't think this title looks like a brag.

Your company name may appear, usually in capital letters, between the complimentary close and your signature, or below your written and just above your typed signature—but it is redundant if the company name appears on the letterhead.

Simplest	*Fullest*
Sincerely yours,	Sincerely yours,
	THE LITTLE WIDGET COMPANY
A. L. Johnson	A. L. Johnson
	Executive Vice President

There is a variation on this standard signature block which should not be used unless the writer's title or department appears on the letterhead:

> Sincerely yours,
> *(hand signature)*

A. L. Johnson: msw

No buts about it, all letters must be hand-signed. If it is necessary for your secretary to sign for you, she writes your name in the space provided then adds her initials, preceded by the word "by," in parentheses: "(by msw)." The use of "per" instead of "by" is archaic, and a forgery without the accompanying confession may put you in a tough spot later on.

Carbon copies need not be hand-signed, but they should bear some evidence that their original has been sent. Your

---

* In business, initials may be used in place of the full first name or names.

secretary may type: "Signed: A. L. Johnson" in the space for your signature, or you may initial the carbon, or she may sign for you with her "by-line" following—whichever is most convenient.

Memos require no signature, but should be initialed to show that they are authentic.

If the letter carries a P.S.—and it shouldn't, unless the postscript contains information not available at the time you dictated the body of the letter, or unless you are making sales-use of this device as an attention-getter—this tag should end with your initials but need not be hand-signed.

In the lower left-hand corner of the letter appear the symbols which remind your secretary now or tell you years later how this letter came into being, what it enclosed, how it was sent and so on.

Unless the writer typed the letter himself, this line comes first:

alj: msw (or ALJ/msw or any such variation: initials of the person who signs the letter, in capitals or lower case . . . colon or slant line . . . initials of person who types the letter, caps or lower case.)

If enclosures go with the letter, the next line says so:

Enclosures: 2
    or
Two enclosures
    or
2 enclosures
    or
Enclosures: 2 pamphlets
  How to Save Money
  Esquire's Handbook for Hosts

(the form is not so important as the fact.)

Then, and this is *very* important, if anyone other than the addressee is to receive a copy of this letter, the eavesdropper must be announced on the next line. The addressee has a right to know who else is reading his mail; the reader of the carbon has a right to know that the addressee has been so informed. The "announcement" may read:

cc: Mr. Joseph Binks
    or
carbon copy to Mr. Binks

Mr. Binks' copy may be sent without a covering letter. All you need do is put a check mark in the margin opposite the "announcement."

Finally, if you want it as a reminder to your secretary, as a record in your files or as a note of urgency in the letter itself, you may add a line saying how the letter is being sent: BY MESSENGER, perhaps, or AIRMAIL SPECIAL DELIVERY.

One item which should *never* appear is the unflattering confession: "Dictated but not read." Your signature followed by your secretary's initials tells the sad story well enough, so why rub it in? If you can't trust your secretary to transcribe her dictation correctly, don't let her mail letters without your seeing them.

The only mechanical problem involved in interoffice correspondence is whether the names of multiple addressees should be listed in the order of their importance or alphabetically. The problem has assumed the proportions of a joke. Crafty politicians have been known to change the order on each carbon of a given memo, so that each recipient will think he is at the top of the list. Cynics have advised eager-beavers to put the boss' name at the top of every list, so lesser addressees will be sure to read the memo; by this system, it matters little whether the boss actually receives a copy! Let your office practice (or politics) be your guide, but consider that the man who is to *act* on the memo deserves the original, or at least a dark and clear carbon.

Given an expert secretary, the mechanics of letter writing will be the last thing to concern you. But if you must or want to give them your attention, a good move would be to sponsor a company handbook on style and form, in order to standardize preferred forms for use throughout your firm.

C O N T E N T

It's good business to make your letters as short as possible, but it's good manners to see that they are not curt. It's good business to state your mission in your first sentence, go straight to the point, give complete information, end with a definite statement of what action is to be taken by whom. It's good manners to add an overlay of friendly interest to the base of business efficiency.

There is no real conflict here, but some letter-writers are so hipped on saying things the short way that they neglect to say them the nice way. "Thank you for your letter of June 16" takes only six letters more than "I have your letter of June 16"—but it is sixty times more pleasant.

Saying something the nice way does not require elaborate phrasing, long sentences, crowded paragraphs or letters that run on and on. In fact, it is as much a matter of attitude as of language. Always assume the best of motives on the part of your correspondent.

Even when you know better, write as if the unpaid bill had been overlooked, the agreement mutually misunderstood . . . as if the complaint were reasonable, the defection unintentional. You'll find that the inquiring letter takes no more effort than the demanding one. The pleasant letter takes few more words than the disagreeable one, and it gets better results.

Clichés like "Begging to remain . . ." and "Yours of the 16th inst. rec'd and duly acknowledged" were, happily, put away with quill pens and celluloid collars. Moderns know better than to use dusty words like "the same," "herewith," "the favor of a reply," "at hand," "regret," "esteemed," "kindly." They don't "trust"; they "hope." They don't "state," they "say." And they don't "take the liberty of."

But the old forms have been replaced by something equally meaningless: tradese. Try not to use technical terms, special slang, trade abbreviations and local-joke expressions. If they're well enough known to be understandable outside your office, they are probably trite.

AND BY THE WAY

Writing good business letters is a matter of detailed and often quite specialized technique. Etiquette intrudes only when you introduce a possibly offensive personal element into business letters, or when you fail to write the letters expected of you. The following reminders slide into this book under one of those two excuses:

1. *Answer all letters promptly*—within ten days at the outside. If you can't fully answer them within that period, the least you can do is acknowledge them and explain your delay. When you are out of town or for some other reason unable to answer your mail, your secretary should handle this chore for you. She has only to write, in her own name, promising to show you the letter as soon as you return.

2. *Let everyone involved know* what action has been taken on a letter.

Suppose you get a letter from Jones, asking a question which Smith can answer better than you. Buck Jones' letter to Smith—but write Jones yourself, telling him you've referred his question to Smith, and send Smith a carbon of your letter to Jones, so Smith will know that it's his move. If Smith is alert, he will send you a carbon of his ultimate reply to Jones, or otherwise let you know that he has held up his end. If Smith is a boob, you had better follow up in a week or so to make sure he *has* answered—for the initial responsibility is yours, as the original addressee of Jones' letter.

3. *Never include race or religion* in an application letter and never ask about them in a job-ad. It may be against the law in some states; it is against good taste everywhere. Where the information is pertinent, and where it cannot be deducted from photographs or schools or names given in reference, it should be handled delicately and orally—not baldly stated in writing.

4. *Don't present a letter of introduction in person*—that is, don't be standing there while the addressee reads what a great guy you are. Letters of business introduction are not encumbered by the same obligations or surrounded with the same rituals as letters of social introduction (see page 335). It's all right to ask for them; it's okay to give them out without first running an investigation on their subjects. The addressee is obliged only to see the subject, and can sometimes delegate that responsibility. The subject is on his own, assured only of a foot in the door.

But in this, business and social letters of introduction are alike: both should be sent ahead, not handed over. A good method is to enclose the letter of introduction with a letter of your own asking for an appointment. Or you may send it in from the reception desk as you wait to be admitted on a previously arranged appointment.

One other nicety about the letter of business introduction concerns your follow-up. You should always write a thank-you note to anyone who has given you a letter of introduction, reporting at the same time how well you were received or what result the introduction produced.

73

5. *Be liberal with your thank-you letters*. **Required:** thanks for all presents and favors. A good idea: written thanks for all written congratulations or good wishes.

Thanks for anything which came to you because of your business may be typed on business paper. It's only when you are speaking neither for your company nor for yourself as a member of that company (as when you're writing a hot political letter to your Congressman, or soliciting contributions to your favorite charity) that you must be careful to use your personal paper.

Almost the only way you can go too far in the practice of writing thanks is to write a thank-you letter for a thank-you letter. So write one whenever the thought occurs to you—and then write a few more in between times.

BUSINESS CARDS

Handed about with less ceremony than social visiting cards, business cards are also less inhibited in design. The major difference between the two types of calling cards is this: on a social card the man's name is preceded by "Mr."; on a business card, "Mr." should never be used.

The most common, conservative card for business is engraved in black ink on plain white board. But printing is acceptable, dark blue is a safe substitute for black, and second colors are sometimes used on promotional cards used by salesmen.

A common size is 1¾" deep by 3" or 3¼" long. In addition to the man's name, centered, the card always carries the name and address of his business; the telephone number may also be included. Abbreviations, numbers and initials may be used as space dictates. If the man is an officer or a department head, his title is usually included. How this information is spaced on the card is a matter of looks and mechanics; there are no inviolable rules.

Here is a sample, unquestionably in good taste, but almost
any variation is acceptable so long as it well serves its in-
formative purpose without offending the eye.

JOHN D. SMITH

Vice President   Little Widgets, Inc.
                                  Terre Haute, Indiana

MIXING BUSINESS WITH PLEASURE

The ideal, supposedly, is to keep your business life entirely
separate from your social life. Working with people is difficult
even in an atmosphere of impersonal objectivity. Hiring and
firing is delicate even without the added strain of friendship.
And after-hours activities are meant to be relaxing and enjoyable—a relief from, not an extension of, business pressures.

But the ideal is seldom realized, or even aspired to, in these
times. The least "humanized" company in the biggest city
has its office party. People who like their work like to talk
about it with people who "talk the same language." And
then there is business entertaining, that half-world where
business and social lives are deliberately entwined, for business reasons.

Whether by choice or by chance, then, there'll be times
when you can't tell if you're working or playing until you
look at your income tax report.

If there is one general rule to be set down for all admix-
tures of business and pleasure, it is simply this: watch your
step. Anything you do can be held against you in both the
business and social world.

As for the specific situations which crop up most often in
this milieu, here are a few guides:

THE BUSINESS LUNCH

Is this treat necessary? A realistic appraisal of your business and your quarry will give you the answer—but don't make the mistake of thinking that all your prospects are free-loaders or even willing guests. More of them than you might think resent the intrusion of business upon the hour which is supposed to be their own, and not a few are leery of attempts to "buy" their favor. Even in fields where doing business at lunch is an accepted and expected part of the routine, it's best always to give the other guy the option of seeing you over his own desk rather than over your expense account. Appearing to respect his time more than his tummy will usually do you more good than a sandbag summons to lunch.

In any case, before you wangle your way into a business lunch, be sure that you have a business reason. People who ask, "Is it all right to talk business at a business lunch?" have wandered far off the track. You should have something specific to discuss, and it should be something too long or too complicated to put into a letter. Ideally, the subject is one which is almost as important to your prospect as to you, one which even he will admit is better treated away from the pressures and interruptions of a busy office.

setting it up

Comes, then, the invitation. Whoever suggests the lunch is the host, automatically. It is as impolite for a guest to struggle over a check as for a host to let his guest pay, so it is important to establish the host-guest roles at the outset. The invitation affords your first chance to clear the way for a graceful check-paying period, so handle it with care.

"I'd like to talk to you about such-and-such," you say. "May I come in to see you or, better, could you spare the time to have lunch with me?"

76

The wording is not important, so long as it a) gives a clear indication of the business at hand, b) makes it easy for him to decline without a lot of lying about being booked for lunch from now until Christmas and c) includes some phrase to establish your host role: "Have lunch with me" comes most naturally to a man of casual speech, but the field is open to anything from "Will you be our guest at lunch?" ("our" meaning your company's guest) to "How about letting Esquire buy us a lunch?" Avoid the vague, "Let's have lunch" and the Dutch-treat phrase, "have lunch together."

When there is no doubt in your mind that the idea of a lunch will be acceptable, your first sally should also mention a specific date. But with someone who, for all you know, is opposed to business lunches, or with someone who is so business-lunched that there is going to be a booking problem, it's better to save the calendar consultations for the next round.

Again, it's your move. He says lunch would be fine; you then suggest a specific date, or open the way for him to name the day by saying something like "I can make it any day next week; what day would be good for you?"

Having agreed on the day, you then suggest the time. If you're clever, you will already have found out what time he likes to lunch. In the absence of an intelligence report, however, 12:30 and 1 are safe suggestions. You shouldn't ask him to make it abnormally early or late just to avoid the rush, because that's your problem—not his.

choosing the restaurant

Now, still keeping a firm grip on the reins, you suggest the restaurant. You should *not* pass the ball to him at this point, because it's your job as host to indicate the price range. Your best move is to mention two places—one the guest is sure to

77

know and the other a less conventional place you can safely recommend.

In New York, the practiced business luncher tries to create a club atmosphere in a constantly changing environment. He establishes himself at a number of different restaurants, so he can offer a choice in keeping with the personality of his guest and the purpose of the lunch. When entertaining a man, he is careful to avoid restaurants with tearoom or lovers' rendez-vous overtones. In general, he tries to offer a choice between a well-known and desirable restaurant and a "discovery" place which may provide an experience his guest would not other-wise have had.

In smaller towns, where the choices are not so numerous, the clever host still tries to pick a place where his guest will be comfortable but also stimulated. In any case, it should be "his" place, not the prospect's "regular" restaurant where the management may inadvertently reverse the host-guest roles.

For his part, the guest may freely choose between offered alternatives—but he shouldn't suggest a place of his own. If he's asked what kind of food he prefers, he may say; if he's asked if he has time for a distant or elaborate restaurant he should tell the truth; but he shouldn't usurp the host's defi-nite duty to set the restaurant level.

handling the mechanics

As in the preliminaries, so in the course of the lunch: the host takes a firm lead. His direction is even more necessary than in a strictly social situation, for he has always to forestall that embarrassing hassle over the check which can undo his busi-ness plans. Thus it is he who makes the reservation—a mini-mum courtesy to his guest and a necessity in a crowded town. He makes it in his own or his company's name, but gives also the name of his guest—just to avoid a mix-up at the door.

It is he who gets there first—and *on time*. If he and his guest don't know each other by sight, he might better go first to the other's office—if he's lunching with a woman, as host or guest, he should make this offer—but door-to-door service as a general rule is an unnecessary and time-consuming extra.

If his guest is late, the host should wait in the anteroom instead of at the table. The exceptions are when the guest is more than fifteen minutes late (and hence might be embarrassed to have kept his host standing so long) . . . when there are other, punctual guests . . . and when host and guest know each other well enough to have agreed in advance to meet at the table.

Once they are seated, the host follows somewhat the same routine as that prescribed for social entertaining, except that he does not necessarily order for a male guest. Certain men may be more comfortable if they are allowed to order for themselves rather than through another man, but they are nonetheless obliged to wait for the host's lead on what to order. (See page 360 for the leading questions.)

"What would you like to drink?" is probably the best opening gambit, because it allows the guest to order a cocktail, tomato juice or nothing at all, with no pressure in any direction. If the guest orders nothing, the business host had better not have a drink; if the guest orders a cocktail, the host had better not cross him up by having tomato juice unless he can offer a convincing explanation amounting to an apology. All this because of the lingering embarrassment and/or stigma which surrounds "solitary drinkers" and teetotalers alike.

Even when he has been given the "big boy" treatment and been allowed to give his order to the waiter direct, the guest will hesitate to summon the waiter for a missing fork, more coffee or whatever. Probably he will also be less willing than a woman would be to ask his host for whatever it is he wants, so the host must be particularly watchful of the service, especially alert to his male guest's needs.

The solicitousness should not be obvious, of course—no man wants to be hovered over by another man—but it should be nonetheless effective.

making talk

If only in the interest of continuity, it's best to wait until after the ordering has been disposed of before launching into your business. But if your guest introduces the subject before that, you should by no means put him off; he is probably trying to save his own time, if not telling you that he has no interest in exchanging small talk with you.

Such small talk, in any case, should not be prying. Besides being boring in the extreme, questions about wives and children ask for information which is none of your business—and, remember, you're here for business. Hobbies and sports make better small talk than families, anyway.

If yours is the kind of business which you think flourishes on friendship, you still owe it to your prospect to maintain his personal privacy if he so wishes. Thus it is better to volunteer information about yourself, in hopes he'll match you, than to conduct an inquisition.

In the business session itself, the worst thing you can be is unprepared. This lunch was your idea, and presumably it serves to save your guest some time and effort, so your man has good reason to be annoyed if the discussion is inconclusive on your end. Maybe you can't set up a sump pump at the corner table, but you can certainly come equipped with all necessary information and papers. Send a set to his office ahead of time if you want him also to be prepared for the discussion.

paying up

Women who take men to lunch resort to all sorts of maneuvers to avoid a public display of money at the lunch table. They pay in advance, they sign checks, they excuse themselves from the table in order to pay up out of sight. But between men there should be no need for high strategy.

If you have played your host role properly throughout the meal, the check will be given direct to you. You look at it briefly, continuing to talk or listen as you were so as not to direct your guest's attention to the process. You put down a large bill, so you won't have to fish through your pockets or count out small change. You figure the tip while the waiter is off changing the bill, so you won't have to pause over the silver tray while your guest sits by in possible embarrassment. And then you simply go.

Whether you tip the hat-check girl for both your hats, or let your guest do it, or go "Dutch" on hats is a matter of no importance. The same thing is true of the cab-fare, if any, back to your respective offices. By rights, being part of the lunch invitation, all subsidiary expenses are yours—but if your guest gets there first there's no harm in letting him fork out some small change.

next?

Most business lunches involve no reciprocity, direct or indirect. He thanks you for lunch; you thank him for his time. The books are closed when your guest has heard you out and you have entered him on your expense account. So you start afresh—second verse, same as the first—if you want to get him across the table from you again.

Business sense will tell you to guard against pressing too frequent invitations on a man who is becoming uncomfortable or feeling obligated over being your constant guest. You may sometimes have to resort to the unattractive convention of pointing out, "It's my *job*" or "It's all on the expense account." But you should never let your guest pick up the check when you have initiated the lunch. If hosts and guests alike would abide by this law of business etiquette, the aftertaste of the business lunch would be more pleasant.

lady's day

When your guest at a business lunch is a woman, your guide on procedure should be date etiquette (pages 261 through 263)—but your guide on approach should be the woman herself.

There is some evidence to support the general male view that a businesswoman wants everyone to think she is lunching with a "new man," not with a salesman who loves her for her job alone. Most likely to fall into this class are the out-of-town buyer, the woman who is doubtful about her sex appeal, the girl who tries too hard to be sophisticated and *any* woman who flutters her eyelashes. For them, the *business:* the exotic restaurant, the soft voice, the admiring stare, an ill-concealed reluctance to talk business, the hopeful suggestion of a brandy after lunch, maybe even the deep and unexplainable sigh when they finally insist they must tear themselves away. (Warning: The act has to be consistent, so be prepared to carry it on even after your business mission is accomplished.)

This routine, however, is a terrible bore and sometimes an affront to the businesswoman who is confident and secure, on both job and sex-appeal fronts. This one doesn't want to be treated like a man, nor taken to a place which features sawdust on the floor and the boys in the back room, but if she suspects that you are wheedling her she will be convinced that your business proposition cannot be sold any other way —or that you take her for a dunce—or both. You'll do better with her if you give her the "ladies first" treatment in an impersonal manner, and let this business lunch live up to its name.

ON THE TOWN

In towns and in businesses where a "night on the town" is the lot of the "customer's man," the business motivation for partying is still carefully concealed. Unlike the business lunch, the business night is ostensibly a social event, for fun only. Although it is often the only thing the principals have in common, business is not discussed.

The procedures are the same as those for a social evening —(see pages 360 to 361)—with one exception. The exception makes etiquette shudder and wives writhe, but this is the consistent practice: the men make the arrangements; their wives just go along.

If the host's wife knows the prospect's wife, it would be pleasant of her to telephone or write a note looking forward to the date their husbands have made. Even when the women have never met, a canny business host may ask his wife to make this move—particularly if there is any problem about what to wear. But this courtesy is unusual.

In the social world, a wife would mark down a hostess if her invitation came through husbands only. But in business practice, men usually ignore the etiquette which requires wives to extend and respond to all invitations for the couple.

Wives are not, however, totally unimportant. If you are entertaining a client and his wife, you have to include your wife or a convincing explanation of her absence. When your wife is along, she assumes some of the obligations of a hostess —helping to manage the conversation, seeing that the other wives are comfortable, and so on—but she shouldn't be expected (or allowed) to run things as if she were Lady Bountiful.

Again, there is no reciprocity in kind. If there is a pay-off in business or good will, this is a secret between sellers and buyers. The opposite effect is the one most often advertised: it is uncomfortable to do business with someone who has exposed himself, the night before, as a waiter-baiter, a bottom-pincher, a sloppy drinker or a general mess. A client who has come a cropper is very likely to develop an active dislike for the salesman who witnessed his shame. And if it's the salesman who made a mis-step, his cause is lost.

That may be part of the reason why taking a customer out on the town has all but disappeared from the big city scene. Those in sales or service businesses, whose out-of-town clients swoop down on them now and then, may offer the facilities of their offices in getting hotel reservations, theatre tickets, transportation. They may see that a bunch of flowers greets the client's wife on her arrival at the hotel. They may suggest places or events which the strangers might enjoy. But they no longer feel a compulsion to wet-nurse their visitors, and they feel no hesitation in saying, "Well, I catch the 6:02. See you tomorrow morning."

This may indeed be a greater compliment to a client than the patent assumption that he can't find his own way around a big city. It involves only one point of good manners: if you're not prepared to fill in a gap thus exposed, never ask a visitor, "What did you do last night?"

IN YOUR OWN HOUSE

When you entertain a business associate at home, the event is strictly social, governed by the rules of social etiquette. The most important requirement of business etiquette is that there be something other than business to sustain the relationship. There should never be an apparent business reason for the social meeting.

This is a limiting requirement, to be sure. It means you have to resist the impulse to "get to know him better" whenever a social move on your part could be misinterpreted. But here's one consolation to you for confining most of your business friendships to business hours: wives have been known to ruin amicable business relationships between their husbands!

There is a further limitation on entertaining business acquaintances who are distinctly above or below you in position or rank. A big-wig embarrasses a junior if he entertains beyond the junior's power to reciprocate comfortably. A junior seems pushy if he entertains his senior without first being sure that his after-hours attentions are welcome.

Inviting the boss to dinner is governed by a definite rule. Your boss must make the first social move. If your boss and his wife have had you to dinner, you may invite them in return. (You probably should, unless you are a bachelor, unless the dinner was a business-good-will affair including other employees or unless the gap between your two standards of living cannot be comfortably bridged.) If you have often met at small parties given by mutual friends, you might stretch a point and assume social equality. But if you have no such definite indication that your boss and his wife are agreeable to seeing you socially, you're stuck with the *status quo*.

When the invitation is in order, it follows the social form: your wife to his wife. They have presumably met before, so there is no complication—but if you want to avoid taking your boss by surprise you may pave the way for your wife's invitation by speaking to your boss at the office. Word your remark so that he'll know that you know that husbands are not supposed to make dates for their wives.

Once the boss and his wife have accepted your invitation, you have only to be yourself as a good, unself-conscious host. If there are other guests, they are better chosen from your non-business circle. Alert them to the fact that you are expecting your boss, if you like, but don't let that be a dominant topic or overtone for the evening. If you have "something

85

other than business to sustain the relationship" you'll be all right.

Good taste and sensitivity, more than a rule, govern the home entertainment of your admitted juniors. If you could possibly be suspected of showing off or rubbing in your superiority, don't do it. And if you do it, don't mix the juniors up with people with whom they can't hold their own.

THE BUSINESS PARTY

Where there's a publicity or public relations department, there's a business party now and then—a cocktail party to introduce a person or product, a luncheon to launch an important announcement, a dinner to commemorate a business occasion. These parties follow, as nearly as possible, the procedures for a similar social event. But because they take place in the special arena of business, they pose special problems.

the guest list

First, the guest list. The purpose of the party will determine this, in the main, but those in charge must be alert to two somewhat paradoxical hazards: cutting across corporate "class" lines, and leaving out the people who are directly responsible for the follow-through the party hopes to inspire.

If the top officers of a company are invited to the same party as their lowest clerks, neither group will have a good time and both may note their hosts' lack of common sense. Still, if a beauty editor is left out of a party which includes her publisher and her editor-in-chief, she will probably resist their later suggestion that she write up the cosmetics her bosses learned about over cocktails and caviar.

There is no particular problem where all concerned are on an executive level, even if some are of management and some of operations. But where the gap between brass and workers is so great as to preclude comfortable mixing, a workable solution is to give two parties. Put the brass party on a general "public relations" level, the worker party on a publicity-service level, but see that the two are of equal plushness.

invitations

Invitations are sent to the guests' offices, whether or not their spouses are included. They are addressed with name and title; the host who doesn't know who holds the job he wants to include certainly ought to find out before dispatching an invitation.

Except for formal parties, when engraved* invitations in the social form are used, the most popular invitation form is a telegram. Letters, printed cards, novelty invitations and telephone calls are equally acceptable; anything goes, in business, so long as it is in character with the party, gives complete information (usually including the purpose) and makes it easy for the guest to reply.

replies

For reasons no different from those of the social hostess, the business host has to know how many guests to expect. The invited should *always* reply, whether or not RSVP is included on the invitation, but he is not required to reply in the same form as the invitation. A telephone call is always acceptable, even for a formal invitation, so most invitations include the name and number of the staff member who will be hawking the guest list. If this person is apparently a clerk or secretary, the invited may have their own secretaries call in their acceptances or regrets. But if no secondary name or reply desk is given, and the reply must be made to the host who signed

---

* In business, printing may be used, instead, but the engraved, third-person forms are followed.

the telegram or other invitation, then the guest should place the call himself. . . . and the host should speak to the fellow-executive in person, *not* fob him off on a secretary at that late date.

Hosts who prefer written acceptances usually enclose reply cards, which have only to be checked and signed, along with stamped return envelopes. If no such card is included, a regular business letter makes a suitable reply.

In view of the cavalier attitude displayed by many business people toward invitations, the host need have no qualms about asking for a reply before a given date. Also, he may telephone to ask if a guest who has not replied may be expected or not. If he doesn't want to risk the prod, and still hasn't had a reply on the day he must give a figure to his caterer he can do nothing but assume that the delinquent invitee *will* turn up.

A vague appreciation of this problem should inspire guests to reply as expected—if not immediately, as in social practice, at least within a week, or three days before the party.

subs and side-wheels

Although the average business invitation is addressed to the individual guest alone, in most cases he may send his assistant in his place. He should not do this, however, without explaining why he can't attend in person and asking his host's permission to send a representative. In business, "asking" amounts to "telling," so it is the guest's duty not to send his secretary or that junior-grade moron from production; his substitute should always be a fitting representative, as close as possible to his own rank.

Again, when the invitation does not make the suggestion specifically, the guest has no right to turn up with an entourage—or even with a "date" or his wife. If it is absolutely necessary that he bring someone, he may ask a bit more freely than he would in a social situation. Most times it would be better to decline the invitation, giving his entanglement as his reason and thus leaving it to his host to suggest that he bring the extra. In any case, he should never show up with extras unannounced.

Just as too many guests make the rude assumption that cost and space are no object in a business party, too many hosts make the thoughtless assumption that business people are perfectly happy to attend evening parties alone. They can't be expected to know which of their guests are married and which might accept more readily if allowed to bring their spouses, but they can be fairly sure that a married *woman* in business has no great love for unescorted party-going. The least a host can do, if he doesn't want to risk doubling his guest list all around, is to be alert to those "regrets" which might be changed to acceptances with a simple "We hope your husband will be able to come, too"—or even, "Our Mr. Associate would like to see you home, if that's agreeable with you."

arrangements

Arrangements are usually left in the experienced hands of professionals, but the host owes it to his guests to select a place sized to the party. If anything is drearier than a small party in an enormous, echoing room, it's a big party in a tiny, airless room.

The host should of course approve the menu, make sure that his guests will not be required to pay for hat-checking or other services, and have the timing of the service clearly understood well in advance.

For a luncheon party, the schedule often amounts to a promise to the guests and is included in the invitation. No guest should be expected to spend more than two hours in the middle of a busy day, so the 12:30 invitation means, roughly, half an hour of drinks, an hour of lunch, half an hour (at most) of speechifying.

For a cocktail party, the timing may be, instead, a secret hedge against "incidents." If the invitations read 5 to 7, it's wise to arrange in advance to close down the bar at 8. About 7:45, then, the waiters would circulate saying something like, "The bar will be closing soon; may I get you a drink?" Coming from a waiter, the warning sounds more like a service than a bum's rush—and the end of a business party is charged up to "policy" rather than to the host's niggardliness.

the business host at work

Like the social host, the business host should see that all his guests are greeted, introduced into conversational groups, served or invited to serve themselves. He should rush to the rescue of any guest he sees alone. He should spend a little time with each. He must protect his other guests from drunks and monologists. But all this is apt to be more difficult for him than for the social host, because often he doesn't know all his guests and they don't know each other.

The practiced business host first memorizes the guest list—names and business affiliations. He can't always stand at the door himself, because he has other duties, but he can always free himself from conversation whenever he spots a guest whom he hasn't yet greeted. He goes up to the new guest, introduces himself (or reminds the guest who he is), holds a brief conversation, then introduces the guest into a group. In making introductions, he gives the guests' business affiliations. Although that is a device frowned upon in social usage, it makes sense in a business group where business is the first, easiest and most natural conversational bond.

The host has one more duty, although to judge by the average business party this is a well-kept secret: he must see that every guest meets the guest of honor. If there is no announced guest of honor, then there is at least a top executive of the host's firm or a principal speaker. The introductions are sometimes complicated—by first-comers who monopolize the guest of honor, by guests of honor who are too important to be steered through the room and hence collect impenetrable walls of living flesh around them in their chosen corners, by a sense of courtesy to the honored guest which precludes breaking into going conversation for constant introductions. But all these difficulties can—must—be surmounted. No guest should be allowed to come and go without having had at least a few words with the big shot.

Where there is a conflict between the wishes of the big shot and the guests' due, the host must simply explain to the guest of honor that the people have been invited solely to meet him. Which suggests another point blatantly ignored by many employees charged with the host-responsibilities of a business party: the people to be catered to at any party are the guests, not the host's bosses! Understandable though it may sometimes be, it is bad manners on the part of the host to concentrate his attentions on his own top brass to the exclusion of his guests. And if the brass have any sense, they'll give more credit for a successful party than for a flattering grease-job.

Where food is served at tables, it is a mistake to let the guests wait until everyone is served before beginning to eat. The host, sometimes with the help of the guest of honor, can set an example which makes better allowances for banquet service and chilling food. Or the company can invest in a waiter for each table, or for each six people, and hope for simultaneous service.

The head table is usually served first. Although this seems a contradiction of the social rule, by which the hostess is served last, it makes sense in terms of efficiency: speakers are able to finish their dessert and coffee in time to collect themselves, so that the "business" part of the party can begin as soon as the other tables have been cleared.

good guesting

Guests leaving a business party should thank whoever has been acting as host and *also* the highest-ranking executive of the nominal host's company. It's pleasant to compliment the host again, next time you meet him, on a well-run party—but a thank-you letter would probably throw the "wheels of commerce" out of kilter.

Like other forms of business entertaining, the business party involves no return obligation. Nothing is required of guests except good guestmanship. But—please note—that includes staying (and staying awake) for the speeches you've been primed to hear.

BUSINESS CLUBS

Clubs presuppose an equality among the members, but even so the junior man in his field does not back-slap and first-name a big shot there any more than he would in the office.

speeches and speakers: the chair

The main etiquette problem posed by clubs is that of handling speeches and speakers. When the speaker is not a member of the club or a personal friend, the chairman owes it to him to:

Give him complete information about his audience, so he will not produce boredom and embarrassment all around with an inappropriate speech.
Give him a definite time limit, well ahead of time so he can

prepare the speech accordingly, then—just before he begins to speak—arrange a mutually agreeable time signal to tell him when he has, say, three minutes left to talk. Advance arrangement is necessary so the pull on the coat-tails will not appear to be related to the interest of the speech itself. And no matter how interesting, no speech to a business club should be allowed to run on beyond the allotted time.

Provide adequate acoustical facilities, and if possible give the speaker a choice between a mike and a projected voice.

Lionize him a bit before and after the speechifying—that is, bring members to him to be introduced instead of circulating the speaker himself around the room . . . center the conversations around the speaker, not around club affairs he has less interest in . . . help to reassure the best and worst speaker alike as to the effectiveness of his speech.

Introduce him *briefly*, with only enough biographical material to establish the speaker as an authority on his subject. Elaborate introductions deny their content; after all, it takes only one line to introduce the President of the United States, so if this speaker is such a hot shot why does it take ten flowery minutes to say so? Introductions which end on laughter put the speaker in a bad spot. Introductions which preview the speech are grounds for mayhem. The chairman should remember that the polite speaker can *never* deny his introduction, however exaggerated and embarrassing, for the denial would be a rebuff to the introducer. Hence—a brief, factual introduction, ending with the speaker's name.

Thank him at least three times: in public, from the rostrum . . . in private, before his departure . . . and in a letter from the club the following day.

All those things are nice to do for "old Joe" as well as for Mr. Eminence, but for a stranger they are absolutely necessary.

If the speaker is a woman, or if the male speaker's wife attends, she is usually presented with flowers to wear. And although the practice is to put the corsage at her place, a smoother method is to send it to her ahead of time. No woman likes to arrange a corsage without a mirror, and most like to dress with an eye to the flowers they will wear.

Head-table arrangements usually put the chairman in the center, with the speaker on his right. If there is a toastmaster, he is on the speaker's other side. The place of honor is to the right of the most important member of the club, and this place belongs to the principal speaker even if his wife is present or other women are consequently relegated to "left-hand" positions.

Introductions are always made standing. The chairman remains standing until the toastmaster has taken over the floor; the toastmaster remains standing until he and the audience have ended the reception-applause and the speaker is ready to begin talking; guests at the head table stand as they are introduced to the audience, unless the chairman has publicly recommended a less time-consuming procedure.

the speaker

For the speaker's part, he owes it to his audience to give them something worth listening to. If he has nothing to say, he should not accept the bid in the first place; nothing is in worse taste—nothing makes an audience squirm more—than an elaborate apology, in false or true modesty, disclaiming the right to take the members' valuable time. If he has indeed been drafted at the last minute, that fact should be explained by the chairman in his appreciative introduction. Audiences make allowances more readily if they are not *asked* to.

Books on speech-making outline helpful techniques, but sometimes they fail to point out the hazards of some of the tricks: racial and religious jokes are here, as elsewhere, in bad taste (and it makes no difference if the joke is on the speaker's own race or religion); any joke in a speech should come up naturally and make a point larger than the point of the joke itself, or it wastes time and insults the intelligence of the audience . . . a pause for applause may be sensible when there *is* applause, but when the audience does not respond naturally, a speaker should proceed without tipping his disappointment; only Milton Berle, if he, can get away with asking, "Is anybody awake out there?" . . . directing the speech to one responsive member of the audience may be helpful in punching up critical points, but if carried to its extreme this old trick serves to make the others feel like eavesdroppers.

members of the audience

The main obligation upon members of the audience is, of course, to listen. It is extremely rude to scrape chairs, hold private conversations and shake your watch as if you can't believe it is still running. If a member must leave early, he will know that in advance and should make proper arrangements: he should make a point of excusing himself to the speaker (or via the chairman) before the speech begins, and he should sit near a door so his departure will be as unobtrusive as possible.

BUSINESS GIFTS

When is a present given for business reasons a bribe, when an insult, when a pleasant and welcome expression of good will? The same package could fall into any one of these three categories, depending on how it was handled.

We're not concerned, here, with promotion items. A sample of the product you sell, a TV hassock imprinted with the time and channel of the program you sponsor, a desk lamp made from a labeled bottle of the drink you market—those things are promotion novelties, not presents. The only mistake you can make (apart from the usual one of assuming that your clients are so lacking in taste as to keep and use junk) is to send such promotion pieces in place of a present the recipient has been led to expect.

When you intend a present rather than a promotion, however, you must be cautious about both ethics and manners.

A present to someone whose favor has acknowledged business value to you can scarcely be misinterpreted if it is a) impersonal b) explainable on the basis of past cooperation rather than expectations for the future c) given generally, to all others who stand in a similar relationship to the donor and d) not extravagant.

One or two of those standards may be watered down, with careful forethought, but when all four are ignored the present is in bad taste and doubtless does more harm than good. It may even be returned, to the embarrassment of both donor and recipient, for a man in business can better afford to seem rude to one person than to seem "bought" to his associates—and his conscience.

W H E N ?

Christmas is the usual occasion for business presents, because general custom relieves people from looking for deeper reasons for a Christmas present.

Weddings, births, anniversaries, illnesses, bereavements, special honors are often hopped upon as excuses for business gifts—but since they are distinctly personal occasions they are risky. It is absolutely necessary that there be some sort of personal working friendliness between the representative of the donor company and the giftee; by rights, the present should be a personal one, and it is completely safe only when in response to a personal wedding invitation, birth announcement or whatever.

Business anniversaries are logical enough, but only where owners or founders are concerned; a hireling doesn't give another hireling a present just because one or the other company has been in business twenty-five years. And because the motive is so transparent, it is not wise to send anything more than a letter of congratulation to someone new on a job, to someone who has just been promoted into a position of business importance to you, or to someone who has just been put in charge of a particular project you're interested in.

The dubious motive cannot be suspected when you send a present to someone who is leaving your realm of influence, of course. Strange how few business gifts celebrate retirements, resignations, transfers to other cities!

W H A T ?

The established methods of keeping a gift impersonal show up both in its selection and in its presentation.

It's a confessed business gift, so it should have something to do with business. Things to use in the office or in connection with work are infinitely better than things to wear or to use at home. But because each man can use only so many desk pads and pen sets and lighters, there is an understandable trend toward less conventional presents.

Even so, things for use at home should be for the business man, not a foredoomed attempt to fall in with his wife's taste in home furnishings. And they should be as impersonal as possible: a gadget for washing his car is better than something for him to use when he is shaving—if, that is, he *has* a car! The point of etiquette here is to avoid an invasion of his privacy, an assumption of his taste or—and this is particularly important in gifts from a man to a woman or vice versa—a give-away to more intimate knowledge of personal habits than a business acquaintance is supposed to have.

Liquor, however welcome it is in many circles, comes under the last taboo. If you know a man well enough to make an exception, you know his company and/or his wife well enough to anticipate their reaction to such a gift. But it is never flattering to a woman to receive a present of liquor, and a single bottle of old Armagnac is always more complimentary to a man than a case of routine stuff.

Whatever the present, see that it's the best of its kind. Instead of a quantity of anything, send the only one or the latest or the hardest to get. The ethical ban on extravagant* gifts rules out a lot of big luxury stuff at the outset; good taste's ban on shoddy merchandise rules out gadgets that don't work, imitations of luxury items, cheap brands. It is better to send a small key case made of good leather than a big briefcase made of leatherette. And anyone who sends a woman a gallon of unknown perfume in preference to a dram of a famous French perfume knows even less about women than he knows about gift-giving.

Whether the same present should be sent to all those on your Christmas list is a moot point. Those who operate in an area of cultivated friendliness—and those who know their "contacts" well enough to know their possessions and enthusiasms—like to send individual gifts to suit individual tastes. When and if they are successful in this personal approach to

---

* It's difficult to reduce "extravagant" into dollar limits, because a $50 present might be appropriate for a customer who pays your $100,000 bills every year, while a $10 present would raise the eyebrows of a writer who proudly deletes all "plugs" from his copy. You can (but probably won't) spend more on a supplier or helper than on a customer, and more on somebody who buys things than on someone who "buys" ideas. But you must always anticipate the twin suspicions: that your company is making too high profits, and that you are trying to buy something that is not for sale. Find out what your competitors are doing and you may have a practical guide.

selection, they score bigger hits; even when they fail, they think they have reflected a little thought and personal regard which is lacking in a shotgun present. But they have added a personal element which is sometimes dangerous. The least precaution they can take is to see that everyone on the list gets a present of equal monetary value.

The "equality" of the recipients is perfectly clear when the same gift is sent to everyone; nor can there be any doubt about the impersonal, business motivation for the present when all members of the Press Club, say, turn up with identical leather notebooks. If this kind of shotgun present seems to you so impersonal as to be meaningless, you may have the notebooks initialed—but get the initials right! Better to give every secretary in town a box of candy, in thanks for checking your listing against her boss' real name, than to send one thing marked "W. H." to a "Bill" whose real name is really "Bill."

H O W ?

If you choose an unconventional or faintly personal present, all the more reason to emphasize the impersonal nature of the gift in the way you present it.

It is not simply from you to him, but from you in the name of your company to him as a representative of his company. It should therefore be sent to his office, not to his house. (Note that this means the present will probably have to pass staff inspection. If it is something he doesn't want, he'll pass it on to some other member of his firm—a more appropriate recipient than a household servant who never heard of your company.)

Sending a home-use present may burden your man with the task of carrying the package home on his commuter train, but that's all the more reason for an office-use present. You should *not* send the present to his home without his advance permission—and getting that permission takes the surprise out of the present—so there you are.

The card enclosed should be from your company, signed by you—with a personal message, if you like. Or it may be your own business card, decked with a seasonal sticker or not as you like. But it should not be a personal gift card signed only by you, without your company's obvious sponsorship.

TO WHOM?

Your gift list itself demands careful planning and checking. No fair sending to a boss and forgetting his assistant, who does most of the work of interest to you. And don't cross off a name which has been on your list for years, even if you've had no business with him this year. You can get into a lot of trouble with omissions. The people you leave out will be hurt; the ones you include will have reason to doubt the purity of your motives.

THEN WHAT?

All business presents should be acknowledged. A pleasant thank-you letter on company paper, addressed to whoever signed the card but including the company in the thanks, is correct. But there is no further obligation on the receiver's part, and if the gift has been deftly given it's bad manners to act as if anything special is expected in return.

CHRISTMAS CARDS

In sending Christmas cards for business reasons, observe the same rules as for presents in checking your lists, guarding against omissions, avoiding blatant advertising, signing company cards in your own name. Send them first class, by all means. And watch out for the "cute" and "smart" cards which just might offend the religious views of those on your list.

(Apropos of religion, Christmas has by now become so standardized—so commercial, if you will—that there is no objection to sending Christmas cards to non-Christians. Comparable neutrality is not enjoyed by other religious holidays, however, so it is not good taste to send cards for holidays which you do not observe yourself.)

INTRA-OFFICE GIVING

CHRISTMAS PRESENTS

Unless you're the boss (in which case you're expected to give money, if you give anything—a raise or a bonus, not a box of bon-bons, please!), your Christmas presents to your fellow-workers are from you, not from your company.

your secretary

The only absolute must is a present to your secretary. It may be anything from the traditional flowers and candy and books to a handbag or theatre tickets. It's for her, not for her desk or her work, but it should not be intimately personal—not stockings or lingerie, say.

If your wife, being a "phone pal" of your secretary, joins in the present—selecting it, wrapping it and signing the card with you—it may be as personal as perfume and outer wearing apparel. But if you alone are the gifter take care not to imply (or advertise) an after-hours relationship.

Five to ten dollars seems to be about par for a junior executive to spend for his secretary's present; seniors may go as high as $20. If you owe her more than that for her diligent

101

attention to your personal business, think of other ways to repay her. Remember that your secretary's Christmas present is up for ladies' room inspection.

your assistant

Your assistant may rate a small present, too, depending on your relationship; you don't want to seem patronizing.

other office personnel

Other office personnel may be included at your option: $1-$2 spent on the people who are particularly helpful and nice to you—office boys, receptionists, switchboard operators, elevator men—may be appreciated but is not expected. The charwoman may look for a tip on your desk Christmas Eve, or maybe your office will take up a collection for the building employees.

your bosses

But NEVER give Christmas presents *up* the ladder. Even Christmas cards are debatable unless a social relationship already exists. If you and your family see the boss and his family socially and have fallen into the habit of exchanging presents for the children, that's something else again, but you will only embarrass your seniors and expose yourself if you include them in your Christmas spirit in any tangible way.

Even a v.p. should all but ask permission before he gives any present to the exec or the president—and then the present should be so special and so unusual as to be obviously worth breaking the rule for. "I brought back a number of ducks; I'd like to send you two. Think you could manage to eat around my gunshot?" Obviously, this kind of casual approach is not available to the junior executive, nor even to the third assistant vice president. It's the exception that proves the rule.

Presents to your seniors' secretaries are almost as suspicious. If the gals have earned such "thanks" it would be better for the junior executives to pool their good intentions and give joint presents.

OFFICE COLLECTIONS

Office collections know no season, and often no good reason, but nothing can be done about them. When the strange girl from billing comes around for your contribution to a wedding present for an unknown Margie, whom you'll never hear of again, all you can do is ask how much "the others" are chipping in, dig down and forget it. In a few weeks, if you look at the bulletin board, you'll see a thank-you note beginning, "Dear Gang . . ." and then if you hurry back to your desk you'll be just in time for the next collection.

If you could get someone to pass this book around in the billing department, Margie's friends might like to know that:

Collections should be confined to people who know Margie.
A nicer way than going the rounds with a coinbox would be to circulate a notice; then those who wanted to join in the present could take or send their money to the collector and those who didn't would be spared the feeling of pressure. And Margie might then feel that the present was a testimonial to more than her buddy's determination.
The accompanying card should be signed in general—with something like, "From all your friends at the office"—to avoid exposing those who missed the collector, accidentally or on purpose.
Those who contributed might at least be told what present was sent. Margie need do no more than write a round-robin thank-you letter, but if she returns to the office and

begins thanking everyone in person, she and her well-wishers will all be mortified if they don't know what "darling thing" she's talking about.

If you have any influence with the front office, you might also suggest an annual "tax" and a general fund to cover all such friendly gestures. It would save a lot of time, and probably some money. It would also mean that old sourpuss in the library got as nice a bouquet at the hospital as the most popular girl on the floor got when her baby was born, but partisans could always add personal (non-collection) presents to the fund's stock greeting.

In any case, executives should not take up general collections for each other, and no one should take up a collection for the boss. Individuals and/or departments can always write appropriate letters; personal friends can always send personal presents to associates when the occasion warrants. Collection-taking is strictly lower-bracket stuff which must apparently be borne as gracefully as possible by its upper-bracket victims.

YOUR "CONTACTS"*

Don't work 'em!

It is never polite to *ask* anyone to "get it for you wholesale." If there are no restrictions on your acquaintance's buying for other people, and if he has no qualms about "working" his own business "contacts" on behalf of personal friends, he may *volunteer* to save you some money. If so, you have only to decide if you are willing to be a nuisance to the

---

* This is an abominable word, which can claim no dictionary listing for the meaning businessese gives it, but it is appropriate for the abominable practice under discussion.

wholesaler, and obligated to your benefactor. But don't fish for this favor.

Anyone who is asked to "get it wholesale" has a perfect right to explain the circumstances which prevent his complying with the request. But since this is often mutually embarrassing, the practice costs a lot of suffering-in-silence. His politeness sometimes costs your friend the money you save, too. Authors, for instance, do *not* get their own books free; if they get a "discount" on them it amounts to little more than their own royalties.

There are many other ways of using your job to advance your personal projects—and all of them are bad. The "original deal boy" is a plague, and something of a fool as well. Even if you think you're doing it subtly, you should be clear-eyed about the limits to which you can go in working people. Sooner or later they'll all realize they're being used—and they'll resent it, if only because you should have thought them smarter.

SEX IN THE OFFICE

Whether you do or don't get involved with a girl in your office, your job is to make it appear as if nothing could be further removed from your thoughts. To stay above suspicion, warranted or no, keep your 9-to-5 relationship relatively formal and impersonal. Don't arrive in the morning and leave at night with the same cute blonde; if you just happen to ride the same train, find some excuse to break it up before you stroll into the receptionist's view. And if you are not so innocent as you would appear, make your meeting places far afield, and make your arrangements in private, on your own time.

Your best protection against the designing femme-fatale in

your office is to be found in the "open door" . . . an average observance of the caste system which prevents your lunching with your secretary . . . and the old stand-by, a consistently impersonal attitude.

There is probably no protection against tears and tantrums, but if you take a bossly and/or fatherly attitude toward these female foibles no one will suspect that they stem from anything more sinister than business frustrations.

You probably ought to know about other pair-offs in the office, if any, because they sometimes effect radical alterations in the "table of organization." But it goes without saying that you should go without saying anything about these supposedly secret liaisons.

THE OFFICE PARTY

Some workers may indeed live for office parties. Most probably just live through them—if they can.

The one answer to all office-party problems would be the abolition of all office parties. But an etiquette book can hardly expect to succeed where sense and wit have thus far failed, so let's assume that this business phenomenon will survive; let's concern ourselves, instead, with the problem of making an office "get-together" more like a party and less like a punishment.

TOP-LEVEL TACTICS

The attitude of management is probably the most important element. Of its several possible approaches, only two hold much chance of success: a hands-off policy, under which the employees may do as they like with a given afternoon off, and an on-the-house policy, under which the management polls the staff to find out what kind of party it wants, then picks up the check. (The poll ought to include an option of party versus an equal division of the money a party would cost—but then we promised not to crusade.)

Under the on-the-house policy, management wisely leaves the decisions and arrangements up to an elected committee, in hopes the result will then better suit the tastes of the employees. The boss should advise only when it appears that the committee has neglected a detail which is important to the smooth operation of the party or the comfort of the guests— and then his advice should sound as much like a suggestion and as little like an order as anything a boss says ever can. He has a right to stick his oar in, because he will be blamed if the party is a flop for some reason which could have been eliminated by money, but his general approach should be "cost is no object so long as the party is fun."

An on-the-house party can be and often is a dinner-dance at a hotel, arranged for as well as paid for by the bosses who are the hosts. There's something to be said for a party which involves no effort on the part of staff members—but those who might be smart enough and nervy enough to decline an invitation from a committee of employees would know for certain that attendance was a must if the invitation came from the boss.

In any case, a boss caught up in an office party should consider these don'ts:

1. *Don't allow the employees to be taxed* for any party in which management plays any part, even the part of honored guest. It's bad enough to have to go to these things without having to pay for the ordeal—and chances are the people who are most likely to enjoy an office party are the ones who can least afford to chip in.

2. *Don't offer your own house or farm* as the scene of the crime. This is usually a well-meant gesture (which might

107

also save the company a little money) but it is fatal to play lord-of-the-manor with your hirelings, or even expose your standard of living to their view.

3. *DON'T MAKE A SPEECH.* If the committee insists that you open festivities with a welcoming address or some such, you may be sure they do so only because they think they should. It's your job to decline, and firmly. If you haven't such strength of character, at least refrain from victimizing your captive audience with platitudes about the happy family and pulling together for a better year next year.

4. *Don't stay too long.* You shouldn't make an elaborate entrance, mill around long enough to pat everybody's head and then depart with a flourish—but neither should you try too hard to get into the spirit of things, because there won't be much spirit until you leave. (Or, if there is, you and everyone else will wish you hadn't seen it.) The happiest move is to slip out. Far better to be thought too good for the party than to cramp everyone's style with your fraudulent-seeming friendliness. Remember that these office parties never change anything, really, except possibly for the worse.

5. *Don't hold anything that happens against anybody.* This is a rather impossible demand, so it adds up to another argument for leaving early.

THE COMMITTEE'S JOB

The committee's responsibilities are not unlike those of any group of hosts and hostesses, with the added obligation of arranging the kind of party the majority wants. To spare hard feelings all around, the committee should definitely decide alternatives by poll. People who have been outvoted on whether to have liquor, whether to include wives or dates, whether to have buffet or table service, whether to dress and the date of the party are much less likely to gripe than those who have simply been ignored. However decided, all such policies should be clearly announced before the guests are asked to sign the "Yes, I'm coming" list.

The date of the party is something which management might reasonably mix into. Workers' families would feel better about the company if it did not send their men home better lit than the tree on Christmas Eve; the workers themselves might prefer to enjoy their hangovers on company time. The boss with a nice sense of public relations might well insist that the party be given the day before Christmas Eve, even if that means he might as well give everyone an extra day off.

Liquor is, of course, the major problem and also the main salvation of an office party. In communities where drinking is not a generally accepted custom, and in companies where the problem is circumvented by throwing children's parties or other inherently non-alcoholic events, all is well. But drinks are expected at most office parties, and the reasonable device of "running out" or closing the bar is usually taken as a further example of management's penny-pinching. So the dilemma stands: if liquor does not flow freely, the tensions are intolerable; if it does, Incidents of Lasting Importance are sure to occur. There is no way out for those in charge; it's up to the guests.

FOR THE GUESTS

For the guests, we can offer three pieces of advice which will almost certainly have no effect:

DON'T GO if you can muster a reasonable, sorrowful excuse. What a perfect day for a trip out of town or an attack of flu or even a crisis which demands your all-night presence at the plant!

IF YOU GO, don't stay too long. Slipping out early might be noticeable and might mark you down as anti-social if everyone did it, but not that many people have that much sense. Never fear that no one else can take over as the life of the party. Fear only that you will make an ass of yourself or—even more likely for a man of any self-control and intelligence—that you will witness someone else's asininity. Remember, what you do and see will be forever held against you.

DON'T DRINK TOO MUCH—which probably means don't drink anything but long glasses of water colored with a little caramel syrup brought from home. You can't afford to be conspicuously sober after everyone else has "loosened up" —particularly since you will later want to claim that you were too tight to remember having seen the Big Blow-up— but don't kid yourself into thinking you can "hold your liquor" well enough to surmount the hazards of an office party.

Next day, or soon after the party, make a point of congratulating the committee members on their good work. They've had a pretty thankless job, and the put-up applause they got at the toastmaster's behest does not remove the necessity for guestly thanks later on. If you stick it out to an acceptable departing hour, of course, you thank your hosts and hostesses as you leave. But if you've tried to sneak out, you won't have called attention to your disappearance by thank yous. In any case, it's nice to do what you can to make the chairmen think their party was a success.

YOUR WIFE AND YOUR WORK

KEEP HER OUT OF IT, if you can.

You're lucky if she knows enough about the ways of the business world to act as a suitable sounding board—or enough about the ways of womanhood to provide needed relief from business pressures. In a company where a certain amount of social mixing is necessary, you're lucky if she is a good hostess endowed with the knack of putting people at ease (a knack which usually includes empathy, the art of small talk and a nice sense of timing in the expression of controversial opinion). It's nice if she wants what you want in your career; it helps if she understands when you have to work hard and late.

But—note—all these qualities operate *AT HOME*.

Your wife should stay out of your office, except by infrequent appointment to meet you there or except by invitation to one of those Open House events some companies stage in order to show wives and kiddies what Daddy does all day.

She should stay off your office wire, except on matters which can't await your call or your return home. And even when the mission itself has your approval, she should *never* deal directly with your employees or fellow-workers.

If she doesn't know these things instinctively, you'll have to risk telling her outright. Explain it in terms of "appearances," a concept women are usually quick to appreciate, and she shouldn't resent the lesson.

For your part, you should avoid dragging her name, activities or opinions into the business day. She's not a skeleton (we hope) to be kept hidden in a closet, but too many men quote their wives too often to hold the interest (and respect) of their associates. It may be true that the road to success is crowded with wives pushing their husbands along—but try not to let it show in your case!

SPORTS

ETIQUETTE

introduction
and primer
for
good sportsmen

In the special world of sports, ignorance is no excuse.

When a man trespasses against the sportsman's code of knowledgeable conduct in and around his particular sports-passion, that man is mentally written off as a wrong guy—or, at the very best, as a good guy not to ask back. Against all evidence that the guest's "mistakes" arise out of innocence rather than a black and evil soul, the sportsman is apt to assume that all infractions of rules, written and "understood," are willful. Although he would sooner retire to the playing fields of pinball than admit it, there are times when the "true sportsman" follows the con-man's code: "Never give a sucker an even break."

This readiness to confuse the helpless innocent with the hopeless boor is tough on sports-newcomers because, when it comes to the unwritten laws, even your best friend won't tell you. It would not be good manners on his part to correct or even to appear to notice your mistakes, and it seldom occurs to him to brief you in advance on things which he presumes that any "gentleman" knows instinctively.

But instinct without experience is not much use to the tennis player on a sailboat, the skater on a horse, the fisherman on a ski slope, the fee-course golfer at a private club. For these tiny, monumental rules are a lot more special to each sport, a lot less subject to sense and sensibility, than the general rules of good sportsmanship.

Those, too, are worth reviewing before you rush into an unfamiliar sport. They are perhaps a little too subtle for comfortable expression in plain English, but the list on pages 117 to 121 may lend a nudge to your natural impulse.

Also included in this introductory section are some general guides to club conduct, good at almost any kind of private "country" club.

But the Pointers in Prevention of Cruelty to Beginners begin on page 124. There you'll find the previously unwritten laws of each major sport, as extracted from the experts who form our board of editors (page V). Next best to "growing up in" the sport, under the kind eye of just such experts, these pointers will put you at ease your first time out. Follow them and you'll be free to worry about your game instead of your manners.

PRIMER FOR GOOD SPORTSMEN

or

MAXIMS TO MAKE THE SPORT GROW FONDER— OF YOUR CONDUCT IN PLAY

"cheatin' proves"

It is axiomatic that "He that will cheat at play/Will cheat you any way." To cheat at love or in business stands a much better chance of being "understood" than cheating at games.

The supplement to this prim little maxim was written by La Noué centuries ago: "The stupid makes a disturbance; the fool laments; the honest man, when he is cheated, retires and says not a word." Only one cheat in a million who thinks he has got away with it really *has*—his victims are merely too nice to challenge him, and too wise to play with him again.

For those with good intentions, this prime rule of sportsmanship says one thing: learn the rules, and then play by them strictly until invited to do otherwise. This doesn't mean, of course, that you should be a stickler for rules-play by others; that can be as disagreeable, as annoying and as "unsporting" as teeing up in the rough or dealing from the bottom of the deck. In many a friendly game, the official rules of play are softened or abridged by unspoken agreement. But as a stranger or newcomer you should not be the one to relax the rules for your own play. You should not only know the rules in order to avoid the unintentional infraction that looks like cheating; you should also be the first to enforce them on yourself. When your golf host says, "Oh take a

117

Mulligan," or when your tennis opponent says, "Let's play that over," that's one thing. When the stranger, the benefactor of such a rules-change, assumes the privilege, that's little better than polite cheating.

win and lose with equal grace

This is part of the ideal, "to love the game more than the prize," but it can be overdone in both directions.

The winner who disparages his triumph can be almost as large a pain as the winner who lords it over his fallen opponent; he adds insult to injury if he implies that he did not deserve to win. The loser who is too hearty is as bad as the loser who is too gloomy; he has to care a *little* or he makes it appear that the game was not worth the winning. The idea is to consider the other person's feelings. A safe pattern is to talk about the game rather than the outcome.

In the conventional exchange of remarks at game's end, the good loser compliments the winner on his *skill* and the good winner sympathizes with the loser on his *luck*.

The responsibility for grace continues on into post mortems, too. That's why you make it easier for winner and loser alike if, as a non-participant, you ask, "Did you have a good game?" instead of, bluntly, "Who won?"

Incidentally, if you have occasion to play less than your best—in order to even the contest or "let" someone else win —it is vital not to let this fact be known, either by being obvious about it or by speaking of it. Winner and loser must always have played their best.

play the game—don't talk it

You don't have to be grim-serious about the thing except with other players who are. But even the most casual of sportsmen is griped by these conversational sins:

118

1. MOANINGS AND GROANINGS. As Sophocles put it:

A wise gamester ought to take the dice
Even as they fall, and pay down quietly
Rather than grumble at his luck

2. APOLOGIES. If you're off your game and are worried for fear you're spoiling the others' fun, you'll only make it worse by talking about it. If your game is just naturally terrible, you'll have warned your companions in advance; it's their own fault if they refused to believe the truth. So just do the best you can, *quietly*.

3. EXCUSES. Okay, so you've brought the wrong glasses or there's a blister on your heel or your head throbs every time you hit the ball. If your malady is as bad as repeated excuses will make it sound, you ought to stop playing; if it's not, shut up about it. And that means *after* the game, too. Who wants to have won or lost to a basket case?

4. TOO MUCH CHITCHAT. A little conversation not related to the game is perfectly all right in most instances, at least when you are not engaged in active play. But a chatterbox is a nuisance, and not always clad in skirts. Remember that there are serious players who like to keep their minds on the game even between shots, and that a little quiet is half the point of some sports. When in doubt, let the other guy initiate the conversation.

5. UNASKED-FOR ADVICE. With a few exceptions, noted under the sports to which they apply, you should let the other man play his own game and make his own mistakes unless he is persistent in his request for instruction from you.

play it straight

Show respect for the sport, its equipment and its playing ground. A lack of the proper respect is evidenced in assorted ways, a lot of them more sutble than blatant destructiveness. Take the matter of language, for instance: the stranger who

119

calls his tennis racket a "bat" or his golf ball a "pill" may be judged to be laughing at the games even if he is not. And a sailboat man who refers to his host's power-cruiser as a "stinkpot" certainly *is* expressing a superior attitude toward motor-boating. Use the correct or "polite" terminology, at least until you're well-enough established to rate using slang.

What you wear is governed by much the same principle. Once you're accepted, and once your proficiency in the sport is recognized, it may be possible to deviate from the norm in your clothing. But when you're new, it's always best to dress up to the customs of the service. That's why the clothes suggested under the various sports are on the conservative side; they're safe, conventional and inconspicuous— all good adjectives to hide behind when you're on trial.

Clowning, even when indulged as a cover for a poor game, is taken as a sure sign that you think the game is as foolish as your behavior. The game is supposed to be worth *trying* to play. If all the trying in the world won't help you, then the least you can do is avoid distracting others with your "cute" antics.

gamblers: put up—and shut up

Pay your gambling debts immediately, on the spot, whether or not the winner protests—and pay them as if they were of no financial consequence, even if it kills you. The stakes (or lack of them) are always supposed to be a matter of complete indifference—way down on the list of reasons why the game is played. Thus there is no admitted stigma attached to saying you'd rather not play for money—except, of course, in games like poker which no one but a woman ever plays "just for fun." But once you've agreed to a bet you must honor it at all costs.

If you find you have lost more than you have in the bank, go ahead and write a check anyway. It will take two or three days for the check to bounce, which will give you plenty of time to solve the problem in the only graceful and gentlemanly way possible: by shooting yourself.

CLUB ETIQUETTE

AS A MEMBER

As a member of a sports or country club, you'll get by nicely with a modicum of attention to the by-laws, the ground rules and ordinary good manners. Clubs differ greatly in their standards of dress and formality, so you need have no qualms about asking the manager or an older member "how it's done here" whenever you're in doubt about procedure. He will not think you a virgin to all clubs (even if you are) simply because you are new to that one; he will like your wanting to conform to the local practice.

About the only trouble you could get into at a club—apart from the obvious man-trap of not paying your bills promptly —would be to act, there, precisely as you would in your own house. That's *supposed* to be the idea to be sure—your club is your second home—but woe to the man who acts as though he owns the place. Your guests have to pass muster with the other members, so it is not enough that *you* like them; the course usually recommended is to invite only those who could be members themselves. And your own behavior is bound to be judged a little more critically than by your family: save your rousing drunks for the home fireside.

AS A WOULD-BE MEMBER

As a would-be member, what you're supposed to do is nothing. You might drop a hint or two, to a member you know very well, that you'd like to join. But except in municipal "clubs" open to everyone, you must not *ask* to be put up for membership. You have to be invited to join. The usual practice is for one member to propose you, another member or two to second the proposal, the board to interview you and the membership as a whole to vote on you—not a gantlet you'd care to run without prior assurance that you were going to make it (nor without the certain knowledge that you can afford it!). If you are ever turned down after such a procedure, you are supposed to accept whatever flimsy excuse you are given without cross-examining your sponsor.

AS A GUEST

As a guest, the first requirement is that you be invited by a member. Since you can't possibly know the rules and charges governing such invitations, you should *never* invite yourself—not even indirectly, and not even though you expect to repay the member whatever your visit costs him. That ought to go without saying, but almost every summer week-end around New York proves that it does not.

Once there as a guest, the conditioning fact is that *your host is responsible for you*—for your behavior *and* your expenses. In most clubs, almost all purchases and transactions are by bill; no cash is in evidence. If a guest is going to pay for anything, he has to pay his host, the member. This is an awkward thing to attempt, in most circumstances, so the no-cash situation only underlines the rules against a guest's ordering or acting on his own. When a guest is floating around without his host—when he's waiting for the host's yacht or foursome to come in, say—he should consider himself helpless unless his host has specifically told him to order a drink or whatever while waiting. In the latter case, the guest may have to sign a check; he should sign the member's name, with his own name or initials in parentheses below so that the record will be clear.

One time when a guest should take pains to pay his own bills is when he has been given, at his nominal host's behest, a *temporary membership card* or a week-long guest card and is thus entitled to come and go as he pleases. Perhaps he lives at the club for the appointed period, taking all his meals there. In such a case, he usually arranges with the manager to sign his own name to chits and to pay them all, as he would a hotel bill, when he leaves. If this is not possible, he keeps a running tab on such bills and sends a prompt check to his "host." He should still, however, remember that he is a guest, in name if not in purse, and if he wishes to entertain his host he had best do it outside the host's own club. (Incidentally, all that applies to town as well as country clubs.)

C L O T H E S

At most clubs, the clothes you wear for active sports are not good enough for the club dining or lounging rooms. Sports jackets and ties are usually required in certain parts of the clubhouse. It will be easy enough for you to find out the ground rules at your particular club—or to provide for a necessary change at your host's club—so the only point here is to emphasize that a rule is a rule, with no personal reflections intended. The member who flouts his club's custom, or makes a scene when he's reminded of it, goes down on the boor list just as certainly as the guest who forces his host to scurry about in search of an extra tie or a pair of spikeless moccasins.

T I P P I N G

As a general rule, club tipping is confined to those who are paid in cash and those who perform personal services above and beyond the call of club duty. Sports professionals are rarely given tips, as such.

In a club where cash is almost never seen, where checks are signed and bills submitted by the month, tips are handled in one of two ways, or both: 1) there is a percented service charge, and 2) there is a Christmas fund to which members contribute. But even in such clubs, where the member can be sure that waiters and barmen and the like are being amply rewarded, regular or occasional tips are sometimes called for in the locker room or its equivalent.

You'll have to scout a bit to see what gives in your particular club. The manager is a good, impersonal source of accurate information. This is only to warn you that the no-tipping-in-clubs rule is not universal, and to suggest that a guest (who won't be around when Santa Claus collects) be particularly alert for opportunities to say "thank you" to club personnel when he has caused them extra trouble.

GOLF

Most golfers agree that the two cardinal sins against their game are:

1. Slow play, or delaying their game
2. Abuse of the course

WHAT THE RULES MEAN

But a great many subtleties are involved. More helpful than the official rules of other sports is the United States Golf Association's booklet, *The Rules of Golf* (25 cents at any golf shop). With the USGA's permission, we here reprint their nine official rules of etiquette; and with the pet peeves of our experts fresh in mind, we footnote those rules to point up the fine points.

1. *"No one should move, talk or stand close to or directly behind the ball or the hole when a player is addressing the ball or making a stroke."*

The best place to stand when someone else is shooting is directly opposite and facing him, at least ten feet away from the ball. Not so good with a fussy player (who might be annoyed at not being able to *see* that you're still), but safe enough if you are out of sight and out of conking range, is straight behind him. Of the two worst places—in the line of the ball's flight ahead or in the line of the player's sight behind—it's hard to say which is the greater ground for mayhem.

Often on the fairway, to avoid delaying the game if your own ball is a long walk off, you may continue on in the direction of your ball while the other player selects a club and lines up his shot. But the minute he gets ready to address the ball, you must stop stock-still—and you should be sure that, at that moment, there is at least a 45 degree angle between you and the ball's expected flight. On or around the green—where your walk cannot be long and where his shot is bound to be delicate—you should make a point of getting into the preferred position opposite him.

Wherever you are, any sound or motion that comes out of you is unforgivable—sneezes, match-strikings and "inadvertent" club-rattlings included.

2. *"The player who has the honor should be allowed to play before his opponent or fellow-competitor tees his ball."*

It's well to have your ball-washing and club-picking all done in advance, so that when it's your turn you can simply step up, tee your ball and drive. But you must not tee up until it's your turn.

On the first tee, there is no "honor"—that is, no order of precedence—except that ladies and guests are often motioned ahead by the host. Thereafter, it's the winner of the previous hole who drives first. Partners who have won the honor as a team usually drive in a consistent order so as not to "change the luck." Maybe one partner drives first on the front nine, the other on the back nine—but it doesn't matter unless it gets into a foolish, "you-first-Alphonse" kind of thing.

On the course, the one whose ball is farthest from the hole shoots first, even if (oh, horrible thought) that makes his tenth consecutive shot.

3. *"No player should play until the players in front are out of range."*

. . . And when you have a blind shot—that is, when you can't see if there are other players over that hill or around the dog-leg—you should send your caddie ahead to signal when the way is clear.

There is only one time when you ever drive before the players ahead have taken their second shots and walked out beyond the longest drive you could imagine hitting. That's when you've been invited to "go through."

The rules give an order of precedence for matches; etiquette and common sense tell you that the nice thing is for any slower playing group, of whatever size, to let any faster group pass them on the course—*if the hole ahead is clear.* (There's no sense in letting those behind you through if they will then only be crowding the next group as they have been crowding you.)

Letting others through is most conveniently (and most safely) done on the tee; but often those ahead will signal from the fairway, then walk over into the rough while the next match shoots through.

It should not be necessary for the speedy whizzes to *ask* to go through. The only time it would be forgivable would be when painfully slow players who obviously didn't know the score were playing to empty greens. In such a case, you might ask, "Do you mind if we go through?", adding your reason for hurry. (A burning house or dying wife is about right.) But then you'd darn well better play out of sight fast.

It is probably unnecessary to add that you say "thank you" to those who let you pass. To "You're welcome," they usually add something like "Take your time; we're in no hurry." They don't want to undo their good deed by undoing your good game with hurry.

4. *"In the interest of all, players should play without delay."*

There must be a special hell for golfers who take too many practice swings . . . who deliberate endlessly about the proper club to use and then, at the very last minute, change their minds and go through the whole process anew . . . who stop to pick mushrooms . . . who line up the simplest putt from every height and angle . . . who walk around the course as if they were in a funeral procession. But until they get their justice in another world, they're hell to play with in this one.

Play at an even pace comfortable to all the players, and be ruthless in eliminating from your game any mannerisms which tend to slow you on your appointed rounds.

One maneuver for speeding up the game, approved by many golfers (particularly when the course is crowded), is "picking up." Sometimes, in a social game, when you've completely blown up on a hole—when you can't possibly win that hole and when the final score is beside the point—it's permissible to pick up your ball. On the face of it, this would seem to be quitting—bad form in any sportsman's book—but in the circumstances it is often more considerate of your fellow- and following players than holing out by the rules. Whether you pick up or hole out in such a sad instance, you have to do it with grace—without embarrassing temper or apologies—and of course you can't later "estimate" your score on a hole you didn't play, for purposes of handicapping or nineteenth hole reviewing.

5. *"Players searching for a ball should allow other players coming up to pass them; they should signal to the players following them to pass, and should not continue their play until those players have passed and are out of range."*

That much for holding up others on the course, but remember that a long, drawn-out search holds up your own game, too. Five minutes is all the rules allow to look for any ball. You'll be forgiven if you look a little longer for one which you know to be in the rough, where you'd have a clear shot to the green, but if you insist on spending even five minutes splashing around in a swamp you'll be rightly unpopular. If your ball had certainly gone out of bounds, you wouldn't do any more looking than was possible on your normal walk to the green; you'd have hit a provisional ball, anyway, in accord with the rules. You might send your caddie back later to prowl around in the parking lot or wherever, but you wouldn't take yourself out of play to save the price of a ball at the cost of everyone else's time.

When a fellow-player's ball is lost, you and your caddie of course help him look for it, but you don't insist upon prolonging the search after he has decided that it's a lost cause.

6. *"Before leaving a bunker, a player should carefully fill up all holes made by him therein."*

This repairing is done with your foot, or with a club head, but the unwritten part of this rule is equally important: don't *make* a lot of holes in a sand trap. Enter and leave the trap from the lowest, flattest place; never walk up or down steep banks. Enter from the flat point closest to your ball; never walk through a trap or take any more steps than necessary in the sand. Walk lightly and flat-footed, so as not to make toe or heel depressions which will be harder to smooth out than flat footprints; never jump down into a trap. And go in alone; get your club from your caddie before stepping into the trap, or leave your bag on the grass outside the trap. It would take you all afternoon to clean up if you held a convention in the sand.

7. *"Through the green, a player should ensure that any turf cut or displaced by him is replaced at once and pressed down, and that, after the players have holed out, any damage to the putting green made by the ball or the player is carefully repaired."*

Probably the rankest dub would not think of turning his back on a fairway divot, but there's more to it than that. Practice swings on the tee dig up turf with spikes and club. Squatting on the green, weight on toes, depresses the putting surface, as does using your putter for a cane. Angry beatings on the ground with a club raise doubts about your self-control as well as about the grass. Throwing your bag down has little to recommend it; you ought never to take your bag onto the green, however gently you might set it down—leave it on the apron, instead. In short, try not to make unnecessary assaults on the course, and promptly repair those you do make.

8. *"Players should ensure that, when dropping bags or the flagstick, no damage is done to the putting green, and that neither they nor their caddies damage the hole by standing close to the hole or in handling the flagstick. The flagstick should be properly replaced in the hole before the players leave the putting green."*

A bit less obvious: don't walk on the green between any one's ball and the hole, lest your footsteps depress the green and deflect his putt. And never set foot within eighteen inches of the cup itself.

Also notice, here, that you are responsible for your caddie's conduct. There's a nice way to correct him: wave him away from whatever mistake he is making at the time, then later tell him in private why you did it. You may be able to get

129

away with being rude to your friends—but you're the worst kind of boor if you pick on your caddies. Even the poorest excuse for a caddie—the kind who really *is* responsible for your bad game—is supposed to be treated with courtesy and consideration.

9. *"When the result of a hole has been determined, players should immediately leave the putting green."*

That is, don't stand about on the green while you mark up the scorecard or discuss the hole. Walk off as soon as you've all holed out or picked up.

10. (*Unofficial*) A strange golf ball is not lost until it stops rolling!

A few more simple "don'ts" might be added:

Don't litter the course with ball-wrappings, broken tees, cigarette packages and whatnot. There's a basket on almost every tee, or a pocket at every hand.

Don't holler. Your friendly greeting to people coming up on the adjoining fairway may prove an annoying distraction to someone on an apparently distant green.

Don't veto the greenskeeper when you tee up. The teeing surface is staked out by markers, changed often for the protection of the turf. You must tee up between the markers or within two club lengths behind them—not off on some private tee of your own.

Don't concede putts to yourself. Always step up as if you were going to putt or—if you're in the line of another's putt—as if you were going to mark your ball. Wait for the other guy to say, "I'll give you that." As a rule, any putt that can be "given" can also be holed out. Except in match play, when the final score is of no consequence and sinking a long putt will not win the hole, few players concede putts over two feet. But most will give you a 15-incher automatically. Even so, assume nothing—putt it out unless invited

not to. And this means really putt it; if you knock at the
ball with the back of your putter and miss the putt, the
miss is on you.

If you're sharing a caddie, don't expect him to tote your entire sports arsenal. The minute you learn that you are to be
a victim of the necessary evil, caddying double, you should
start unloading your bag—removing at least the extra pair
of shoes, the practice balls and the copy of *War and Peace*
from its bulging pockets. If your bag is one of those super-
dreadnought leather jobs, your conscience might also impel
you to shed some of the fourteen clubs allowed you by the
rules—or switch to a light canvas bag for the day.

On the course, the double-caddie usually goes to the ball
with whoever will shoot first. The other player can either
pluck a choice of clubs from his own bag before the parting
of the ways or carry his bag himself. Only when his lie is admittedly unpredictable should he delay the game by waiting till the caddie has time to accompany him to his own
ball.

Don't be a bore about the score. Most golfers keep track of
their own and their fellows' scores automatically, without
a lot of audible counting and reviewing. Some don't even
need a scorecard to tell them how everybody stands. If you
are not so practiced, or if your strokes are so numerous as
to require an adding machine, just be as quick and quiet
about it as you can. One man will have fallen heir to the
scorecard—he's often the guest or stranger, because the
card's notes on yardage and ground rules are helpful to
him. On the walk from green to tee, he'll say, "Scores,
please" . . . or "You had a four, didn't you?" *That's* the
time to give your correct score—not stroke by stroke on the
hole itself, and not halfway down to the next green. If
you've really forgotten a stroke, and if the scorekeeper is
pretty sure your mistake is not deliberate, he'll give you a
gentle reminder. But only a genuine dub can get away with

recurrent mistakes. Anyone else will be scored as he calls 'em, and suspected accordingly.

Don't volunteer advice, unsolicited. The rules and human nature are agin you. If you know a course, however, and your guest does not, it's nice to point out the hazards and help the stranger estimate distances. The rules of golf don't approve but guests do if you say, for instance, "There's a creek over that hill, so we often take a two iron here and shoot short of it. A good drive may land you right in the drink."

Don't take a "Mulligan" or "lunch-ball"—even if the extra tee shot is common practice in your group—if others are waiting behind you on the course.

WHAT TO WEAR

In recent years, wildly patterned, open-necked, short-sleeved sport shirts and bright-hued slacks have turned up on the most proper of men and links. In some clubs, knee-length, tailored shorts are perfectly in order on the golf course (but some still prohibit shorts to men and some to women). Still, anywhere in the United States, the conservative dress for golf would be:

Shirt: Long-sleeved, opaque sport shirt or unstarched, button-down collar and button-cuff broadcloth shirt, in solid color or white, or in a very quiet design with a conventional color like blue or brown predominant. The shirt is usually worn open at the neck for play, with a wool or cotton knit tie, bow or four-in-hand, for club house meanderings. Silk scarves are on the effete side. Any kind of shirt should be tucked in, all around!

Trousers: Gray flannel and tan gabardine rank first. White linen or duck are all right in a resort atmosphere. The bright browns and blues are a tetch "daring"; the fashion-plate plaids and their brethren may be a handicap among strangers; and you can't get by with the trousers to your pin-stripe suit. Slacks are worn with belts, not suspenders, of course. And maybe you can find some place besides your pants pocket for those six extra golf balls.

Shoes: Regulation leather golf oxfords with spikes are the old standard but leather shoes with rough ribbed rubber soles are just as good. They're usually brown. Two-tone shoes and suedes are turning up more than they used to, but they're still in danger of looking corny—like pointed toes and fancy perforations and other deviations from the conventional blucher or moccasin-type shoe. Sneakers and crepe soles indicate that golf is not your game.

The two practical rules are: don't walk around the course in leather-soled shoes unless they are spiked, and don't walk on clubhouse rugs and floors (except in the locker room) in spikes.

Socks: Wool or heavy synthetic, as bright as you like. If they're black or thin or ribbed they'll be suspected of doubling at the office.

Extras: A pullover sweater, soft and light and of course roomy, comes in handy. Wear it outside your belt. A poplin windbreaker is good to have for rain or cold. It is not necessary to wear a hat, but if you do, see that it is not a city business hat. Snap brims in cotton or unbound felt are good, and visored caps are okay if they are not reminiscent of the city-editor's green eyeshade: see that the bill is not too long and pointed, and duck those isinglass insets if you can. Dark glasses are perfectly okay, so long as they are not those extreme models that belong on a motorcycle or a swishy beach. Golf gloves are a matter of choice and calluses—but when they cost so little it's foolish to "make" one from an old dress glove.

All in all, you don't want to look as though you're bound for a cocktail party or one of those gentlemen-of-leisure tableaux. Your clothes should be casual and functional. Nor do you want it to seem that you raided the storeroom for your leftover Army fatigues. Your clothes should be clean and pressed, and not pressed into service from another sport.

In the clubhouse, the same sort of clothes are appropriate for all but the fancy affair. You have only to change to a fresh shirt, add a tie and an odd jacket, slide into clean socks and moccasins, and you're fit to be dined.

MONEY MONEY MONEY

On principle, a guest at a country club should pay his own green fee and his own caddie. The fees are not inconsiderable. The host is doing quite enough when he extends the privileges of his membership to you and probably buys you drinks and lunch besides. More golfers would get to play more courses if every host could be sure that his guest would pay; and more guests *would* pay if they could be sure that they were expected to, or at least that their gesture would not make a scene or be interpreted as an affront by the guy what brung 'em.

The difficulty lies in the club "chit" system.

At a club where cash can be used, or where a non-member can pay directly for certain things, there is no great problem. When the member signs you in and reaches down for the $5 or whatever the green fee, you simply step up with the money as if it's the most natural thing in the world and the way you always do it. If he demurs, as he probably thinks he must at least once, you are insistent. You can advance an elegant theory or make a bum joke about how you're going to win it all back from him on the round, but no matter how you do it —even if you have to play the eccentric to get away with it— you must pay. Having won that encounter, you can expect no trouble when it comes time to pay off your caddie. You're on such firm ground by then that you can even ask your host how much it will be all right to give the boy as a tip.

At a club where the green fee appears on the member's monthly statement instead of in a cash transaction, there's no future in attacking the problem in the pro shop. If your host is not someone you know well enough to hand money to, before or after he signs you in, your move is to pay the caddie fees—his and yours both. Presuming a club where caddies are paid in cash, somewhere between the eighteenth green and the caddie shop, this is a simple maneuver. You merely get to the caddies fustest. Again, the conventional objection of your host is easily overriden by firmness. You can be good and firm because you know that he knows you're right.

Where even this method of evening up is closed to you, as in clubs where caddie fees are on the bill and tips are not allowed, you are pretty helpless until you get your host out of the club. You won't be able to buy a drink, either, so the best thing you can do is to play host at dinner off the premises. Or, if such a dreamy possibility is open to you, settle then and there on the day when he will come to play at *your* club. (And none of that call-you-sometime routine; it has to be clear to you both, for your mutual peace of mind, that you are determined to take some of the edge off the large fat bill he's going to get for this day of golf.)

When you're a guest-on-your own—a possibility in some clubs, where a member can write or telephone authorization for you without putting in an appearance himself—you pay as you go, if you can, or send the member a prompt check covering all things charged to him. You'll know exactly how much you've cost him, because you'll have had to sign chits with his name.

Between contemporaries or close friends, all this involves less footwork than it seems. The "host" may say, when first suggesting the day, "I thought we might get up a Dutch-treat foursome at my club"—or he may simply assume it. In that case, guests should make some air-clearing remark at the first opening—that is, at the first evidence of cost—something like, "We'll all chip in for this." And they should follow through, at parting, by pressing a large bill on the guy who has been signing the checks. (Unless you can really figure your share, it's a good maneuver to offer a bill much too large. The "host" can get credit for a balk simply by balking at the amount, and that makes it graceful for him to say how much is *not* too much.)

Apart from an even split of expenses, somebody usually likes to "buy a drink." Custom decrees that the loser (and/or the winner, in a money game) buy a round after the game. When the loser is a guest at a no-cash club, his course is determined by his relationship with the member-host. To a friend or contemporary, he can say something like, "I want to buy a drink. Is my money any good around here, or should I just pay you, instead?" Like "Have you stopped beating your wife?", a question so phrased offers little out to a host who thinks he must protest. When the member is older or richer or stranger, the guest might be more comfortable with a suggestion like, "Where can I exercise my loser's privilege and buy a drink? Could we stop at the Such-and-Such on the way back to town?" A genial host then has the option of telling the guest how he can buy a drink right there at the club, or of accepting the offered alternate.

There are exceptions to the rule that the guest *must* pull his own weight, but these are usually obvious. When you're an impecunious college student roped into a game with your girl's affluent father . . . when you're a client on the course with a kowtower on an expense account . . . when you're a junior clerk invited out by your paternal and rich boss . . . when you're a golf pro or some other such hot shot with whom it is an acknowledged honor to play . . . or when you are obviously being repaid, this day, for a lot of prior hosting on your own part . . . of course you just relax and watch the bills roll by. But remember that your host's senior years or bucks are not enough, of themselves, to remove the necessity for your firm gesture. The relationship, the form of the invitation, the *sub rosa* purpose of the game all tip you off. When in doubt, try to pay. When there's not the slightest doubt, insist on paying.

Tips pose another money problem for guests, especially in clubs where guests can't be expected to know the rules and policies which govern the members. A safe rule is to give the boy in the locker room $1, even if your member-host does not. A club member probably gives the locker room attendant one or two dollars a month for his services—cleaning his shoes, sending his clothes out to be pressed, telephoning the starter to reserve a tee-off spot, being there with the extra towel, etc. A guest pays higher, then, for a lesser service—but a folded dollar bill is the least he can tender.

Caddie tips, where they are allowed, vary, but a safe minimum is 25 cents for a caddie-fee under $2, 50 cents for a fee over $2. When they have shared a caddie, both players tip as if for individual caddies. In tournaments it is customary to tip at a much higher rate; in the semi-finals or finals, even at your own club, two and one half times the regular caddie fee would not be over-generous. In a national tournament, you probably wouldn't tip any less than $5 a round, even in the early rounds.

Golf pros are not usually tipped. They may have been in the "servant class" in England, but over here they're social equals—and golf superiors! They expect you to pay no more than their fixed fee for lessons, their caddies' fees when they play with you. (But they don't mind winning your money—more than you'd usually bet—in play!) If you know your pro well enough, you might buy him a drink and send him a book or a bottle at Christmas-time. The one sure way to lose your face and his faith—as sure a way as "stiffing" a tippable person

—is to buy your golf equipment at a bargain basement instead of at the club pro shop. (And don't think he won't *know;* he sees your clubs more often than you do.) If it really riles you to pay his high prices, think of the extra expense as the tip you would otherwise be giving him.

The caddie master is not tipped. As one veteran put it, "When it's raining gold pieces, he doesn't even get damp."

If the assistant pro is more of a starter and a club-cleaner, he may get an occasional buck from members but he's no concern of guests. A parking lot attendant might be tipped now and then by a member; the usual quarter would be ample for a guest unattended by a member. Other club personnel are tipped only in cash clubs; there, they expect to be tipped by whoever pays the bills they tender, at rates which parallel top-hotel tipping.

Golf bets are pretty casual things—the most popular form being the $1 Nassau ($1 on the first nine, $1 on the second nine and $1 on the eighteen). As such, they are more flexible than, say, card-game stakes. The man who's up at the ninth may very well offer to give the other an "extra" on the second nine; the loser at the halfway mark might even *ask* for such an extra bet so he could even up if he won the back nine. Neither move is necessary, of course, but neither is a sign of a poor sport.

When your handicap is involved in fixing a bet, it's not fair to exaggerate your game in either direction. If you haven't an official and valid handicap, the safe thing is to give your last score, or your best and worst recent scores, along with an honest estimate of what you consider your usual game. Never mind the editorializing: everyone knows this course is strange to you and no one cares that you had a hard night last night.

PLAYING WITH A LADY

. . . let your gallantries be in inverse ratio to her golf skill. Unless she's a dub, and doesn't care who knows it, she doesn't want you to be her caddie or her pro or her judge. You might wash a ball for her now and then, and you would automatically help her across a ravine or let her precede you across a bridge. If you were both caddieless, you'd carry her bag sometimes—but only when you were going her way and when you felt like it. You'd let her drive first off the first tee, and you might let a woman partner drive before you on every hole, but you wouldn't make a Thing of it. If she were using the ladies' tees out in front of your tees, for instance, you'd naturally shoot first and then walk to her tee with her.

By and large, a woman is just another golfer. You owe her as much courtesy and respect as you owe a fellow-male, but very little more.

IN THE GALLERY

The etiquette of golf applies to non-participants as well as to golfers, so when you're merely walking around take care to be quiet, to stand out of the golfer's line of sight, and so on. Your consideration for the players should be matched by consideration for the course: stay out of traps and off greens, no matter how well you're shod . . . don't *run* with the trampling herd on the fairways . . . and don't litter the course with papers.

Comparable consideration for your fellow-spectators tells you to kneel when you're in the front row of the gallery. The ropes and marshals will usually dictate your other movements, and determine whether or not you may use the clubhouse.

But perhaps one more word is in order: a golf tournament is not a baseball game. Your cheers should be confined to mild applause—and then only when the noise will not distract another player. Your jeers should be strictly secret. And your nearness to the golfers does not give you license to strike up a conversation.

AFTER THE GAME

Try not to be one of those golf bores who give the cartoonists so much fun—and golfers so much agony. A certain amount of post-morteming can't be helped, may even be enjoyable, but watch out for the three biggest traps of the nineteenth hole:

Your yen to play the whole 18 over again, stroke by stroke. The recitation is no less unforgivable when directed at a fellow-player. He has a built-in defense—he can play *his* game right back at you—but he doesn't like it any better than the innocent bystander who hadn't the privilege of seeing you in action.

Your wails about what might have been. The first time you hear yourself saying, "If I'da . . ." say "Excuse me," instead, and send yourself off to the showers.

Your natural inclination to exaggerate—the length of the putt you made, the shortness of the putt you missed, the angle of your lie on number seven, *anything*.

And you'll stay in bounds better if you stay out of your cups, but then that's *another* sport!

TENNIS

Tennis, anyone will tell you, is quite a proper game. Perhaps because the tennis court is a goldfish bowl . . . perhaps because tennis-philes consider the sport a crucible of character

140

. . . or maybe only because no one can play tennis *alone,* your manners matter.

WHAT TO WEAR

Your manners begin with what you wear, the most obvious evidence of your respect for the sport and its environs. Although "natural" or "sand" or "off-white" are almost as correct in anything but tournament play, white—from top to toe—is traditional. And it must be *clean* white.

Your shirt may be a white cotton-knit T-shirt or a white sport shirt, usually short-sleeved or with sleeves turned up and always tie-less. An old sleeveless undershirt won't do.

Shorts and slacks are equally acceptable, but shorts should be of the tailored, knee-length variety known as Bermuda or walking shorts. Nothing is quite so eyebrow-raising as a pair of short and shiny basketball shorts—unless it be those form-fitting swim trunks (which oughtn't to appear on beaches, either). Trousers are usually of white duck or linen or flannel, preferably not resembling seersucker as a result of lying in a heap on your locker floor. The shorts probably have a self-belt; a plain white belt is better than a "novelty" belt on the trousers.

Your shoes, perhaps the most important of all, should be white from top to bottom—white, oxford-type sneakers with white soles. Watch out for those edged soles that will damage the court, and unless you're an orthopedic case stay away from high shoes. P.S. *Clean* your tennis shoes once in a while!

Clean white sweat socks are the norm. Those knee-length, cable-stitched jobs are better saved for your dress shorts.

Once the game is over, gray flannels and a tweed jacket will take you anywhere. Add a tie and you'll be dressed for all but the formal affair. Moccasins are preferred but sneakers are all right to wear off the courts. Shorts, when dressed up with a jacket, are as good as slacks. On the average club porch, over an after-game drink, the jacket is not necessary—but a shower and a dry shirt usually are.

THE SPORTING GESTURE

On a par with clothes as a criterion is the Sporting Gesture. The afternoon's pleasure of your opponent, your partner and sometimes the players in the next court can depend on your approach to the game, as expressed in the "little things." Here are some pointers to bolster your general feeling for sportsmanship.

1. *When the game begins,* the question of who is to serve first and from which side of the court is usually determined by flipping a racket. Someone calls for the rough or the smooth side, and if it falls your way you choose either court or service. Nobody expects you to give yourself the worst of it. But if the game has a more casual beginning, take care that you do not accept both the first serve *and* the best court. If you've been invited to serve first (and you should never just *assume* that privilege), walk automatically to the court where the sun will be in your eyes or whatever.

2. *By the rules, you change courts after the odd games—* 1, 3, 5, *etc.* So no pouting when your opponent walks over to take the court you've just got used to, and no protesting when he comes to take the sun in *his* eyes for a while. Politeness doesn't enter in, here.

3. *As you stand ready to serve, there's no point in calling out, "Are you ready?"* You can *see* if he's ready or not, and the formalized exchange has therefore come to be in a joke-class with that other inquiry, "Tennis, anyone?" If by ill chance you serve to someone who, it turns out by his action, was *not* ready, you add insult to injury if you then ask, "Weren't you ready?" If he was so far from ready that it's obvious to all, you may simply say, "Sorry—send that back and

we'll start over"—leaving no room for argument. Or you might just make it easy for him to win the *next* point—without making a speech about it. But the best way of all, of course, is to look before you serve.

4. *Your first serve,* in a social game with a person whose game is of unknown quality, ought not to be burned in. Save your aces for someone who shows, in the first rally, that he's got a good chance of returning some of them. The idea is not to be patronizing—only to have a game with an opponent instead of an exhibition with a ball-chaser at the other end.

5. *When the first ball* served to you is out, *don't* hit it back. Let it go by and stand ready for the next, lest your bat at the ball be interpreted as a real try or—more likely—lest you break the rhythm of the other guy's serve. If it is necessary to roll a faulted ball out from under foot, do it as quickly as possible.

6. *You are the linesman* for all balls hit into your court, but it is stupid and annoying to holler "good" or "out" after every shot. Your opponent can see all but the close ones as well as you can. Play the good ones; let the obvious outs go by; call only the close ones.

Similarly, you can tell from your opponent's attitude or obvious assumption whether your own ball was good or not. You can't question his decisions (unless he calls 'em in your favor and you know better). If he's blind or dishonest, the best you can do is avoid playing with him again.

The "let's play-it-over" routine involves a lot of backing and filling and should be resorted to only when both players are honestly in doubt. When a rally has obviously been ruined by some outside force—as, for instance, when a ball from another court bounds in to interrupt your play—you "play a let" almost automatically. Otherwise, it's simpler to give the other fellow the benefit of any doubt.

7. *Annoying to all* but once-a-season players is another verbal mannerism—that of calling out the score after every

point. It's particularly irritating when, as usually happens, it's the winner who makes such broadcasts. Anyone who plays tennis can keep score without a lot of public announcements to help him. If an occasional progress report is necessary, let it be given by the guy who is trailing.

8. *Don't call an opponent on a foot-fault.* What's the difference, anyway?

9. *When returning balls to the server,* after a point has been scored, remember two things: he needs and wants all three balls in his hand when he serves . . . and he doesn't want to have to chase after them. Collect all balls on your side of the net after the point, and return them one at a time but in series. If one of the needed balls is on another court, don't ask for it until the other players have finished their current rally (and don't return their balls to them when they're in mid-point, either). Don't chase after a wayward ball if your path will cross the line of sight of neighbors in play.

The best way to return balls, unless you can throw accurately, is to *roll* them back.

10. *In the absence of definite club rules* which take the responsibility off your shoulders, playing tennis while others are waiting to use the courts can be an uncomfortable business. The ultra-polite finish their current set of singles, then invite a pair of the late-comers to join them in doubles—or finish their doubles match and then retire. Those who are more conscious of their own rights and less nervous about the gallery play three sets, at the most, then either quit the courts or break up their own combination to admit some of the others. A minimum obligation is to play, not just bat the ball back and forth, when others are waiting.

They also serve who only sit and wait. They shouldn't ask to break into a going game, at least not until it is apparent that the others intend to play until sundown no matter what. They should decline offers to join in a game if they are not up to the kind of tennis they've been watching; tennis is a game which sinks to the level of the poorest player. And while they're waiting they should sit still and be quiet.

11. *Relative quiet is a pretty good rule for players, as well.* Gay conversation is strained when shouted from one end of a tennis court to the other, and one-word comments in the "whee" or "sob" class are best swallowed. Once in a while a compliment for a particularly good shot is all right, but if you remark on *every* play you'll bore your opponent and distract your neighbors. Many a tennis player wishes that the words, "too bad, old man," could be expurgated from the language, so rejoice if that English-film-type of sporting talk does not flow off your tongue.

P.S. It's easier, but no better, to talk to the players at your end of adjoining courts. Each court is, or should be, an island unto itself. Don't go on the make for the girl in the next court . . . don't assume that you can get chummy with strangers simply because they're playing alongside. Just play tennis in a friendly kind of way and let it go at that.

12. *Billy Talbert, the best doubles player* in America, says, "Playing doubles is an art. With players of equal skill who understand each other, it can also be a pleasure." Which ought to point up the fallacy in the popular presumption that doubles is "easier" than singles. Skill aside, it takes a lot more diplomacy; you have to keep your partner happy.

One good way to make him unhappy is to hog the shots. If you're not accustomed to playing with each other, it can't do any harm to say, in the beginning, what area you expect each of you will cover. Done nicely, almost tentatively, this pre-game conversation is as much in order as the bridge-players' prior huddle on systems.

Even so, there'll be times when you run for a ball you later realize should have been returned by your partner, or vice versa. Keep the remarks at a minimum; your attitude and re-form will be forgiveness or apology enough. If you discover that your partner is wont to stand in the middle of the net when you serve or has some other such annoying mannerism, you may suggest a place you like better, or not, depending on how well you can pull it off. But probably the best way to play doubles is just to relax if you're underpartnered, ask advice if you're overpartnered.

13. *When playing with a woman*, follow the "ladies first" routine in changing courts; hand her balls and towels and drinks of water and so on. More important, at least if you want a contest, is to adapt your game to hers: play the kind of tennis she can keep up with. When your doubles partner is a woman, you will usually take the more active court—the left, that is, if her backhand is weaker than yours. But be careful not to hog the shots when they're clearly hers, any more than you would with a man. When one of your doubles opponents is a woman, it's unsporting to concentrate on her if she's the weaker player. Don't avoid hitting her way, of course—that's no fun for her—but don't pick on her, either.

THE GUEST

The guest at a tennis club makes no effort to pay for anything, but he should be sure to supply his own racket and it's nice to take at least three new balls to any tennis date. (And don't expect to take them back home with you!) Tournament players want new balls for each new set, at least; everyday players should throw in new balls as often as necessary to maintain the weight and surface.

For extra service from the club's locker room attendant, a guest might tender a dollar's tip, as inconspicuously as possible. If he were the guest of the club rather than of a particular member—for tournament play, say—he would tip the locker room boy $5 or maybe $10 for a week of superservice. But that is the only tipping situation at a tennis club, and the guest of a member is a guest all the way.

He should arrive with his necessaries compactly packed in

a duffle bag or its equivalent, and he should leave everything but what he will need on the court in his locker or in the club safe. Loose change, watches and superfluous stuff left on court benches are a nuisance.

The guest at a private tennis court has an extra obligation —to be on the alert for ways in which he can help care for the court. A lot of rolling, raking, lining and weeding is involved in the upkeep of a court. Unless the host is obviously well staffed with caretakers, a guest should not expect to play and run. Much of the work must be done immediately *before* play, so it's a good idea to arrive early and pitch in, as well as to volunteer your help after the game.

THE SPECTATOR

The spectator at a casual, social match should stay out of it. Except on invitation, he is not welcomed as linesman, referee or commentator.

The spectator at a tournament will save his neck if he sits at one end or the other of the court he wants to watch. He'll save his face if he sits *still,* not jumping up and down as at a football game and not walking around during play no matter how hungry he is for a hot dog. His movements may distract the players as well as his fellow-spectators.

He is supposed to applaud only good shots, never errors. That is, if his favorite aces his rival, a decorous handclap is in order, but if the rival falls on his face or hits a ball out of the court, silence is requested. In any case, applause should be saved for the times between points, not let loose during actual play.

YACHTING

SAILING

There are three basic ways to assure that you will never be invited back aboard a sailboat:

1. To wear hard-soled shoes or otherwise threaten damage to carefully kept decks.
2. To be a sloppy strewer, in this world where neatness is a necessity and space is at a premium.
3. To get in the way—or to *make* work, as by falling overboard.

Thus, most of the following tips are designed to prevent your tripping up in those general areas.

try this for size

Suppose you are invited for an afternoon's sail or a cruise on a yacht. (Her owner will doubtless refer to her as a "boat," though strictly speaking a "boat" is a craft which is carried aboard a ship. A privately owned craft—either sail, power or steam—is correctly, if a bit pompously, called a "yacht.") The first, best thing you can find out—if you can do it without blurting out a direction question—is the size of the boat.

On a "yachty" boat—one of those 60-foot jobs with a paid crew and almost ocean-liner accommodations—you won't lift a finger except to encircle a glass, so your clothes are to look at instead of to work in. They're on the dressy side of country clothes: white flannels with blue coat and tie, gray flannels with tweed jacket, or long, tailored shorts, with coat and tie, such as you might wear to a cocktail party. If you were going only for lunch at anchor, with no sailing involved, you could go straight from the office and not be uncomfortable. If you were going for a cruise, you'd take evening clothes, spruce-up

148

stuff to wear ashore and almost as many clothes as if you were boarding the *Queen of Bermuda*. For any overnight trip you'd take (or later send) a "house present" to the boat. You'd be formally correct with the hands. You'd be careful not to invade the engine room and crew's quarters without invitation, and not to usurp the owner's chairs—those on the starboard side of the quarter-deck and on the starboard bridge wing. When you said your farewells you'd tip the stewards and cook as you would the servants in a comparable private house (see page 387).

But yachts under 50 feet in length, and yachts without a professional captain and crew, put you in another boat altogether. You're going to *work*. Even if you are the rankest of rank landlubbers, the captain will have a ready answer to the question you *must* ask, "What can I do to help?" If you can't be trusted with anything else, you'll draw the jobs requiring beef or the spit-and-polish detail. Therefore, your clothes must be and look functional, indestructible and many dunkings removed from the yachting department of the sporting goods store.

gear for "small" boats

To wear: T-shirts or cotton shirts open at the neck . . . slacks or knee-length shorts in duck, denim, khaki or some such material which can't be hurt by a soaking . . . wool sweat socks . . . white-soled sneakers not so worn that they're slick on the bottom (for safety's sake) or, best, a kind of canvas-topped, rubber-soled shoe called "Topsiders"; they have a special tread to give you traction on wet decks. Crepe soles will pass, but you must never set foot on a painted or varnished deck wearing leather soles or hard-rubber heels. . . . If you want a head covering, make it a seaman's hat, a billed fisherman's cap, a beret (if you can get away with it) or a narrow-brimmed cotton hat. Four nevers for your hat: it should never blow off; it should never be a hard hat of any description; and it should never never be an imitation of the emblemed yachtsman's cap which only yacht club members may wear. . . . The safest colors for sailboat wear are white, tan, gray and blue, but no one will criticize a plaid shirt and checked shorts if they look like they mean business.

To take: A change of the same kind of clothes in case you get doused . . . a warm sweater and/or a windbreaker for the night you get becalmed after the sun has gone down . . . bathing trunks if a swim is possible (and wear them under your pants if dressing room space is going to be nil) . . . raingear if you're going on a cruise: oilskins, waterproofed nylons, slickers and sou'westers, or rubber coats and pants . . . dark glasses and suntan oil if you're at all sensitive to glare (but *never* get sun oil on the deck!) . . . dramanine pills if there's any chance you'll whoops with the waves . . . your own toilet goods so you won't have to borrow . . . a watertight cigarette box if you want to smoke instead of chew . . . and, if you're likely to wind up in a yacht club, some coat-and-tie version of flannels; tailored shorts are less generally acceptable at night, except on British-influenced shores.

To pack in: A soft, collapsible bag. Hard luggage is as unwelcome on a boat as hard shoes, and storage space aboard is too limited for large suitcases. If you are off on an extended cruise, you can probably arrange to store suitcases at the home club.

for smooth sailing guests

Before taking off on a cruise, it's nice to ask what you may bring for the larder—or, better, if you think your host might protest too much and duck your blank question, volunteer something specific. "May I supply the beer? . . . or . . .

"Would a cold turkey be in the way? I've got one on order and hate to let it molder in my icebox." The point is that keeping a boat costs a lot of money, and sometimes the added supplies needed for guests can turn out to be the famous last straw. Still, it's better not to just show up with bulky purchases which may duplicate your host's provisions or strain the limited stowage space. Even an unheralded bottle of bourbon is not always a wise idea; the captain may not be that kind of a sailor. You should either ask or forewarn your host, unless you are so familiar with the boat and its captain's whims that you can safely trust your own judgment.

If you want to send a thank-you present—a good idea, at least after an extended trip—it's best to send it later, after you've seen what the boat needs and has room for. *One* hand-tooled log goes a long, long way.

Chances are you'll meet your host on his boat or at his club. If you know enough about sailing to be useful, get there a little early so you can help ready the boat.

If you are expected to get out to a mooring on your own, you'll probably find that the club launch is alerted to take you out to the boat. You do not tip the club launchman.

If the boat is alongside a dock and you have only to step aboard, one warning: don't set foot on the boat until you have been greeted and invited aboard by your host. That is, if he's not in sight, call out to him or wait until he comes to greet you. (Incidentally, if the boat is flying a little square blue flag the owner is not aboard.) If you are going aboard at the same time as your host and the other members of the party, it might help to know that the captain is supposed to go first, with the others following in order of "seniority." (In leaving the boat, custom decrees reverse order: juniors first, captain last.) But a man may precede a woman in order to help her.

Once aboard, you'll be shown a locker or wherever the owner wants you to keep your gear—and there your stuff must

151

stay. Never leave your shaving things in the head, your extra sweater lying about, your possessions of any description in the cockpit.

Don't disarrange the ship's gear, either; you'll soon note that there's a place for everything. If you use a can opener, rinse out a glass, peer through the binoculars—put them back where they came from and are supposed to be stowed.

Your neatness should cover the water around you as well as the boat. Before you throw a beer can overboard, punch holes in both ends so it will sink. If the item you want to dispose of won't sink, don't throw it in the drink in any harbor. And whatever you cast into the sea, throw away from, not into, the wind.

Cigarettes pose a problem of safety as well as neatness. Watch out for the ashes that blow into someone else's face or—worse—into sails made of synthetic and highly combustible materials. On racing and sailing boats, you never smoke when stopping light sails or when furling sails. Take your cue from the captain on when and where you may smoke, then do it with a little more thought than is normally required on land.

The owner and captain is the absolute master aboard his boat. However he may disguise his orders as suggestions, they are *orders,* to be followed immediately. The more polite he is, the more considerate of your inexperience, the more alert you'll have to be to his wishes. And if he seems *not* polite— if he tells you to get the hell below during some difficult maneuvers, or if he won't let you do anything more than stick your rear end out over the weather rail—don't take it to heart. He's responsible for the safety of boat and passengers, and often there's little time for the amenities.

For similar reasons, you shouldn't engage him in conversation when he's busy—and remember that he doesn't have to *look* busy to be mulling over an important decision. Let him start the small talk, suggest the Cook's tour, offer to let you take the tiller, indicate when it's convenient and safe to break out the beer. (Control yourself; he may belong to the "no drinking till the hook is down" school.) Having let him know by your specific offers and your watchful waiting that you are interested, and ready to do whatever he asks, don't then pester him for lessons or lore. He'll be sociable when and if he can—but the option is his.

Sailors are apt to flinch when you call ladders "stairs," bulkheads "walls," the head "the can," the bow "the front of the boat," the galley "the kitchen," a bunk a "bed." The very least you should know is that a boat is a "she." You can learn the essential terms with a little attention—including that "Ready about" or "Hard alee" shout that means "Watch out or the boom will bean you!" It's better to be quiet, however, than to sprinkle your talk with a lot of terms which are obviously foreign to you—and it's always better to ask than to bluff.

Above all, don't hesitate to *ask* if you don't know how to operate the plumbing. The head takes a lot of hard pumping; it will *not* take foreign objects, so its lid ought to be kept closed against accidental invasions. Another good rule: be conservative in your use of fresh water. The faucets will probably be such that you couldn't let the water run if you wanted to—but let that be your cue to use the water sparingly.

If you swim off the boat, make a point of swimming *against* the current. You'd be surprised how quickly you can be swept away from the boat, and how annoyed the captain will be if he has to come after you. Particularly on a boat with a lot of varnish work, you should be careful not to drip all over it with your wet feet and suit. Take a towel to the rail *before* you dive in, then dry off in one spot when the swim is over. Don't, of course, dry your towel and suit by draping them over lines, rails or spars.

But probably the worst thing you could do would be to go for an *accidental* swim. As Arthur Knapp, Jr., author of *Race*

Your Boat Right, put it, "Anyone who falls overboard during a race deserves to have his head shrunk and mounted on the mast." Whether it ranks as a nuisance or a tragedy, an accidental dive is no more welcome a break in a non-racing, casual sail. The best preventive, next to proper footgear, is to follow the old sailing adage: "One hand for yourself and one for your ship." *HANG ON!*

When the boat has tied up once again, perish the thought that you can say thank you and goodbye. Usually, the deck has to be washed with fresh water and the bright work wiped down with a chamois . . . the salt has to be polished off the brass . . . the sails have to be furled and made ready for the next day or perhaps carried ashore. Even if there is a paid hand, the good guest sticks around and does his share of such work.

If you sail with the same skipper often during one season, and hope to be invited out again, remember that sailing has its winter work, too. Save up your elbow grease for off-season week-ends—and don't be alarmed if your pleasant friend at sea turns out to be a martinet or a fussbudget in the boat yard. He's still the captain, and he knows exactly how he wants each detail handled.

POWER BOATING

Guestiquette on a motor cruiser differs from sailing etiquette only in dress and duties. Your guiding principles should still be neatness, deference to the captain, care of the boat and attention to safety. But if you're going out just for the ride, not for fishing, you might dress a little more respectably: you won't have any rough work to do, and there's less chance you'll be drenched by a wave.

The most help you can be to the captain will be to keep out of his way and refrain from dropping lighted cigarettes into the gas tanks. You'll have a sociable, drinkable afternoon —boring in the extreme to the sailor, idyllic for the guys who think sailing is more like work than sport.

HORSEBACK RIDING

If you are going to be around but not of the horsy set, you will need only: casual country clothes . . . polite respect for the sport . . . and an alert awareness of the nature of the horse.

On the latter score, you should know that a slow kind of quiet is the first requirement for visitors to a stable. Even the steadiest of horses can be frightened by sudden motions and strange noises. You should never raise your arms abruptly in front of a horse; behind him, it's well to say "steady" or something equally soothing, so as not to startle him. Don't surprise him, ever, or he may surprise you even more.

If you're going to ride as well as admire, you must know a good deal more. First, of course, how to ride—and the best way to learn that is from a qualified professional or a patient amateur, not from your host or his groom on a country weekend.

But let's assume that you are a proficient rider. You can get along with horses just fine; all you need is a few pointers on how to get along with horsy people. Here's how:

CLOTHES

Out of respect for the sport and the other riders, dress correctly.

Riding is tradition-ridden; the restrictions and refinements on riding clothes are so conventional, so divorced from "fashion," that they have changed little in the last hundred years. You can be sure that this world has not been breathlessly waiting for you to show it how to be "different."

The correct dress for *informal* riding in an English or flat saddle must be chosen, then, from this limited list:

Brown leather boots. With regular riding breeches, you may wear riding boots, field boots (a kind of boot which laces over the instep) or puttees and ankle shoes. With jodhpurs, a kind of breeches which extend down to the ankle, you wear jodhpur boots; they may lace or strap around the ankle, or have elastic gullets on their sides. Their tops should be worn *under* the jodhpurs.

Regular riding boots should be high on your leg, and they should *fit the calf*. Have ready-made boots cut down if they are too large in the leg.

All boots must be polished. Trees help them to look and last better.

Breeches or jodhpurs that fit, so closely in the leg that you can just bend the knee in the saddle, but full enough in the seat and crotch to prevent binding. The correct flare or "peg," a fullness along the outside seams from hip to four inches above the knee, is hard to describe—but horsemen can see deviations coming a mile away. The outside seam should *cross over* the upper leg above the knee, so the seam and buttons or laces run down just *inside* the kneecap.

Put yourself in the hands of a good tailor or clothier, one who wouldn't think of letting you wear breeches that wrinkled at the knee or—horror of horrors—buttoned on the outside of the leg.

Materials are circumscribed: whipcord, twill, Bedford cord, cotton or wool gabardine. Colors are even more so: the best colors are beige, eggnog and russet, but most light or rusty shades of brown will pass. Green, red and black are considered too hideous to mention.

For riding saddle walk, trot and gaited horses, you wear

something called a Kentucky jodhpur, cut like frontier pants, with no flare, but made in the same materials and colors as the English jodhpur and breeches.

Cotton or light wool socks. They should go up to and under the ends of your breeches. Silk socks (and talcum powder) ease your way out of riding boots. There is no special sock made for riding.

Spurs, if any, should be blunt. They're worn high, just under the ankle. Don't wear them if you are not secure enough in your seat to keep your heels down and away from your horse until you mean to use them. They are not necessary except for dress.

Riding coat. This is something special, not just a country tweed jacket. It is shaped at the waist, flared below, cut longer than an ordinary jacket and split in the tail so it won't catch on the back of the saddle seat. It has slant pockets with flaps. Good ones have rubberized linings in the skirt to protect them from the horse's sweaty flanks. Colors and patterns vary, but browns predominate, usually in pepper-and-salt or herringbone weaves.

In cold weather, you may wear the coat with a turtle-neck sweater or with a shirt and vest. The shirt is an ordinary flannel or cotton job, with collar attached, worn with a wool or knit tie. A white linen or piqué stock requires a neckband shirt, also white. (A stock, by the way, should *not* be worn in the manner of an evening muffler—one loop, and the ends overlapping each other down into the vest. Instead, tie a square knot, cross the ends right over left, then pin stock and shirt together with a gold safety pin.) A stock-substitute for everyday hacking is a gay silk foulard, worn like a muffler.

The vest may be fawn, yellow, Tattersall in any colors to complement your riding coat. Except with a stock, when a vest is a must, you may wear a coat without a vest, but you must never wear a vest without a coat.

In hot weather, you may wear a linen or salt-sack jacket or

ride without a coat. Then, your collar-attached shirt may be worn open at the neck and with sleeves rolled up.

In rainy weather, you turn up the "storm collar" on your coat and button it there. There are plastic hat coverings, raincoats in special shapes and rubber riding boots—optional, all.

Hats vary, and you don't have to wear one at all if you prefer to go informal and bareheaded. The best hat for hacking around the countryside is a snap-brim felt—or a tweed cap. The best hat for jumping is a regulation black hunting derby; it is higher in the crown than its street mate, and it has a protective lining of cork or steel. It is attached to your coat by a hat guard or cord.

Gloves are customary except in hot weather. String gloves give a good reins-grip; yellow and white are preferred. In winter, pigskin and doeskin rate with lined string gloves.

Clothes for formal riding are something else again. But before it occurs to you to ride in a horse show, you'll be beyond the point of wondering what's right and what's not. And before you let yourself get involved in riding to hounds, you'll need a separate book on that stylized sport, anyway. If you're going to pay the "cap" or day's fee and do no more than tag along after the hunt, you may dress in "ratcatcher" by making a selection from the preceding list—except that jodhpurs are considered incorrect even in the remotest part of the hunting field. Members of the hunt club will be wearing scarlet with hunt buttons if they have been invited to do so by the Master of Fox Hounds. Otherwise, they will appear formally in black boots, black hunting coat, hunting derby or silk topper, carrying a hunting whip with thong.

Garb for riding in a stock or Western saddle is totally different from the riding clothes we've been describing. You have more leeway in choosing your reinforced Pendleton pants or Levis, plaid shirts, neckerchiefs, fancy cowboy boots. Perhaps the only caution is to avoid looking as if you'd be more at home on television than on a horse. Ever tried trampling on new clothes, or bleaching your blue jeans, so as not to look too new a dude?

CONSIDER YOUR HORSE

A primary rule is to walk him for the first and last half mile of your ride—the first to limber him up, the last to cool him off. Just about the worst thing you can do is to gallop in, with your horse all in a lather, then stride off blithely; someone else has to walk him around the stable yard to cool him off. A meticulous rider *leads* his horse in, at least the last few hundred yards, with girth loosened and stirrup irons up, so that the horse's circulation will be restored gradually under the saddle. The minimum, if you would be known as "a horseman and a gentleman" is to bring your horse in cool, dry and quiet.

You may let your horse have a few swallows of water after a ride, but take the bucket out of his stall or loose box for an hour after that.

Some horses go better on a loose rein, others when "fully collected." Some do better in a Pelham or a full bridle, some in a snaffle. So ask the owner how you should ride his horse, and ask whether or not the horse jumps. The owner will think you very knowledgeable, and the horse will have reason to agree.

The horse's idea of good manners for riders probably includes a thank you—in the form of cut-up apples or carrots after he's back in his box. Better make sure it's all right with his owner before you give him sugar. And don't feed him when he has the bit in his mouth: you'll frustrate him, if not choke him.

CONSIDER YOUR FELLOW-RIDERS

Take care not to startle others' horses by clucking to your own horse, waving a crop or fly whisk about or snapping a hunting whip near horses who may not be broken to its pistol-like crack.

Not only because horses are easily disconcerted, but also because their impulse is to follow the leader, you should never trot or gallop past another rider. When you meet or pass other horsemen on the road, you should slow to a walk. Otherwise, if you brush breezily by, you may catch legs and upset yourself. And when a rider in your group dismounts, as to close a gate, you should stop until he has remounted.

For the same reasons, you should never put your horse at a fence unless you are certain that all riders behind you plan to take the same jump. You'll get no thanks if a horse follows your lead when his rider is not ready for jumping.

If you are leading other riders, don't change gait without notice. Just before you stop or slow to a walk, you should raise your hand as a signal. And before you move into a trot or a canter, call out to make sure the others know. In leading a trot or canter, you should try to keep the pace steady—not so slow that the others will be bored, but not so fast that they can't keep up comfortably. If you know the country, try to arrange a long walk, a long trot, a long gallop—then repeat. Too frequent changes of pace can be annoying.

Ride to the left of a lady, a child or a less experienced rider —so you can reach out and help, if necessary, with your free right hand.

Consideration for other riders should include their opinions, too. Don't get into arguments over the various schools of riding; you might as well argue over religion. Your best bet is to listen politely and keep the peace. Find out what the *horse* likes, in any case.

The technique of helping someone else to mount is simple: stand near the horse's head on the "off" side, holding the horse by his noseband and pulling down the "off" stirrup leather to counterbalance the rider's weight as he mounts from the left or "near" side. Sometimes a less experienced or a rather short rider needs more direct help. To "give him a leg up," you stand with him on the left side of the horse. He takes up the reins. As he bends his left leg at the knee, you grasp the lower part of his left leg, and as he springs upward off his right foot, you help propel him.

When anyone tightens the girth for you, when you are in the saddle, hold the saddle skirt up for him until he has finished.

CONSIDER YOUR NECK

The most experienced horseman habitually checks certain points about the horse's tack before he mounts, so no one will be offended if you take a moment to see that the reins are clear and arranged snaffle-curb-curb-snaffle, the girth snug, the curb-chain and throat-latch neither too loose nor too tight, the cheek-straps of the right length to hold the bit correctly. And it's only sensible, if you're going to jump, to make sure that the horse's martingale is long enough to allow for its stretching out his neck to balance himself.

On the ride itself, no one will think you a tender-heart if you make it a rule always to *walk* on macadam roads and wooden bridges . . . down steep hills . . . across land pocked with holes. In fording streams or crossing ice, it's safest to kick your feet out of the stirrups; then if your horse falls you'll be able to dive away from him. A generous horse's length between you and the rider ahead is a good interval to maintain. And if you find yourself getting near a horse who wears a red ribbon on his tail—*don't:* the ribbon means he's a habitual kicker.

Just remember that there's nothing fuddy-duddy about caution on horseback. Quite the reverse. The daring young man on the flying steed is acceptable only when he rides his own horse, alone, on his own land—and where's the fun in that for a show-off?

CONSIDER THESE, TOO

There are a couple of other ways to lose friends and horse's influence in this world. One involves cigarettes. Around stables, "No Smoking" signs are to be taken literally. If there are no signs, you are nonetheless expected to know that matches must be handled carefully around hay and horses. When you smoke on horseback, a more important concern is the woods. Just remember your Boy Scout training—break matches in two and snuff out cigarette stubs on your heel before casting them away.

The other involves hounds. The worst possible thing you could do would be to let your horse kick a hound. So if you meet up with hounds (not "dogs" please note) move your horse to the near side of the lane and then turn him to *face* hounds until they've passed. It's then perfectly all right to continue your ride; you needn't wait until those riding to hounds have also passed.

TIPPING

Only the ubiquitous problem of tipping remains to rattle the guest.

If your host maintains his own stable, and if you ride more than once or without your host at any time, tip the groom who attends you. Do it when you leave, and make it folding money. A dollar would be fine for no perceptible trouble; better make it at least $2 for anyone who has tacked up for you three or four times. If there are several grooms, if you feel no special identity with any one and if you've done a lot of riding over a week-end, you give the head groom or stable manager a few dollars "for the boys." He himself does not take tips—at least not so you can notice it.

If your host boards his horses, you do not tip.

If your host hires a horse for you, you tip the stableboy half a dollar or so, on your return, assuming that your host will have paid the actual fee.

If you yourself hire the horse, you tip the stableboy 50 cents over the fee. And if you want the horse reasonably fresh the next time, maybe you'd better make it a dollar.

If your host takes you over to see hounds in kennels, he will do any necessary tipping of the kennelman. If you should make such a visit on your own, modest folding money repays the kennelman for showing you around; you never tip a huntsman or a whipper-in.

SKIING

Whether your skiing is a sweet dream or a nightmare, your guide to good ski manners is an appreciation of safety factors. Most bad habits on the ski slope are as dangerous as they are annoying.

PLAY IT SAFE

The primary rule is to ski within the limits of your skill and experience: never try to ski over your head.

Bravado may get you a pair of broken legs. Maybe you're willing to take that chance, but your fellow-skiers are not. On a ski slope, one accident is apt to make another, and anyone who is not in complete control of his skis at all times is a hazard to others.

163

That's why slopes are ranked. Stay on the novice or intermediate or expert trails, as your skill dictates. Stay far away from jumps unless you know exactly what you're doing. And remember that the show-off maneuvers of reckless experts are no more welcome on novice slopes than the derring-do of jittery beginners is welcome on expert trails.

The rule has a corollary: don't dare anyone else to ski over his head, either.

The dare is usually unspoken, a smug assumption that everyone in the group skis as well as you do. Hide it if you think there's something amusing or heinous about a lower-slope man. With a novice who is self-conscious about his limitations—and particularly with a girl, who may fear you'll demote her on your list if she doesn't try to keep up with you —it's best to let the least skilled skier in your group set the pace.

If you later want to go off on your own, for headier stuff, there's nothing to prevent your asking to be excused for a try at the expert trail, but never assume that the others are "game" if they're not qualified.

Maybe "complete control" is many lessons and seasons away, for you. Then the first and best thing to learn is how to fall. It's always better to fall than to yell "track," scattering more sensible skiers.

After a fall, fill in the hole you've made in the snow before going on. Like empty cigarette packages and other such unforgivable litter dropped on a slope, a hole is a danger. That's also the reason why no one should ever walk across a slope on foot.

When someone you don't know falls in a peopled area, your own responsibility is to skirt him on your way by. His own friends will help him, if he needs help, and the Ski Patrol will be on hand in a matter of seconds. Well-meaning bystanders will only complicate the situation.

On a lonely trail, however, or in any situation which you

can see is not already under control, the thing to do for an injured skier is to stay with him while someone else goes for help. If there's any chance he has broken a bone, don't move him; just keep him warm with whatever clothes you can strip off yourself and keep him awake until the Ski Patrol arrives.

The lethal look of sharp ski poles tells you why the windmilling skier rates high on the list of slope scourges. The poles' dagger-like ends should not be pointed at unsuspecting passersby on the ski train, either. Pack all your equipment neatly and compactly so you can keep it out of the way, en route. (See that your equipment is complete and in good shape *before* you leave home. Ski-waxing in the train aisles is not much more endearing than borrowing small necessaries on the slope.)

The ski lift is dangerous only when it inspires show-offs to swing and bounce their way uphill. But even in its safest form it is apparently a major field of operation for boors. The skier nobody likes is the one who cuts in on a patiently, politely waiting line. Almost as annoying is the guy who crowds up against those ahead of him, engaging them in a ski-tangling joust. "Take your turn; don't crowd or dawdle or clown" may sound like elementary advice, but ski slopes are cursed with elementary offenders.

CLOTHES

Clothes for skiing are governed less by tradition than clothes for, say, riding and tennis. Fashion has its place here, and the man who turns up in the "latest thing" from his ski shop is not necessarily a snowbunny.

The mark of the know-nothing, then, is not too bright but too many clothes. Exercise keeps the skier warm, so good ski clothes are lightweight, not bulky. They're designed mainly to keep the skier dry while allowing free motion.

165

Here are some practical pointers. They're obvious to anyone whose skiing has progressed beyond the department-store dressing room, but perhaps these reminders will help you get together an outfit that lets you keep your mind on your skis.

1. *Your cap* should be snug so it can't blow off. Ear flaps and head binders are effective against wind and snow. A peaked cap is not so good if you expect to do much falling on your face.

2. *Goggles* are almost a necessity—skiing with tears in your eyes is not recommended—but see that they are ventilated as a prevention against vision-clouding mist.

3. *Your throat* is your most exposed area, so keep it warm with turtleneck sweater or scarf or whatever works.

4. *The most practical mittens* have wool linings, detachable so they can be dried immediately after use.

5. *A silk sock*—or a light sock of equally smooth material —is the best prevention against blisters. Under the silk sock you might wear a layer of hand lotion or soap, a further blisterproofing. Over the light sock, you wear a heavy wool sock, with its top tucked under your ski pants and your pants then tucked neatly into your boot.

6. *You'll want something—a polo coat or a parka*—to put on over your ski clothes when you're standing around, inactive in the cold. (The parka is no good for actual skiing because the hood fills up with snow when you fall.)

What you wear for the indoor sports of a ski lodge—drinking, dining, square dancing—depends somewhat on the lodge. Women have begun to turn up at the fireside in sequined slacks, jeweled sweaters and other fancies known as evening ski clothes. Some men can get away with wearing slipper-socks and Norwegian sweaters. But you'll seldom go wrong if you pack your uniform of sports-jacket, gray flannels and moccasins. White shirt and knit tie would be your dressiest addition; open-necked flannel shirt would probably pass in most places.

NO STUFFED SHIRTS

One thing not to pack in your bag: your stuffed shirt. The atmosphere in most ski lodges is one of camaraderie. A girl will probably schuss with the guy what brung her, but she won't stand on introduction ceremonies before joining in the general gaiety. If she's your girl, you might as well be prepared: she'll probably fall for the ski-pro, he of the magnificent tan, the intriguing accent, the close-cropped blond hair and the way with women. As he circulates among the guests, playing the role of host and mentor and general menace, he may join you at your table. Don't expect him to pick up the tab. It's supposed to be an honor to lose your girl to this modern counterpart of the dancing master, so resign yourself to accepting gracefully.

HOSTS, GUESTS, GIRLS

Because of the traveling and over-nighting involved, skiing can be an expensive sport. There are few pure host-guest relationships, so when you are invited to join a week-end ski group you should expect to pay your way. Most lodges, even those which are run on a club basis, deal in cash. Tipping is handled as in a comparable hotel. So you should have no difficulty in paying for your own room, buying your own lift-tickets and holding up your end in the food and drink department.

When you invite a girl to join you on a ski week-end, however—and this you can safely do when the lodge is run on the dormitory style which bunks men and women in separate quarters—the expenses are all on you. You buy even the train tickets. She brings nothing but herself and her ski equipment. Girls who are part of a regular gang of week-end skiers may insist on paying their own way; a girl you know well may volunteer to share expenses; but these arrangements are as special as a Dutch-treat night on the town.

The "date" relationship continues on out to the ski slopes, in that you look out for her and keep her company as her ski skill requires, but you are not expected to carry her skis or dry off her equipment unless she's a befuddled dub.

Even with a dub, it's wise not to make big talk about what the first Alp said to the second Alp when the Tyrol got a glimpse of your superior ski-form. When you're lying on your face, you'll wish you hadn't said so much. It's bad enough to eat snow, without having to eat crow besides.

SKATING

When skating on the mill pond, with all the room in the world, you'll need no more "etiquette" than you would for a stroll down a country lane. When skating at a public rink, follow the rule of "skate and let skate" and you'll be all right; everyday common sense will tell you not to skate against heavy traffic, not to crowd onto the sharp heels of other skaters, not to spray ice over old ladies or ply your hockey stick across the space reserved for figure skating.

But when skating at a club—particularly at one of those old, revered skating clubs which can very easily out-tone the toniest town or country club—you may need a more precise knowledge of the ways and wishes of good skaters. Here it is:

ICE NICETIES

1. *Nobody*—not even the frailest-looking damsel or the dodderingest old gentleman—really likes to be helped up

from the ice after an ordinary pratfall. Somewhat nonsensically, since even champion skaters fall, hard and often, most people are momentarily embarrassed by a flop. You only prolong the embarrassment if you step in with a well-meant helping hand when it is not really necessary. When it *is* necessary—as for hard falls, for your own dance partner, for the very old or the very green, and for falls you yourself have caused—give your help quickly and unobtrusively. Don't make a point of the unfortunate fall.

2. *Club members* and guests feel free to greet each other in passing on the ice, considering that, even if they don't all know each other, "the roof is an introduction." But some are out to skate, not to chat; they don't like to be detoured to the sidelines for a lot of yakety-yak. A skater who is seriously practicing his jumps and spins may wish to postpone even a distracting "hello."

Understanding this, you will save your long conversations for the clubrooms. Equally, you'll feel no hesitation about skating off from a chatting group whenever you feel like it. A simple "see-you-later" kind of parting remark is enough; if you want to skate, not keep a winded and windy dowager company, no excuses or apologies are necessary.

3. *Most club skating sessions* are labeled in advance, either for figure skating or dancing.

Although there is no set pattern or direction for figure skating periods, and you just go wherever you want to go, you'll find that most people skate and jump and spin to their left. It's best not to buck traffic, if possible, although any direction is permissible.

Where another skater has marked off an area in which to practice his figures, *don't* set your skate-blade within his boundaries. Figure practice requires *fresh* ice; the moment you mark it with an irrelevant whorl of your own, you go down in his black book. The people who don't seem to know

169

this, who think that the figure skater needs only the end of the "patch" where he is currently working, are matched in numbers only by those who cross the skate-drawn lines by accident. But whether the trespass is due to ignorance or ineptness, it's a real sin in the eyes of the figure skater. Once marked up, the ice will not be "fresh" again until the rink is reflooded and refrozen—by which time the frustrated figure-skater will be through for the day. That's why he hates to see any skater skid across fresh ice at any time. Somebody might have a better use for it!

4. *Respect for the ice* is the determining factor, too, in the general rule that you don't smoke while skating. Some teachers do, but unless they're super-careful with ashes and butts they attract frowns.

5. *Among good skaters,* the learner's best policy is to maintain his own direction at all times, leaving it to the more competent to avoid *him.* The beginner who rushes for the rail, in a well-meant attempt to get out of the way, is harder to dodge at high speed than the one who stands still or continues on a predictable path. Still, even a true wobbly should know better than to skate into the line of a jump already started down the ice. The world's best skater has trouble changing direction in mid-air!

6. *At an informal club session,* you will probably be able to select and play the music. Any skater may take off a record or put on a new one without ceremony, but the process rates two words of warning: a) Make sure, before you approach the record-player, that no one is "doing his program"—that is, practicing and timing a set routine he uses in competition. And b) don't play "The Skaters' Waltz"; it's all used up. As a matter of fact, waltzes are best saved for dance sessions.

7. *Dancing on skates* is a stylized thing; you had better take lessons, to learn the definite steps each dance requires, before venturing forth at a club dance. Free lancing is not welcomed if it upsets the patterns of others.

CLOTHES

A man is by nature saved from most of the clothing hazards of skating. Unlike the average girl, he wouldn't think of tying bells on his skates, folding his socks over his skate-tops or turning up in a department store's idea of a skating costume, no matter what. All he needs to know is that there is no such thing as a "skating outfit," as such.

Ski pants are not worn unless they're indigenous to the environment, as at a ski resort where almost everyone on the ice is about to go skiing or has just come in from the slopes.

Slacks, sport shirts, pullover sweaters, invisible socks and skates usually make up the informal costume for figure or free skating indoors. Outdoors, a heavy sweater and perhaps a cap might be added, but a skater usually has more trouble with overheating than with cold.

For dances, jackets and ties are usually required. Depending on the club and the pre-dance festivities, you might wear an odd jacket and a knit tie, your good blue suit or even your dinner jacket.

Whatever the occasion, don't strip down to your T-shirt when your exercise begins to tell. And don't tuck your trousers into your skates, if only because they'll spoil the snug fit of your boots.

SKATES

Wherever you skate, hockey or figure skates are your best bet. Speed skates are outlawed as a hazard almost everywhere. And whatever the skate, you'll do better if it really *fits*. Part of the right fit is the right lacing up. That's why it makes no sense for a young gallant to lace up his lady fair's skates for her. If she's any kind of skater, it will take her six tries to get them laced just right herself; chivalry will only bring the count to seven.

She doesn't want you to hold her hand, either—unless she'd like it on the street as well, that is, or unless she really needs to be held up. Currier and Ives postures are a bit out of date, on club rinks at least. Disappointed? You can always go "sparking" in a nice, dark movie instead of skating at the club!

SPECTATING

When you're a spectator at a skating competition, the only thing required of you is quiet during the compulsory school figure. There should be no talking when a "figure" is being performed; applause should be saved for the periods between figures. A skater likes an enthusiastic audience as well as the next sportsman, but if he has to choose between cold silence and a cheer that might jar his really serious concentration, he'll take the quiet. During free skating he likes enthusiasm and applause—but grandstand coaching is always out of place at the rink side.

SHOOTING

It is considered impolite to shoot your host in the back, or to burden your hostess with making funeral arrangements for you, so much of the etiquette of shooting is inextricably bound up with safety rules.

There are two guys that *no* one wants to go hunting with: the one who doesn't know how to handle a gun with absolute safety to everyone and everything except the appointed target . . . and the guy who *does* know how, but gets drunk.

S A F E T Y   F I R S T

Therefore, the best thing you can do is to practice, so consistently that they become second nature to you, the Ten Commandments of Safety as recommended by the Sporting Arms and Ammunition Manufacturers' Institute:

1. Treat every gun with the respect due a loaded gun. This is the cardinal rule of gun safety.

2. Guns carried into camp or home must always be unloaded, and taken down or have actions open; guns always should be encased until reaching shooting area.

3. Always be sure that the barrel and action are clear of obstructions.

4. Always carry your gun so that you can control the direction of the muzzle, even if you stumble. Keep the safety on until you are ready to shoot.

5. Be sure of your target before you pull the trigger.

6. Never point a gun at anything you do not want to shoot.

7. Unattended guns should be unloaded; guns and ammunition should be stored safely beyond reach of children and careless adults.

8. Never climb a tree or a fence with a loaded gun.

9. Never shoot at a flat, hard surface or the surface of water.

10. Do not mix gunpowder with alcohol.

There are a few fine points which vary with the particular game and circumstances. For example . . . in shooting ruffed grouse, which stay in heavy cover and are the devil to catch, you might seem to violate Commandment Five by taking a blind snap-shot. But you would never take such an unaimed shot if there were the slightest chance that other unknown hunters might be around, and you would always be sure that your gun's muzzle pointed upward at least 30 degrees.

But regardless of various small exceptions, the spirit and

the underlying principles of the Ten Commandments prevail. Woe to the hunter who does his own editing of the rules. He will find that his companions are not very "polite" about correcting—or ditching—him.

MANNERS, FOR "LUCK"

The hunter's particular brand of sportsmanship is conditioned by his desire for good hunting—today and ten years from today.

Toward good hunting in the future, he takes the conservation laws very straight and imposes a few of his own. It's not "cute" to shoot more than your limit, to shoot the mothers of tomorrow's bag or to shoot today a quarry which would give a hunter better sport a little later on. Also, he is meticulous in his respect for others' land: he knows how few careless or messy hunters it would take to persuade a farmer to close his property to shooting. He always asks specific permission to hunt over privately owned land. He is careful to close gates, steer clear of outbuildings and livestock, avoid littering the land with papers and empty cartridges. And he makes a point of his thanks when he leaves: he offers the farmer a part of his bag. (If this hurts, he can be glad he's not in Europe, where he would have to pay for the privilege of shooting and then buy the birds he shot from the land owner.)

As for good hunting today, he wants it for the others in his party as much as for himself. Getting it covers a lot of bases: from clothes to demeanor, from taking turns to taking the inherent discomforts without bothersome griping.

CLOTHES

Clothes? The experts describe their hunting clothes as "horrible" and point out that Hemingway can shoot better in a ragged T-shirt and bare feet than the average sporting department customer can shoot in all the "right" garb. But you notice that their clothes, horrible or no, are functional. The function is often specific to the particular kind of shooting.

For duck hunting, for instance, the hunter's clothes should be inconspicuous. Their colors should blend naturally with the landscape, so browns and woody greens are the best; blacks and light colors show up too much. Their texture should be soft and dull, so as not to reflect light up to duck eyes.

For upland shooting, on the other hand, the hunter wants to be visible—to other hunters. The game is in front of him, rather than overhead, so his light-colored jacket is a safety measure which doesn't spoil the hunting, and its hard texture serves a definite function in repelling burrs as he walks through fields.

For one kind of hunting you might want leather boots, for another rubber, and for another a hob-nailed shoe. In one situation the most important part of your costume might be a sun helmet, in another, long woolen underwear. So your best bet, at risk of sounding like a debutante, is to ask your more particularly experienced companions what they're going to wear—or at least to find out precisely what you're in for so you can put it up to a good sporting goods store.

One general standard, however, applies to all hunting clothes. They should be comfortable, and they should allow the freedom of motion necessary in gun-handling.

E A S Y   D O E S   I T

In almost all kinds of hunting, you have to be quiet. The degree depends on the game and its nearness to you. While waiting for ducks that may or may not come over your blind any minute, quiet conversation is safe enough—but once the birds are in view, silence. While tracking elephants you know to be miles away, music and laughter will do no harm. But while waiting for wild turkey to fly up from their roosts overhead, the very least sound will ruin the show.

You have to be as careful with your movements as with your voice, in most instances. Geese may spot you just from your turned-up, shiny nose; a deer will flee at the tiniest crack of a dry twig. But keep your mind on your prey and you'll be all right, particularly if you understand something about his habits and his talents for detecting hunters.

SMOKING

Smoking needs special mention. It's probably obvious that the light of a match in the pre-dawn will tip your lair as surely as a brass band or a round of practice shots. But remember, too, that animals can *smell* smoke. When the wind is blowing from you toward your quarry, better not smoke. Even if *you* don't mind driving in to the specialty butcher for your day's bag, you can't afford to take chances with the others' chances of getting a good shot. (Needless to say, you'll ruin the hunting for years to come if your smoking is so careless as to start a forest fire.)

WHO SHOOTS WHEN?

Taking turns, in shooting, is pretty automatic with the experienced marksman, but a novice might, with all good intentions, hesitate over a shot that was his or grab a shot that was another's. Often the hunters will agree, well in advance, who is to have the first shot; thereafter, they'll alternate. Otherwise, it's the target that makes the decision. Any bird is your shot so long as he is in your quadrant; wait till he gets there, and if someone else hasn't picked him off first, in *his* quadrant, he's yours until he passes into the range of the guy on your other side. This is the safe as well as the courteous system.

An animal once shot at by another, whether missed or only wounded, is his to kill no matter how much easier it might be for you—unless, that is, you're shooting in self-defense or on the particular invitation of the guy who muffed it.

UNSPORTING SHOTS

Of one thing you can be fairly certain: if the shot is a lead-pipe cinch, it's probably nobody's. There is a hunter's conspiracy against easy shots. In addition to the proverbial "sitting duck," any small bird or animal who hasn't a sporting chance to escape is not a sporting shot. A large animal may be shot standing, but when the true sportsman is lucky enough to have a static quarry he uses that advantage to assure a shoulder shot instead of just banging away at first sight.

When pass shooting is used—that is, when you sit still and wait for the game to come to you—it's not sportsmanlike to shoot as the birds glide to alight on water or roosts. When they're taking off from such spots, you should give them time to get up speed before picking them off.

Wild shots are also frowned upon—and often they are illegal, as well. Never shoot into a flock of birds, willy nilly, in a generalized hope of bringing something down! (And if you do, you "butcher," don't expose your bluff by revealing your surprise when you get something besides tail feathers.)

DOGS

When dogs are involved in the hunting, it's important to appreciate two things: no dog can be touched or ordered about by anyone except his owner or handler . . . and any bird retrieved by a dog belongs to the dog's master. (If it's a

177

bird *you* shot, you just have to wait for the owner to rectify the dog's error.) You shouldn't take your own dog on a hunt without the specific permission of your host or the other dog-owner. When you know your dog is going to be among strangers, it's best to perform the introductions—by way of practice runs with the other dogs—well in advance of the actual gunning trip.

CRIPPLES

The hunter is almost as careful about his quarry's feelings as about his companions'. There may be other than humane reasons for it, but a prime rule of hunting is never to abandon a cripple. If you've hit but not downed an animal or bird, you are honor bound to go after him until you find and kill him. Even if the side hunt takes all day, you've got to do everything in your power to recover a cripple. The others just about have to go along and help you, so such an inaccurate shot penalizes everyone in the party! That's one reason why hunters are pretty fussy about estimating range. If you're too far away, pass up the shot rather than risk making a cripple. (And if you're too close, wait until the game moves into the correct range rather than down a mutilated morsel of meat.)

GUESTING

As a guest, you take your own clothing and gun, of course, but the only other thing your host does not supply you, normally, is your ammunition. Take plenty!

You tip your host's gamekeeper or guide as you tip other members of his staff on a week-end visit. If you're assigned a personal guide and spend all day with him, you probably give him $5. For a general sort of helper, who did little more than clean your gun, $2 for each day's shooting would be plenty. If you found yourself involved in a production, with more helpers than hunters or birds, you'd give the head man $20 or so to portion among his staff. When you can do so comfortably, however, it's always best to ask what's par for the course; no two shooting set-ups are exactly alike.

The host has nominal title to all game shot by his guests. He will almost always insist that you take whatever you want, or divide the bag equally among the group if the luck has been spotty, but you shouldn't blithely assume that you're going to take home everything you shoot.

DUTCH-TREAT

The pure-guest role gets rarer and rarer with the passing of big estates. More common than the week-end at a hunter's lodge, these days, is the Dutch-treat hunting trip. Each man takes his own food or a contribution to the party's lunch, and expenses are divvied up. At one of those hunting preserves where the hunters pay a fee and go out with hired guides, dogs and the works, the expenses can run into something like $50 or $60 each, for a day's sport, so the Dutch-treat arrangement will doubtless be clear at the outset.

ANNIE OAKLEYS

A woman who shoots is just one of the boys, entitled to no special privileges or courtesies. You wouldn't expect her to carry a deer home without your helping hand, but she wouldn't expect you to give her the first shot or your last shell. A woman who can't shoot safely is better left behind —not behind a gun.

BIG GAME FISHING

In the hands of a savvy and considerate host, not even an old bent-pin fisherman would catch angry glares from experienced anglers. So let's start with a few pointers for the big fish on a big game fishing boat. Here's what a host should do to avoid embarrassment for and trouble from a neophyte guest:

THE HELPFUL HOST

... *mixes advice with his invitation*

In extending the invitation, or getting up the party in a Dutch-treat kind of situation, the host should make all arrangements perfectly clear. And if the guest has any doubts about where to appear at what time, what to bring or what to wear, it is better that he *ask* rather than get lost on the way, turn up late, "have to get back" just when the fishing is looking up or find that he must raid the boat's supplies for things he should have brought.

The knowing host will anticipate these questions, particularly as they concern clothes, for he is the one who knows most about his own boat and the probable weather. Maybe he'll take it for granted that his guests know about shoes that give traction and don't mar varnish (see yachting etiquette, page 148), but if he's ever had all the blankets on his boat soaked because people used them for raincoats and sweaters, or if he's ever sacrificed a good sport shirt to the cause of keeping a guest from sunburn, he'll suggest: sleeves and trousers that can be rolled down against sun and glare, a change of clothes as a precaution against dousing, a raincoat and hat if a storm threatens, some warm outergarment in case of wind or chill.

180

. . . *"introduces" his tackle*

Before a guest reaches the fishing grounds, the host should see to it that he is shown what to do and how to do it. There will be at least fifteen minutes, probably an hour or more, before the boat gets out into good fishing waters; there's plenty of time for the guest to be indoctrinated—casually, gently rather than pedagogically, but thoroughly.

A check-out on the tackle is the bare minimum, a necessity to everyone who is going to handle the equipment. The average "green pea" has no idea that a good big game fishing outfit costs more than $900; the best trout fisherman in the world may not realize that it might take $100 to replace even the lightest rod and reel on the boat. In lieu of displaying his bills of sale, the host should simply show everyone how the tackle works and what can be expected of it in all the situations which may arise.

A danger to the neophyte is that even a knowing host will begin in the middle, showing you the idiosyncracies of his particular equipment but skipping over two basic points which apply to all deep sea fishing gear:

1. *A rod* can stand the strain of a big fish's pull only if it is free to bend. Thus it must always be held aloft, never braced against a rigid obstruction which will force it to break (and maybe disqualify a record catch). If you use the stern of the boat as a fulcrum, with your weight pulling at the rod inside the boat and the fish pulling at it deep in the water, you'll learn this lesson the hard way. But if you keep the rod-tip *up,* you may never know that a good rod can cost about $250. (The reel may cost as much as $600, so—if you were faced with such a Hobson's choice—it would be cheaper to brace and break the rod than to let the fish take the whole outfit down to the bottom of the sea with him!)

2. *No deep-sea fishing line* is as strong, at the beginning of the fight, as the fish it can catch. Thus if you put the drag

on too quickly, when the fish is running, you'll break the line. If you don't know what kind of fish you've hooked—or if, knowing that, you don't know his fighting style or whether to expect a deep dive or a high jump—don't ad lib. Do what your adviser suggests, immediately; save your "better ideas" for another day. And don't pout if your host sets the drag at the outset, so you *can't* bust anything.

. . . *previews a strike*

Before the first fish is hooked, the experienced host will give his guests a preview of what each one is expected to do when someone gets a bite. Ideally, he will explain why split seconds count . . . why one of the most important questions of the day is that initial one, "Will he take the bait the first time?" But again, in case he begins in the middle out of mistaken respect for your intelligence, this background may help you to understand why he or his captain orders you about with seeming rudeness at the first call of "Strike!"

1. *In catching a big fish,* the novice angler is about third in importance. More telling are the boat and the guide. With a boat that can perform and a guide who thinks like a fish, the dubbest dub might break a record.

There can be only one quarterback. Only one person will talk to you and advise you when you have a fish on the line. He's the smartest fisherman on the boat, and what he says goes. Whether he's the paid captain or your host, his role has been settled in advance. Do what he says, and do it fast. If you want to know why he says, "I'm going to bring the boat around, now—take in some slack," ask him *later.* Don't clutter up the intricate proceedings with unnecessary conversation while you're fighting a fish.

2. *If you're out for big fish,* there will be only one line overboard at a time. If you're fishing for smaller ones, like school tuna or bluefish, four of you may fish at once. But

while you're angling for a 75-pound white marlin, perhaps a 700-pound blue marlin will come after the same bait. When such a big fish shows himself, all but one must reel in. If the fish hasn't already made the decision, it's the quarterback who decides which anglers will bring their lines in and which one will have the chance at the big boy.

3. *Then everyone* not pregnant to the situation must get himself and his gear out of the way. The clever host will assign a specific retreat to each guest. If you haven't been told exactly where to go when a big fish is hooked, simply move back out of the cockpit and out of the captain's line of sight: he must have clear vision at all times between himself and the angler and the fish. Stay off the bridge and don't ever touch the controls. And wherever you go, to get out of the way, take your rod with you! Don't leave it in its holder or drop it on the deck.

TEN POINTERS TO GUESTS

Now, here are some "unwritten laws" which even the best host won't spell out for his guests:

1. *Don't bring or ask to bring uninvited guests.* There is not "always room for one more." A boat has only so much space, and everyone needs more room than you'd think—for good fishing.

2. *Take along your own lunch* unless your host tells you he has made other arrangements. He has enough in his larder to get by if you show up empty-handed, but he'd prefer to avoid the nuisance of replacing his "emergency stock"—and the bother of serving you your meals. If you have your own lunch, you can eat whenever you feel like it without disturbing anyone.

With a host and a boat so fancy that you'd feel corny showing up with a sandwich and a thermos, take a case of beer or Coke, a bottle of liquor, or something for everyone to eat.

But first let your intentions be known. It's always safer to inquire. (Page 150, in yachting etiquette, may help you over the hump of how to do it gracefully.)

3. *If you prefer to take your own tackle,* talk it over with your host first. Make sure his lines or outriggers can handle your "pet," that you won't be spoiling his plans by fishing your way. For, normally, the boat supplies all the gear and the bait for the day.

4. *Keep your suntan oil on yourself,* not on the tackle— and especially not on the deck, where it could cause a fast-moving mate to slip. Shark waters are no place to toss someone in for a surprise swim, particularly when there's a fish on the hook!

5. *Be neat, yourself,* but don't "tidy up" about the boat. Leave things where they are, however out of place they seem to be. When the mate reaches for the gaff, he wants to find it exactly where he left it. And if he doesn't—well, you've heard about the fish that got away?

6. *Don't expect to turn the boat back* if you develop a sudden case of seasickness. Fishermen have little patience with anything that interferes with fishing, but if politeness overcomes his contrary wishes and your host suggests going in, you absolutely *must* refuse. And suffer your misery as unobtrusively as possible.

7. *Don't make the mistake* of treating captain and mate as if they were servants. They are professionals, and the fact of their employment by your host does not diminish his respect for them. He knows—and you'll soon find out, if you get them down on you—that they are important to the day's catch. A little appreciation, a few words of admiration and interest, non-patronizing good manners and, above all, a sharing of the credit for catching your big one, will go a long way toward improving the day's "luck."

There is, however, a little paradox here: captains and mates are tippable. You offer them some of your lunch, as you would any friend sitting near you, but you thank them with cash, as you would the cook and chambermaid in your host's house. No tip is necessary or expected after a single day's fishing on a private boat (but no captain or mate will refuse the prize you offer in exuberance over catching a big fish, either). After a cruise, however, a tip is standard. You might give your host's captain $10, his mate $5, after a particularly good week-end of fishing. On your return from a two-week junket, you'd more likely start with $25 and $10. The "rates" are just a little higher than comparable tipping in a private house—and that because these are pros who just *might* have "principles" for anything under $5.

8. *If you sight a fish* that's too big for your experience, offer to turn your rod over to your host rather than lose the fish. The good host, who wants you to catch a big one, will refuse your offer in most cases. But if the fish might set a record, and if it is apparent that he will get away if not expertly handled, your host may snap at your offer—may even make the suggestion, in abrupt action, himself! In any case, he'll appreciate your deference, and if you wind up with an empty hook your regret won't be complicated by remorse.

9. *In case of accident* to any of the tackle (except lines) you owe your host a replacement. As is true in any other sport, you make the replacement as soon as possible, as exactly as possible and with as little prior conversation as possible: everyone *knows* that this one is on you, so there's no point in promises and demurrals. However, if your host *volunteers* that he is insured, that it was an old rod he knew would break any minute, or that the accident was due to his own or his crew's negligence, you have a perfect right to believe him. He is under no compulsion to say such things, the replacement rule being widely accepted as it is. So if he insists, he means it. You may let it go at that.

10. *Don't expect to take a fish home* just because you caught it. It's the host who divides the catch—and his division

is governed by a lot of factors you may not understand (see page 187). So just sit back and wait to be given that fish you're so proud of.

CHARTER-BOAT FISHING

Charter-boat fishing imposes a few "unwritten laws" of its own, most of them built around consideration for the boat captain. At first gulp, you might think that the fee he charges to take you out on his boat for a day of fishing covers everything and allows you to issue a few orders, as well. But a fishing boat is a very specialized piece of equipment, expensive to operate and maintain. And a charter-boat captain is a very special guy, independent in everything but means.

He's a sportsman at heart. He'll never win a $10,000 championship or be asked to endorse a bourbon; he'll probably end as a private boat captain; but he goes on fishing because he loves it. Because his living depends so much on things beyond his control—things like weather and sportsmanship and luck—the following "little things" are important to him. (They're important to you, too, if you want to be cold-blooded about it. Charter captains are a clannish, itinerant tribe. If you let one of them down in the Bahamas you may find that the fishing is not so good at Montauk next season!)

1. *Tips,* over and above the day's fee, are a generous thing to think of. On the East Coast, par is about $5 per day for each of the mates. The captain's tip is apt to be based on the success of the day: after a fine day, with a lot of fish and a lot of good work by the captain, you might give him $10 or so. If you caught a record fish, you might be inspired to tip more exultantly. But you wouldn't expect him to faint in gratitude. He knows a man who always gives the captain and crew $200 when he catches a big one, and he's heard

of the angler who celebrated a record by giving the mates $2,500, the captain a pair of new motors for his boat.

If you're one of a Dutch-treat group on a charter boat, it's wise to agree on the question of tips in advance. If you're a guest, you can count on your host's doing the major tipping along the lines indicated above—but if you've had good luck, yourself, you might very well add an independent tip of $5 or more.

Outside the U.S.A., particularly in South America and the Caribbean, it's easy to overtip. And that is frowned on by other fishermen as much as a "stiff" is scorned by captains. Your best bet is to inquire in advance. Ask the manager of your hotel, the dockmaster or an official of your fishing club what amount will be suitable.

Fish are sometimes a supplement to, sometimes a substitute for, a tip. In any case, you should not take home more fish than you can actually use. Leave the bulk of the day's catch aboard, for the captain and the crew to sell. In some ports, it is the custom for the boat captain to keep the catch, above what you can use personally. In Nova Scotia, for instance, the giant tuna are always kept by the crew; but their expectations, at six or seven cents a pound, are reflected in lower charter rates.

If you don't know the local customs or the policy of your particular captain, ask him on the way out. And if he leaves it up to you, leave him all fish which would otherwise spoil in some photographer's studio. (You can be sure that he knows precisely how much fish an average family can use, particularly away from home!)

If you've had a good day—if, for example, you're leaving behind most of a 500-pound swordfish, worth 50 cents a pound—the fish is tip enough! Additional cash is optional, in fact, whenever the market value of the fish comes close to the amount you would otherwise have tipped. But if the captain has figured on the catch anyway, or if the fishing has not been so good from a pounds-and-money standpoint, play it safe and tip as usual.

2. *Lunch and drinks* are never included with the charter. If you ask the captain to lay in supplies for the day, expect to pay him—and not at supermarket prices. If you bring your own, bring enough for the captain and the crew, too. They'll have brought sandwiches in their pockets, but if you can offer them some of your fried chicken, you'll find that it does no harm in assuring a pleasant day. *P.S.* Leave the left-over beer and vittles aboard.

3. *Major damage* to tackle is on you. The captain expects to pay for broken lines, but you should expect to pay for any lost or broken rods. Ask him, at day's end, what you owe him.

Boat damage, on the other hand, is not your financial concern. Knowing that most charter captains don't carry insurance you will sympathize, but you won't pay for mechanical failures which are not your fault.

4. *A reservation* is a contract—not legally, perhaps, but humanely. If you cancel a reservation, however far in advance, you should always offer to pay for it in the event that the captain cannot replace your charter. Leave it up to him. He'll try for a replacement, bill you only if he loses the one thing he has to sell: a day of fishing.

Similarly, if you have cut a charter-day short, you should ask the captain how much you owe him. He may charge you a little less than the full fee because he has used less than the full day's gasoline. But by rights you owe him for the complete charter once you have made the reservation and/or put out to sea.

FRESH WATER FISHING

The worst kind of fisherman is a hog—a hog of fishing waters and a hog of fish. Let conservation, no less than consideration, guide your conduct on lake and stream.

CONSERVATION

In the matter of conservation, official limits are unreliable guides to how many fish you may acceptably take home. The limits set by game laws or club rules are maximums, seldom approached by the conscientious sportsman. The purist often goes home empty-handed, as a matter of principle rather than luck. His sport has been to fish, not to dispense his catch to the neighbors. Without question, he puts back every fish he does not need. And in the rare fishing ground where by-laws prevent his returning a fish to the water—(a few clubs operate on the theory that a hooked fish is a hurt fish and should not be put back)—he may cut short his day's sport rather than take more fish than he has immediate, personal use for.

A bulging creel is suspect on another score. The avid angler, who can foresee the day when he won't know where his next fish is coming from, deplores the kind of tackle which makes it easy for the unskilled to haul in fish. Particularly if you are using unconventional or "foolproof" tackle, then, travel light on the way home.

And you might as well fish with trap and net as turn up with a spinner or a worm among dry-fly trout fishermen. A polite fisherman will take pains never to ridicule your tackle or your methods. He will pretend to believe that anything goes, and that the "right" way is any way that fools the fish. He may even apologize for his own "eccentric" adherence to old-fashioned techniques. But it's all an act of good manners! So when you're new, when you're a guest and when you care about the opinion of others, play it safe. Use the tackle and lures your host suggests. Inquire about club ground rules or customs, then fish up to them without comment. And whenever you're in doubt, do it "the hard way."

CONSIDERATION

The best gauge of one fisherman's consideration for another is the space he gives him. The unwritten law of lake and stream is: "Finders keepers." Whichever fisherman got there first has prior rights to all fish within reasonable casting distance.

This means not only that you must give him at least seventy-five feet clearance on all sides, but also that you must avoid disturbing the water in his area and, regardless of the peace and space you allow him, avoid picking off fish on their way to his chosen spot.

If you and the man who got there fustest are in some wilderness not yet discovered by the nation's other 16,999-998 licensed fishermen, by all means follow the old rule: one rod to a stream. But if you're fishing an area where you can't possibly put other fishermen out of sight, mind these don'ts, at least:

Don't cast across the water being fished by another angler.
Don't wade through a pool being fished by another. If you encounter another fisherman while you're stream fishing, detour around him.
Don't fish directly across from another on a narrow stream.
Don't cast into the mouth of a small feeder stream on a lake if another man is already fishing the feeder.
Don't let your boat disturb the waters near another fisherman. Above all, don't run your outboard close astern to a trolling boat.

190

PRIVATE WATERS

When you want to fish private waters, by all means get prior permission. Permission will seldom be refused—in fact, navigable streams and state-stocked ponds are not legally private, regardless of houses built on their shores—but the courtesy of your request will smooth the waters.

AS GUEST AT A CLUB

As a fisherman's guest, you supply nothing but your own equipment except by prior arrangement. Your host takes care of lunch and all expenses. (At a club, the expenses include pound or unit prices for every fish you take, so guard your greed—and realize that "your" fish belong to your host!) He won't, however, expect to supply you with fishing equipment, so get it straight at the outset what clothes and tackle you'll need. As Ray Camp, outdoor editor of the *New York Times,* puts it: "There are three things—maybe four—that no man will lend to another: his dog, his fishing rod, his gun—and, possibly, his wife."

CLOTHES

Practical considerations, not etiquette, govern the clothes you fish in. The fish can't see colors or hear rustles; fishermen can't object to the most battered, talisman hat. Fishermen's wives and club officers may have their own objections to muddy boots and fishy jackets, however, so you will need a change of clothes whenever you expect to wind up at a table instead of at a campsite.

YOUR GUIDE

Your guide on a fishing trip is not a servant, to be bossed about, nor a country cousin, to be patronized. Treat him like a somewhat senior fishing companion—with respect. Call him "Mr.", if he was introduced that way, until he decides to favor you with your first name. Better not drop names and fish stories in his direction; he'll be impressed only by performance. And when you tip him at trip's end (at the rate of $2-$5 a day), give him the money as his due, not as if you were bestowing a favor.

BILLIARDS

OF SOUND AND HURRY

A delicate game, this, requiring concentration and patience. Let that knowledge govern your conduct around a billiard table. Almost any noise but the sound of cue on ball is suspect in a billiard room, from the irritating grinding noise some people make when they chalk a cue to loud talk.

When you're not shooting, sit down—preferably out of the player's line of sight—and be quiet. Even the flare of a match or the clink of a glass can be a major distraction, and if you're involved with a really serious billiard player he won't appreciate unnecessary conversation between shots, either.

It's not a speed sport; a man can justifiably line up a shot two or three different ways, so long as he doesn't then choose to shoot it in the way that was obvious to everyone at the outset. Because no one's in a hurry, there's no sense in stepping up for your turn before the other guy has clearly and definitely missed the billiard. Don't anticipate—wait and see.

A game of billiards is not an athletic event, either, so keep your coat on. It's all right to tuck your four-in-hand tie into your shirt, to avoid its touching balls or table when you lean over, but otherwise you should be able to go out into the street or on to the dance right from the table. Perhaps this is the primary difference between "poolroom" and private house or club billiards.

A "gentleman" will not call your fouls, nor question your verdict on whether or not you made a particular billiard, so you are expected to lean over backward to be honest. Actually, you can *feel* fouls that no one can see; you must call them on yourself. When you're not sure whether or not you made a billiard, step down; someone else will speak up if he thinks you made it.

When you see an opponent about to play the wrong ball or make some other error subject to penalty, point out his mistake *before* he shoots. Don't call fouls on anyone but yourself in social play.

Certain poolroom mannerisms can mark you down in the gentleman's game. For instance, a serious player calls his cue a cue, not a "pole"—but he speaks of a "natural" and a "kiss off" as slangily as they do in the corner saloon. Like the Englishman who takes a bawth in a bathtub, the billiard player who frowns on some words but adopts others cannot be precisely predicted. It's safer to follow the leader. At least, don't try to display your familiarity with the game by word of mouth unless you're pretty sure you learned the lingo at a "proper" knee.

Also, the conventional sharpy techniques of looking for a bet are out of place in a social game. If there's money on the game, see that it doesn't influence your play or your manners —unless to make you even more careful about the etiquette of billiards.

THE PROPERTY'S RIGHTS

Many of the unwritten laws are designed to protect the game's equipment. It's best not to smoke while you're shooting, not only because the cigarette-stuck-to-lower-lip look is not being worn in private rooms but also because a falling ash can burn the table. You should park your cigarette in an ashtray, your drink on a side table, because that inlaid wood around the edge of the table does not take kindly to scars and rings. Keep your chalk in your pocket when you're not using it; perhaps it can't damage the table edge, but it can be in the way. And if you use talcum on your hands, wipe off the excess—not on the table—before you shoot. Little specks of powder on the green are annoying to the neat and the expert alike.

The rules allow you to sit on the edge of the table so long as you keep one foot on the floor, but your host might like you better if you keep such shots at a minimum. The table is a scientifically balanced and leveled instrument, so of course you should never sit on it just to be sitting somewhere.

A cue, too, is carefully balanced. You should never bang a cue about or lean on it. When you're not using it, it should be in the rack or held firmly in both your hands, not propped against the table or planted anywhere where it could be jolted into a fall. And of course an ivory ball is not designed for a game of catch.

Consider, when you're shooting, that the cloth on the table costs $70 or $80, and that you'll have to replace it, over all hostly objections, if you tear it. If not the money then the scene involved should keep you from attempting a massé shot you can't manage or otherwise taking chances with the table top.

AS A CLUB GUEST

As a guest in a club you pay for nothing, tip no one, unless drink waiters are paid in cash or unless your constant host is so good a friend you can split expenses without a fuss.

AS A SPECTATOR

As the spectator at a championship match, where you can't change your seat just to get out of a player's line of sight, just be extra-careful not to make distracting motions or sounds. The contestants would like it if you knew how to applaud appreciatively—for difficult shots well made, not merely for spectacular ones which send a lot of balls running around the table—but that takes a knowledge of the game. To live up to the etiquette, however, you need only common sense and consideration.

CARDS

BRIDGE

Bridge comes in two sizes—the "afternoon" variety, in which chitchat and refreshments are at least as important as the game, and the serious kind, in which a poor or inattentive player can lose friends fast.

For both kinds, one rule applies: *Don't play if you don't know how.*

If yours is the "afternoon" brand of bridge, where you don't know if a card is "good" until you see what happens to it in play, stay out of games with good players. If they insist upon pressing you into service as a fourth, even after you have seriously and positively described your shortcomings, what happens is their own fault; but that won't make *you* feel any better, and in their fury they too may forget their share in the affair. When you are so drafted, do the best you can; don't compound your felony by apologizing or clowning. But it would be far, far better to avoid the game in the first place, for the simple reason that your mistakes are not yours alone: your partner suffers at least as much as you.

It's simple enough to say "no thanks" when a hostess suggests bridge. She'd much rather cope with you on the loose than foist you off on another guest who *cares*. If you find yourself in a group where Bridge is the Thing, better to take some lessons—or find some new friends—than to ruin evening after evening as a fifth wheel or as a bridge-table terror.

Certain persistent bridge-table habits annoy almost *all* bridge players, so regardless of the quality of the game you find yourself in you'd better heed these don'ts:

1. *Don't post-mortem,* at least not after *every* hand, and if pressed into comment on the preceding play stick to the most general terms. Any and all variations of, "If you had played the nine instead of the Jack" can be quick death. Never say how a gone hand *should* have been played, even when the misplay was your own. And never, never criticize your partner. If he did well, say so; if he did badly, act as if you'd have done the same; and if you're determined to give him lessons, save your instruction for another time.

2. *Don't wander around when you're dummy*—or talk irrelevancies, or coach your partner with quick intakes of breath, or criticize him with eyes raised to heaven. When ya gotta go ya gotta, and when you're dummy is the best time to leave the table if you can do it unobtrusively, but you're *supposed* to stay seated and keep your eyes open. The rules give you a few duties. You are supposed to protect your partner against revoking by asking things like, "No spades, partner?" when he sluffs or trumps—but *don't* overdo it; don't ask too often or too emphatically. You have a right to straighten out the dummy hand or push it all closer to your partner when necessary—but don't edge individual cards toward him or anticipate his play. You're supposed to watch the play, but not to look into opponents' hands. You've got

a job, so you shouldn't just vanish—especially if, on your return, you are going to ask, "What happened?"

3. *Don't snap or riffle cards,* or slam or loft them onto the table, or bend down the corners.

4. *Don't play out of turn*—or, more exactly, don't be *ready* to play out of turn. You shouldn't pull a card out of your hand before you see the play up to you, no matter how sure you are what's coming.

5. *Don't throw the remains of your hand down with, "The rest are mine."* It's almost as annoying to play out every hand to the bitter end, regardless of its obvious outcome. But when you lay down you should describe your plays: "I lead over to the dummy with this and then lead out the trumps, so the rest are mine." In so doing, don't mess up the cards. Give slower players a chance to absorb what you are saying, and die-hards a chance to challenge your assumption.

6. *Don't study every play;* you shouldn't have to. The good player makes a plan at the outset, then plays quickly and precisely; long study is forgivable only in tournament play. His good opponent may do a little thinking before *his* first lead, but thereafter he too has a plan or is quick to adjust to the way things are going. If you're not that quick or practiced, you'll be forgiven a slower rate of play throughout—but you'll drive the others to distraction if you pore over your cards *every* time around, or if you hold half-audible meetings with yourself over *every* lead. The person who plays that way is usually guilty, too, of changing his mind. Play the wrong card, if you must, but play it definitely. Put it out, let go of it and remove your hand from the center of the table. You can't take it back, so why hesitate as if you wanted to?

7. *Don't be totally oblivious to your "unconscious" mannerisms.* The others aren't. Some will be annoyed by your off-key whistling, others by your drumming on the table. Some will wish you didn't continually rearrange your hand.

Some will begin to tense up if you use a bridge cliché at *every* opportunity: just one "not through the Iron Duke" lasts quite a while. And almost everyone will curse inwardly if you cover a trick with the winning card, without first making it possible for everyone to see what has been played.

8. *Don't just push away from the table to call a halt to a money game.* Whether you're winning or losing, you ought to give at least one rubber's warning of when you intend to cash in and go home. It's easy enough, even when you're a big winner; all you need is, "Sorry, but this has to be my last rubber."

9. *Don't hog the bidding,* even when your partner is obviously inadequate. You're not good enough to play bridge single-handed, and your partner's not that bad, anyway. If you're stuck with a hopeless boob and *must* adjust your game, do it as subtly as possible so it will not humiliate your partner, or set you up as a show-off.

Generally, the rules of good sportsmanship apply to bridge as much as to other games, but there is one major difference. In bridge, you aren't expected to announce your own crimes. That is, if you have unintentionally led from the wrong hand or failed to follow suit, you are not expected to call the penalty on yourself. Therefore, it is perfectly in order for your opponent to call you on an error or rules violation. If he's nice, if he sees it in time and if this is an extremely informal game, he tells you your mistake when there is still time to correct it; he doesn't deliberately let you make your next play and then claim a penalty. But if it's a tight game or if your error is too far gone to correct, he calls for the penalty—and you comply gracefully, neither imagining a personal affront nor mentally impugning his sportsmanship.

On the same general theory, you are supposed to guard your own hand from your opponents' view. If you hold the cards out so he can see them, he can either memorize your hand very quickly and make good use of the information, or scrupulously look away. He can't very well ask you to pull in your hand, because that would seem to be a righteous display of his own honesty.

As in other games, it doesn't pay to be fanatical about the letter of the rule book. Wait and see how strictly the others play before exacting or even displaying your knowledge of a penalty. But be ready to comply cheerfully and gratefully with the "local ground rules." And whenever you assume one of your rule-given rights—as, for instance, to re-shuffle the cards before you deal—do it gracefully, unpointedly.

A good basic thing to remember is that the rules of bridge are not made to prevent cheating—it's bad manners to think so—but only to provide for an orderly game.

P O K E R

The only way to get any real fun out of poker is to win, and the foundation of the game is deceit and misrepresentation, so the normal considerations of etiquette are largely ruled out.

All the same, there are five bad habits certain to make you *persona non grata* in any game—and two gambits it's best not to try in a new group without first sounding out the regulars.

The five dangers:

1. *Playing out of turn* Mr. Hoyle (so often cited and so little read) says that a player must bet, pass, raise or drop out only when his turn comes. The player who signals his move, or makes it, ahead of time gives another an unfair advantage, legitimately resented by the other players. Jumping the gun is a definite infraction of the rules, but since there is no practical penalty that can be imposed on the offender, the habit rates as a sin against manners rather than law.

2. *Being ambiguous.* Make your intentions perfectly clear

whenever you pass, bet or raise. There are several ways of indicating, for example, that you pass: you may say "check," "pass," "by me" or something equally clear, or you may simply tap the table to indicate the same thing. But then, when the man after you bets, don't protest that your table-tap was simply a nervous habit, or that your "check" had a question mark after it. Be definite—and final.

3. *Daydreaming.* "How many cards did you draw?" . . . "What did you turn over?". . . "Is it up to me?" These are questions you should ask very sparingly, if at all. It's your responsibility to keep up with what is going on, not the others' job to give you regular reports. Nothing is more irritating than inattention at a poker table—particularly to a heavy loser.

4. *Stalling.* The champion louse of poker is the guy who, once he is comfortably ahead, uses every kind of delaying tactic to protect his stack. He goes to the kitchen to build himself a leisurely drink; he starts the yawning and migod-my-wife-will-kill-me-if-I-don't-get-home routine; he lapses into an anecdotal mood while casually but ever so thoroughly shuffling the cards. To such a churl is directed the old poker player's lament: "The winners crack jokes and the losers cry, 'Deal!' "

5. *Free-loading.* In a game that is held regularly at the home of one of the players, the usual practice is for each player to contribute, or for the pots to be cut, to pay for the food and drink. Even if the host is generous and well-heeled, and even if he's a consistent winner, each regular should make a point of making a free will offering now and then—a flagon of twelve-year-old stuff, say, or the side of a cow.

The two cautions:

1. *Lying.* By this we mean deliberately misrepresenting your hand verbally. For example, suppose you're in a five-card stud game, with the ace, ten and eight of clubs showing

before the last card is dealt. You implore the dealer to give you another club, implying that you have a club in the hole, when actually your hole card is the ace of diamonds. If your fifth card turns out to be a club, another player with two pairs, three of a kind or a straight may well concede to the apparent flush.

Whether misrepresentation of this sort is permitted or not is purely a matter of convention. In some games, you're welcome to lie your head off; in others, you must tell the truth or keep quiet. So you'd better find out, when you enter an unfamiliar game, what the local attitude is.

2. *Sandbagging.* That's another name for checking-and-raising. There is nothing in the rules against it—it's a very useful and perfectly legal weapon—but in a few circles it is considered highly unethical. Again, better find out the ground rules before you try it.

OTHER CARD GAMES

The customs of bridge apply more or less to other games played with partners. Where you're on your own, as in poker, you have much more leeway on the *style* of game you play and are much less apt to ruin everyone's game if you're in over your head. Even so, being a good winner or loser matters a great deal, and your attention to the code of paying gambling debts promptly is vital. *"In cartum veritas."*

If you're a spectator at any card game, better known as a kibitzer, heaven help you. You can do no right!

SOCIAL

ETIQUETTE

shall we join the ladies?

Money and ability may obscure a man's rough edges in business . . . sportsmanship and skill may excuse a lot in sports . . . but when it comes to the world of women, Etiquette is All. You can't fly by the seat of your pants in the social skies.

But if an adherence to "form" is a concession in the woman's game, it is also a tool in the man's game. Good manners are good strategy, whether your intentions are honorable or not—and perhaps especially if you don't know which they are. Etiquette has the happy effect of keeping women at a distance or bringing them closer, as you will, between the "please" and the "thank you."

Here, then, the tools—and the "rules":

THE WAY YOU LOOK

When it comes to the amorphous subject of men's clothes, etiquette runs headlong into questions of individual taste, local custom and, sometimes, fashion.

Strictly, perhaps, an etiquette book should tell you little more than which suit to wear for what occasion: what short-hand on the invitation means white tie . . . what to wear when you're married and buried . . . what your hostess means when she tosses off the phrase, "Don't dress."

But—like his manners—a man's clothes are apt to be taken as a key to his character. It's a foolish criterion, on the face of it; but, on the face of it, what else has a potential date or employer or hostess to judge by in this frenetic world of first impressions?

A guy who wears pointed yellow shoes may not *be* a sharpy . . . a man who drapes his too-full polo coat over his shoulders may not *be* a queer . . . a man who flashes a luminous tie may not *be* corny. But if a man *looks* sharp or queer or corny, the people he meets may not stick around to discover the truth hidden by his off-beat clothes.

It follows, therefore, that you owe it to yourself to dress well. If you don't give a damn about clothes, dress well so that no one will give your clothes more importance than you do. If you believe that "clothes make the man," dress well so your clothes will "make" the right man.

In either case, perhaps your best general guide is this quotation from the ubiquitous Lord Chesterfield: "Take great care always to be dressed like the reasonable people of your own age, in the place where you are; whose dress is never spoken of one way or another, as either too negligent or too much studied." A modern P.S. might add: "Take care that the care you take is not obvious." You and your companions

206

will be more comfortable if you limit your "care" to the selection and upkeep of your clothes. When you wear your clothes, wear them as if they were of no concern to you.

They will be "of no concern" if, in addition to the little points tossed in throughout this chapter, they conform on the two big points of men's clothes: fit—and fitness.

F I T

. . . makes all the difference in the world in the way you look in your clothes. The slow changes of fashion have a little to do with it, but not much. The current trend is toward a narrow, natural look, as against the broad-shouldered, V-man appearance of some years ago. But neither fashion in its wildest extreme could condone the collar that stands away from your neck, the sleeves that make you look shirtless or the trousers that trip you up as you walk.

suits

If that new suit, which otherwise suits you, doesn't pass the following check-points, look with malice in the looking glass before you leave the fitting room:

Collar of suit jacket—should fit low and close around the neck, exposing about half an inch of your shirt collar in the back. No matter how wildly you move your arms, it should not gape or fall away from your neck. And it should stick with you when you sit down, too. (A correct fit in the collar will automatically solve some of the other problems of an ill-fitting jacket—lapels that don't lie flat, for instance.)

Sleeve of suit jacket—should expose about a half inch of your shirt cuff when your arms hang loose, more when your arm is bent. In no position of your arm should the sleeve fall over your hands, concealing all linen. Nor should it ride up so high that the top edge of your shirt cuff is visible.

Bottom of suit jacket—should be parallel to the floor all the way around when the jacket is buttoned. (And remember that you button only the top outside button of a double-breasted jacket, only the middle button of a single-breasted jacket.) This is a special hazard for the man who stands erect before the fitting-room mirror, then collapses into a slouch when he steps out into the world. See that the fitter sees you in your *natural* posture.

Jacket length—should give adequate coverage of the seat when you lean forward as well as when you stand upright. A jacket any longer than necessary to fulfill that function is considered theatrical or zooty—these days, at least—but regardless of the whims of fashion it is well to remember this design principle: the greater the distance between the bottom of your jacket and the floor, the longer-legged, and hence the taller, you look.

Jacket waistline—is not fitted, in a single-breasted jacket, but hangs straight from the natural shoulder. In a double-breasted jacket, or in any jacket which has unnaturally broad shoulders, the waistline may be slightly tapered—but never snugly, never noticeably, and never in any *extra* darts or seams; the fitting must be done in the regular side and back seams of the coat. Even if your companions cling to the V-look, and you are therefore impelled to label the newer, narrow look as "eccentric" or "New Yorky," take care that your buttoned jacket is not so waist-fitted as to force its lapels to bulge when you lift your shoulders.

Matching vest or contrasting waistcoat, if you choose to wear either, should be fitted so it does not gape where it meets your shirt. Have a daytime waistcoat fitted the way you'll wear it—with its lowest button open.

Length of trouser—should provide a slight break above your instep when you are in an easy standing position. If you're of college age, you may wear your trousers a little shorter, so they hang free instead of resting gently on your shoes. But if your socks show, your trousers are too short. And if the pants leg is festooned over your shoe—man, you made the pants too long!

Width of trouser leg—is slightly subject to fashion change. The trouser width should appear to be about two thirds the length of the foot. Odd slacks for sports wear may be fuller, trousers for dressy suits may be narrower, but that is a happy medium.

Pleats in trousers—are optional. Let your contours be your guide! If you choose pleated instead of straight-cut trousers, you have a choice between reverse pleats, which throw the fullness to the side pockets, and inward pleats, which give you greater fullness in the hips. The inward pleats are one inch deep at the waistband and the fold becomes the crease in the trouser. The outer pleats are one-half inch wide at top and taper for six inches to no pleats at all. Whichever pleats you prefer, see that they provide the right fullness for comfort and for ease of putting your hands in the pockets. A good test for comfort is to sit in a chair.

shirts

Line of collar—should slope forward, conforming to the line of your collarbone, and should fit close to your neck. Your collar is too tight if wrinkles appear across the collar in front and if you feel constricted. It is too loose if it gapes widely at any point, particularly in front. The answer is correct size, learned by measuring the neck with a tape measure, held with moderate looseness along the line of the collar. In ready-made shirts, it is wise to select the next half-size: that is, if the measurement is 15¼ inches, select size 15½. Never try to squeeze your neck into size 15. Custom shirts, in fabrics controlled for shrinkage, may be made to the exact measurement.

Height of collar—depends on the length of your neck, of course, but if your collar reaches your natural hair-line in back it is theatrically high. On a man of average build, the lower part of the shirt collar rests on his collar bone in front.

Length of sleeve—should reach the wristbone, only. And it should be held there—so it neither slides into your palm nor sneaks up into your coat sleeve—by button or cuff-links. A proper check is to have measurement made from the center back, just beneath the collar, to the wristbone. This figure, which ranges from about 32 inches to 37 inches, is your sleeve length and should be specified exactly.

outercoats

Collar—should be fitted the same as the suit collar, high enough to cover the collar of the suit but low enough to show a narrow strip of the shirt collar where weight and thickness of the outercoat allow.

Sleeve length—should be adequate to cover the sleeves of jacket and shirt. A guide is the point of the break of the wrist when your hand is turned inward.

Coat length—should never be longer than just below the knee, but may be shorter in unfitted, unbelted styles. Even in a poplin raincoat, however, anything shorter than *two* inches above the knee has an undergraduate look.

Waistline—is slightly fitted in most urban styles, should not flare even in the most casual of country coats. Fitting standards follow those for the suit jacket, above, but in this case the fitting should be done with all buttons buttoned.

hats

Fashion currently prescribes narrow brims. Common sense always dictates a hat-shape not noticeably different from your face-shape: that is, the fatter the face, the fuller the crown and the more the brim. But good fit, regardless of other considerations, depends on having the hat sit firmly yet comfortably on your head without burying you in it. Ideally, the back of the hat rests just below the back bump of your head. Never put the hat on "dead center." Rather, tilt it to one side or the other, leaving about one fourth inch between the bottom of the brim and the top of your ear on the low side. But you can usually count on this: if it feels good, it looks good.

evening clothes

Length of tailcoat should extend to a point two inches below break in knee.

Waistline fit of tailcoat should be shaped at the natural waistline, but not so tight that coat front bulges.

Length of waistcoat should be enough to cover top of trousers. A tab on the inside, to be fastened to a button on the inside of trouser waistband, helps to hold waistcoat in place.

Width of cummerbund—about 6½ inches.

Fit of dinner jacket—same as suit jacket, page 207.

Width of cuffless trousers—by current narrow standards, 18½ inches at bottom. Always worn with braces.

formal day clothes

The club jacket is fitted by the same standards as a daytime suit jacket, the cutaway like a tailcoat, formal day trousers like evening trousers.

211

CLOTHES CARE

To keep your clothes looking as well as they fit: The die is cast in the fitting room, but even the best-fitting clothes can look like rags and bags if they are not treated to proper upkeep. A poor cleaner can spoil the whole effect of your suit by pressing a knife-edged crease in the jacket sleeves or by mashing down the lapels; always instruct him to "roll 'em." A crowded closet can put permanent pleats in the straightest unpleated trousers; give 'em room! A shoulder pad poked out of line by a sharp and misplaced hanger can ruin that "natural" look you thought you'd assured; use smooth and shaped wooden hangers!

Here's the minimum care your clothes need if you want them to look (and last) better:

1. *Rotate your suits.* Never wear the same suit two days in a row if you can possibly help it. Give it a chance to hang out, and breathe, and reshape itself while you wear your "other suit."

2. *Brush your suits* before and after each wearing.

3. *Hang up a suit,* with jacket buttoned, as soon as you've taken it off, but don't put it away until it's had a chance first to air. If you're married—that is, if you share your closet with her out-of-season coats and the household vacuum cleaner— let your worn suit hang on the closet door for a few hours, or overnight, before putting it away. If even your closet door is crowded, one of those standing valets might be a good investment.

4. *Have your suits cleaned as seldom as possible,* and have them pressed without cleaning NEVER. You'll be surprised how long good daily care prolongs the intervals between cleanings—and thus makes your suits last longer.

5. *Don't overload your pockets at any time.* If you have too much stuff to be accommodated, without bulges, by inside

chest pockets and side pants-pockets, consider carrying it in a briefcase instead of straining your suit—and your silhouette. And, of course, empty your pockets after each wearing of the suit.

6. *Store your hats separately,* not "nested," so the air can circulate around them. Brush them as regularly as you brush your suits. Have their sweat bands changed when they begin to show why they are so named. And keep the hat bands clean, too! A new band on a nicely broken-in hat is apt to be conspicuous, so it's better to spot-clean the original band as you go than wait until your wife starts campaigning in favor of a new hat.

7. *Rotate your shoes,* for the good of your feet as well as for your shoes. Keep trees in them when they're resting. Keep them shined, for leather-preservation as well as for appearance. Have them regularly re-heeled, even when they look as if they could "get by" for another few wearings. Keep on hand at least one spare set of laces for each pair, so that you'll never be forced to venture forth tied in knots. And use a shoe horn when you put your shoes on, so as not to break down their backs.

FITNESS

. . . is a matter of wearing the right thing at the right time, and also of wearing the right things with each other. Both have become more difficult as life has become less formalized.

Clothes which were once considered suitable only for "the country" now turn up regularly in "the city"; the dividing line between casual and business clothes is as meandering as the line between country and city. No one expects the commuter to change clothes between office and city cocktail party; no advertising man wants to look like a banker or vice versa; not even a stickler for the "old way" insists upon being any more uncomfortable than necessary in hot weather.

And as the men's clothes front has become increasingly muddy, the man's clothes have become more a matter of individual taste and circumstance, less a matter of rigid rules and "form."

The same is roughly true in the matter of putting the right separates together to make a right whole. There remain some hard-and-fast rules—that the tie worn with a tailcoat must be white, for instance. Some of the old taboos still prevail—the pox on green suits, say, or the association of horse-blanket-plaid suits with race-track touts.

But fashion and freedom have conspired to give men more variety from which to choose within the limits of acceptability—and, thus, more ways to go wrong in the assembly of a cohesive costume.

for freedom without license

Let's see if we can erect some general guideposts in the path of this "new freedom." These are safe and sure:

Avoid exaggerations of current fashions. Even at the height of the "bold look" popularity, it was not good taste to wear the very widespread collar with the oceanic roll and the enormous Windsor knot. No matter how far the current "narrow look" goes, you will not want to look corseted, or undernourished, or "foreign." Take new fashions, when you take them, in their least obvious form—and take them one at a time. When they represent radical departures from the norm of the past, wait a while until you see if they are boons to the well-dressed man or only booms for their manufacturers.

When you move into a new environment, walk the clothes fence until you've had a chance to look around. An alert college boy on a new job will wear his "best" gray flannels, tweed jacket and pork-pie just one day before he realizes that what is dress-up at college is dress-down at his office. An aware cosmopolite turned commuter will wear his blue suit to only one suburban party before he senses that city clothes seem stiff in his new territory. And if such newcomers were even more sensitive—if they anticipated a possible change in standards—they'd look or ask beforehand. Whether your motive is to avoid self-consciousness for yourself or for the others, the safe course is always to appear to "belong"—that is, not to look "different," especially if you are.

for business as usual

Conventional business clothes, for spring, winter and fall, almost invariably consist of:

1. *Matching coat and trousers.* Slacks and odd jacket, although they often turn up at the office on half-holidays or at the studio almost any day, are still considered too casual for business-like business. But a suit worn to town need no longer be of a hard-finish material. Flannel is better than cashmere or doeskin . . . a smooth tweed rates better than a rough one, a herringbone better than a big hound's tooth check. . . . but at least you are no longer limited to worsted and serge. Darkish grays, browns and blues still have a marked edge on light or bright hues.

2. *A matching vest* has an edge in very conservative circles, a contrasting waistcoat in self-confident ones, but the middle way is: nothing between shirt and jacket, either single- or double-breasted. Sweaters are still reserved for sportswear.

3. *Shirt and tie.* The shirt may be white, a solid light color, checked or striped, but it should not be a blackish solid, or made of wool or cotton flannel, or cut on sport shirt lines. Collar-styles, named in order of their increasing dressiness, are: button-down, rounded tab, longer-point spread, short-point spread. Strictly speaking, the buttoned cuff is for sportswear; French cuffs are better for business. Pleated

bosoms are best reserved for the blue suit and the off-hour; they should never be worn with a casual suit. And patterned shirts with detachable white collars make you look like a street-car motorman at *any* time of day.

Whatever the collar style, it should stay put, close around the neck. Plastic stays should keep collar points flat and straight inside your jacket; collar pins should keep a tab collar in place without bulging or wrinkling; but no such device should be obvious.

The tie may be either bow or four-in-hand, but it should be knotted to fill the front-spacing of the collar: a wide knot on a rounded-tab collar is as bad as a skinny knot on a widespread collar. The long end of a four-in-hand should completely conceal the short end, and neither end should be visible above or outside the buttoned jacket; thus, those who go vestless should be particularly careful to buy *long* ties—and, vest or no, a tie-clip helps hold down the front. Both ends of a bow tie should be hidden by the bow, but if you can't manage a buoyant butterfly it's better to switch to a four-in-hand than retreat to one of those too-perfect ready-tied bows.

Best tie materials for business are silk or synthetic, woven or knitted. Most cotton ties and wool ties are less dressy; they look well with flannels and tweeds, but the tendency is to dress up such once-casual suit materials with less-casual accessories.

4. *Smooth leather oxfords, with leather soles, in brown or black.* Black is all right but no longer required with dark blue suits; a dark brown shoe goes with any business suit you own. Crepe soles are definitely for casual wear only. Rough leathers—reverse calf, buck, suede—still do not belong on city streets, despite manufacturers' confusing tendency to city-style such country materials. Light, white and two-toned shoes still look corny (and soon dirty) in most city surroundings; even in hot weather, the now-acceptable mesh shoe is best in

dark and uniform shades. The toe-capped oxford, although gradually being encroached upon by city-styled bluchers and moccasins, is still the first choice; sandals are never-nevers.

5. *Dark socks that stay up,* whether by means of garters or elasticized tops: If the latter, make sure that they are high enough to hide your hairy leg even when your trousers are hiked up by knee-crossing. The socks may be of lisle or light wool or wooly synthetic mixtures; silk and silky synthetics are better reserved for evening, very heavy wools for sports. Solids and patterns are equally good, but the dominant color should be a dark one; your brightest Argyles are still more fitting with slacks than with business suits.

6. *A dark hat in a smooth finish.* In some parts of the country, light and/or fuzzy hats are standard, and there are places where a bare head is not a sign of immaturity, but the big-city norm is a dark gray or brown felt snap-brim or a black homburg. Hat bands are usually grosgrain. Sometimes they are in a contrasting dark color—black on a gray hat, for instance—but more often they are in a deeper tone of the hat's own color. "Novelty" bands and feathers are risky.

7. *Brown or gray leather gloves.* Mocha and capeskin are all right, but chamois and doeskin are too-too for business wear.

8. *An outercoat,* single- or double-breasted, woolen or worsted or covert, patterned or plain but with gray or a dark color predominant. A city overcoat is usually slightly fitted, not belted, but a raincoat may be either belted, half-belted or cut straight. With any outercoat, a scarf is necessary. It may be wool or silk, light or dark, figured or plain, fringed or hemmed—but the monogrammed white silk is better saved for evening and the bright yellow cashmere is perhaps a bit too casual for business. In any case, the scarf should be crossed. The scarf looped or tied in an Ascot, like the turned-up coat collar, looks a little "cute" in daytime hours.

for summer business

In the summer, all the above would still be correct but not comfortable. The conservative translates the winter rules into summer materials: gabardines, tropical worsteds, seersuckers, cords, lightweight suitings of all kinds in natural or man-made fibers. He still avoids too light, ice-creamy shades; he still wears dark and citified accessories; he switches to straw but still wears a hat; he skips vest and gloves but still wears jacket and tie. He may substitute seersucker jacket and gray flannel slacks for matching suit, but only because ordinary seersucker trousers wrinkle so readily.

The general effect of good summer garb for business is one of cool, efficient neatness.

after hours

The city "uniform" for an after-five date or a cocktail party is a dark blue suit, white shirt, silk tie, blue or black socks, black shoes. But the rule requiring black shoes with a blue suit after dark has all but tottered, and anything which rates as good business dress also fits gracefully into the afterwork or Sunday scene, summer or winter. When in doubt, lean toward the simplest and most formal of your daytime clothes—the kind of thing you'd wear on the day you'd scheduled a meeting with the client or lunch with your boss. But never fear that you will be "underdressed," at any informal city affair, in a smooth tweed or dark flannel, particularly if it's dressed up a bit with a white shirt and town accessories.

outside city limits

All the above restrictions, loose as they are, collapse when you move off concrete into village, suburban or country life. There, you want to *avoid* the "city look," but if your business clothes are single-breasted, in soft materials, rather than double-breasted pin-stripes and hard worsteds, there is no reason why you need build a separate wardrobe for your hours of relaxation away from the office. The main difference will be in the way you accessorize your basically casual clothes. The following clothes, too off-hour for the office, rate as "dress up" in the country. That is, they go to the Connecticut cocktail party as well as to the Long Island polo game:

Odd jackets—in flannel, shetland, homespun, tweed, gabardine, cashmere, even corduroy. Lightweights, including linen and cottons, in summer. The single-breasted style is preferred for all casual clothes.

Waistcoats—in chamois, suede and other soft leathers, as alternates for the Tattersall checks and plaids which double for business. Brighter, lighter colors are possible. Wool pullovers and coat-style sweaters, too. In fact, the matching vest is almost the only type which doesn't go.

Trousers—in flannel, covert, gabardine, doeskin—plus denim and duck for sportswear. They usually are in solid colors, worn with patterned jackets, but checks and plaids are safe enough if they're not too brilliant, and if they're worn with solid jackets. Bermuda-length, tailored shorts are fine for sportswear; worn with knee-length socks, they go to cocktail parties in some areas.

Shirts—should be in soft fabrics like flannel, gabardine, oxford. Collar may be plain or buttoned down; cuff should be buttoned.

Ties—may be bow or four-in-hand, in woven materials: knits, wools, repps, cottons. Silky ties are for dressy evenings only.

Socks—in wool or man-made fiber, and in colors as bright as you please. They shouldn't slop into your shoes even in this environment, so you still need either garters or elasticized tops.

Shoes—thicker-soled, rougher-topped than your city shoes. Brown brogues and moccasins predominate. In season, white leathers or fabrics, but never with hard soles. Still no open-toed sandals!

Hats may be supplanted by caps. Soft or rough snap brims in felt always look good; the pork-pie style is in its element in the country. Summer calls for bold native straws, puggree bands.

Gloves—in pigskin or buck, wool or string.

Outercoats—single-breasted overcoats, but not in the dark solids you'd choose for town. Double-breasted polo coats, trench coats. Three-quarter length, lined windbreakers. Rough and sturdy materials in unfitted styles always your best bet.

Jewelry—Silver, leather, wood—often with sports motifs and figures—rather than the dressier, heavy gold.

dress clothes: when?

Formal and semi-formal clothes leave less leeway for individuality, hence less room for error. Follow the following lists and your problem in this department will not be what but *whether* to wear. It's everybody's problem—the more so since cutaways and top hats have moved farther and farther back into the closet—so you should never be afraid to ask. But here are some general guides to the wearing of the fancy-pants.

Evening clothes. When the invitation to any evening event is engraved—as for weddings, dances, receptions, banquets, etc.—you may wear tails but you don't have to. Black tie is taken for granted unless "white tie" or "decorations" is specified on the invitation—except that you should never wear a dinner jacket into church. "Black tie" means your black or midnight-blue dinner jacket in the winter. In the summer, the winter garb is still acceptable but you'll be more comfortable in a lightweight white dinner jacket, worn with winter's black or blue trousers.

Thus you see that your regulation dinner jacket is good anywhere, at any time, except on those few occasions when tails are a must. Even for some of those—particularly semi-public ones, like business banquets, or huge private ones where you have no official function—you can usually slide by in a dinner jacket if you don't own tails.

According to standard etiquette books, the dinner jacket is the norm for dinner at home, or informal dinner parties at another's home. The host may wear a smoking jacket with his evening trousers and shirt, but his guests, to take the books literally, turn up in dinner jackets. This may be true in secluded islands of wealth and tradition, but your average dinner hostess will clout you with the casserole if you bring anything dressier than a blue suit to her pot-luck. If she doesn't *say* black tie, *don't* take it for granted.

In any case, evening clothes are never worn before six P.M., and never on Sunday night. For ocean voyages, there's an extra "never": you don't dress the first or last night out.

Formal daytime clothes. Members of the wedding party at a formal daytime wedding must wear a cutaway, as the groom does. Pallbearers at a big funeral may be asked to wear cutaways. Guests at a formal diplomatic function, fraught with honors and protocol, should dress up to the occasion in cutaway or its sack coat variation. But with these exceptions, rarely encountered by the average joe, a dark blue suit is entirely acceptable as a substitute for formal morning or afternoon clothes.

Guests may, of course, wear formal clothes whenever principals present will be wearing them. They're quite correct for church or a Sunday stroll. But they are by no means necessary except at official ceremonies, and then only for those who have an official function of some sort. A young man who is a mere guest will doubtless always feel better in a blue suit, even if he has a perfectly good cutaway at home. But he should give the blue suit the full treatment: white shirt, white handkerchief, black shoes and socks, his dressiest, least flashy silk four-in-hand tie (black or very subdued solid color for a funeral; anything but black for a wedding).

dress clothes: what?

FULL DRESS

Tailcoat—Black or midnight blue worsted
  Peaked lapels only, faced in satin or grosgrain
Waistcoat—White piqué
  Single- or double-breasted, with bottom edge in V or in straight line
  Fastened with self-covered buttons or separate studs, the latter usually crystal, white pearl or white enamel, made to match the shirt studs
Trousers—Worsted to match coat
  Double stripe of black or blue satin, faille or braid; to be strictly correct, this striping is different from that on dinner jacket trousers—but few will notice if one pair of evening trousers does double-duty
  Cuffless
Shirt—White piqué in neckband style, with stiff single cuffs and detachable stiff white wing collar. Starched bosom of white piqué
Tie—White piqué bow, to match shirt bosom and waistcoat. Straight club or butterfly shape
Socks—Black or blue, to match coat, in silk or silky synthetic
  May be clocked, but only in same color
Shoes—Black patent leather only
  Pumps, with or without flat grosgrain bows, or oxfords without toe caps
Hat—High silk hat or high collapsible opera hat. No fedoras,

no homburgs, no derbies—nothing but a top hat will do

Gloves—White mocha, chamois, or doeskin, buttoned
(White kid gloves are worn indoors only, and the practice
of dancing with gloves on has just about died.)

Outercoat—Black, oxford gray or dark blue wool, with or
without velvet collar

Double-breasted or single-breasted with fly front

The opera cape is still correct, but it's almost extinct

Accessories—White suspenders

White silk scarf, worn crossed or in a single loop tie. Initial or monogram (optional) in white, black or gray
only

White linen handkerchief in breast pocket. Should have
hand rolled hem. Initial (if any) in white, black or gray
only

White or red carnation for jacket lapel, white being the
more formal. A small white gardenia may be used instead of a carnation for a wedding or very festive occasion. No fake boutonnieres, and no boutonniere at all
if you are wearing a decoration

A pocket watch—to be strictly correct—but many men
now ignore the ban on wrist watches with formal clothes

A thin key chain, not jeweled, strung from change pocket
to side trouser pocket

Studs and cuff-links to match. (See Waistcoat, above.) Tiny
rose diamonds, small white or smoked pearls are acceptable; colored stones jar the "white tie" effect

"BLACK TIE"

Jacket—Black or midnight-blue worsted. In summer: white
linen, tropical worsted or blended fibers

Single- or double-breasted

Peaked lapels on double-breasted jacket; either peaked lapels or shawl collar on single-breasted jacket

Lapel or shawl facing in satin, grosgrain or dull silk. Summer jacket may be without facing, if you prefer

Waistcoat—Black or blue, in worsted to match jacket or in silk—plain, ribbed or self-figured

Single- or double-breasted, with or without lapels. Fastened with self-covered buttons or separate studs to match the shirt studs

The waistcoat is not necessary with a double-breasted jacket, and these variations are acceptable with either style jacket: a black or blue silk cummerbund, instead of a waistcoat; in summer, with a white jacket, this may also be maroon, worn with a maroon tie—but plaids and checks are considered peculiar outside Miami

Trousers—Worsted to match coat

Single stripe of black or blue braid, or material to match jacket lapels

Cuffless

Shirt—A range of formality, from the old white piqué with stiff bosom, stiff single cuffs, stiff wing collar through the soft shirt with pleated or plain bosom, attached fold collar and double cuffs—right down to a plain broadcloth shirt with no starch, no studs and sometimes no cuff-links. The remaining rule: it must be white. But it can certainly be soft and comfortable

Tie—Black or blue bow, butterfly or narrow, in dull silk, repp, satin or grosgrain. With summer-white jacket, bow may also be maroon

Socks—Black or blue, to match trousers, in silk or silky synthetic

May be clocked in same color or in white

Shoes—Black patent leather only

Pumps or oxfords, same as for full dress

Hat—Black or blue homburg, only, in winter. In summer, a fine Panama or Milan

Gloves—Gray mocha, chamois or buck
   Button or slip-on
Outercoat—Black, oxford gray or dark blue wool, with or
      without a velvet collar.
   Double-breasted or single-breasted (Fly-front optional)
Accessories—White, black or black-and-white suspenders
   White silk scarf. Initial or monogram, if any, in white,
      black or gray only
   White linen handkerchief in breast pocket. Initial, if any,
      in white, black or gray
   Red or white carnation for jacket lapel, red being the usual.
      No feather-boutonnieres. With a decoration ribbon in
      the buttonhole, no boutonniere
   Pocket or wrist watch—or none
   Watch chain—same as for full dress, if worn, with addi-
      tional possibility of gold
   Studs and cuff-links—same as for full dress, with possibil-
      ities of gold, sapphire or other colored stones, black onyx

FORMAL DAY CLOTHES

Cutaway—Black or oxford gray, in worsted, cashmere or
      Cheviot
   Peaked lapels, plain edges
   Bone or cloth-covered buttons
Waistcoat—Usually double-breasted, but may be single-
      breasted
   To match coat, or may be pearl gray or buff doeskin; also,
      in summer, white or tan linen
   Fastened with self-covered buttons if it matches cutaway;
      otherwise, bone or pearl buttons
Trousers—Black-and-gray striped, or black-and-white, in
      worsted or Cheviot. Stripes may be close-set or up to
      one inch apart

225

Cuffless

Shirt—White only, with stiff single or double cuffs, pleated or plain bosom, wing or fold collar

Tie—Gray, black or silver-gray silk; plain, figured, striped— Ascot, four-in-hand or bow—with the following limitations:

> An Ascot is worn only for a wedding, and with a wing collar. A funeral calls for a black four-in-hand and a fold collar

> A four-in-hand and a bow may be worn with either wing or fold collar

Socks—Black or dark gray, in silk or lisle or wool

Shoes—Black calf oxfords, with or without toe caps

Hat—Black silk top hat

Gloves—Gray mocha

Outercoat—Black, dark blue or oxford gray worsted, with or without velvet collar

Double-breasted or single-breasted

Accessories—Gray or black-and-white suspenders

White or gray scarf

White linen handkerchief

Boutonniere, except at funeral: white carnation, white bridal flowers, dark red carnation, or whatever is suitable to the occasion

Pocket watch—or none. But again, many men wear wrist watches in the face of old traditions

Key chain, as for formal evening wear

Studs and cuff-links to match: gray pearl, gold or gray enamel

Black stick or umbrella

Spats (optional)—Gray felt or doeskin in winter; white, gray or tan linen to match similar waistcoat in summer. Spats are correct but not necessary at weddings, should never be worn at funerals

FORMAL DAY VARIATION

(less formal, more modern)

Jacket—Single-breasted sack coat in black or oxford-gray worsted. (Double-breasted also acceptable.)

Waistcoat—To match jacket or of pale gray or buff
Single-breasted or double-breasted
Fastened with self-covered buttons, if matches jacket; otherwise, bone or pearl

Trousers—Same as for Cutaway

Shirt—White, with fold collar, stiff cuffs

Tie—Four-in-hand or bow, in black or black-and-gray silk, striped, figured or polka-dotted

Socks—Same as for Formal Day

Shoes—Same as for Formal Day

Hat—Black homburg (preferred) or black derby

Gloves—Same as for Formal Day

Outercoat—Same as for Formal Day

Accessories—Same as for Formal Day, except
—no spats
—wrist *or* pocket watch
—stick optional

incidentally . . .

Jewelry—if not plain, heavy and absolutely functional—is dangerous. The safest pieces are the least conspicuous ones: the gold safety pin at the collar, the small initialed clip on the tie, the flat gold squares at the cuffs, the pigskin watchband, one or two small pearls at the evening shirt front, the undecorated watch chain.

A ring is just about the only pretty that a man can wear without looking pretty-pretty himself, and even a ring ought to mean something—like a wedding ring, or a signet ring bearing a coat of arms he's really entitled to. Except for wedding rings, more often worn on the fourth finger of the left hand in this country, all men's rings should be worn on the little finger—left hand, if you want to make hand-shaking less painful.

Your instinct will warn you away from too many mono-grams, too delicate engraving, too fancy shapes, too obvious stones. So the above "rule" is mentioned not so much to hamstring you as to stiffen your resistance to presents from the other sex.

Mourning for a man consists merely of a two-inch black armband, usually felt, sewn to the left sleeve of each of his jackets and coats, midway between elbow and shoulder. A man in mourning generally leans toward dark suits and ties, white instead of colored shirts, but there are no widower's weeds for him. A man might wear such a band for six months after the death of a member of his immediate family, three months after other blood relatives had died. But more and more people make no point of their grief; they think the armband, however "correct," imposes an unnecessary strain on others. They wear the armband and the blacks only to the funerals of family members.

A handkerchief in your left breast pocket is completely optional with daytime clothes, but if you choose to wear one it should be spotlessly clean—i.e., not used as a handker-chief. It may be folded in a square or rectangle, with merely the top edges sticking out of your pocket, or it may be grasped in the center and thrust into the pocket with points showing as they fall. But the precise six-point fold of other days is now considered suitable only for department-store dummies.

what goes with what?

In the coordination of clothes, your two guides should be color and pattern.

As to color, you may use either different shades of one color or contrasting colors which complement each other. A one-color scheme is easier, and always in good taste, but if you find it monotonous from day to day you'll mix 'em up a little: a gray suit, say, with a blue shirt, a maroon-ground tie, maroon socks, brown hat, brown shoes, brown gloves. That sample is a conservative one; you could safely throw in one bright color, probably in the tie. But the rule of safety is to use only one light or bright color, wear not more than three dark or grayed shades at once.

The best of taste, because it steers clear of foppishness, avoids matched "sets." Your socks may be keyed to your tie, your breast pocket handkerchief to any color you're wearing, but they shouldn't be cut from the same bolt if they are to appear outside the haberdasher's window.

Correlating patterns is a little more complicated than matching or contrasting colors. Here's a simple rule of thumb: when one article of clothing is of strong or positive design, all others should be neutralizers. Plain or solid colors are certain neutralizers; small patterns are, too, if they are subdued and grayed. By this rule, a plaid waistcoat or a brightly figured tie or a striped shirt or a checked suit would each be worn with solids.

Actually, striped or small-figured ties look very well with Glen Plaid suits, a noisy sport shirt can easily take Argyle socks, and the right man can concoct a right combination of checked shirt, plaid waistcoat and figured tie. But if you haven't either an unfailing eye or a carry-all manner, settle for one accent at a time.

PERSONAL GROOMING

Having achieved fitness and fit in your clothes, there remains only one more stumbling block: personal grooming.

Thanks to advertisers and your fellow bus-riders, nobody

need tell you about the importance of daily baths, deodorants, dental care, frequent shampoos, close shaves and fresh linen. But etiquette has a word to say about these footnotes to the neat-and-clean look your good clothes demand:

your hair

. . . should clear your ears, cheeks and collar at all times, and that means the day before you have your hair cut as well as the day after. The perfect look conjures up no visions of barber chairs, present or absent. It is achieved by having your hair scissor-trimmed every week or ten days, and staying far, far away from clippers at all times.

No one will notice whether you part your hair on the right or left side, or, as with a crew cut, not at all. But if you turn up with a center part someone will be sure to look down for your high-button shoes.

If your hair stays in place, no one will care whether or not you wear a dressing on it—so long as the dressing is not obvious to nose or eye.

No one cares that you are bald, unless *you* seem to. Balding men who wear their remaining hair long, or try to arrange a few strands to serve for many, advertise not only their baldness but their vanity.

Lest your vanity show at the other extreme, you'd better not wear your hair long and thick on top, either—particularly if it falls into pretty waves, or into your pretty blue eyes.

your perfume

. . . is something you probably think you don't wear. But most of the toilet preparations you use are doubtless perfumed, and chances are that their various scents conflict with each other. You have three alternatives, each better than the olfactory hodge-podge which usually results from ignoring the sniff question: 1) You may use matched toiletries, all carrying the same mannish scent; 2) you may shop around for completely odorless soaps, lotions, creams and talcs, and go forth in your native scent (guarded, please, by a deodorant!), or 3) you may top off an unscented toilette with small doses of a controllable cologne.

"Spicy," "leathery," "woodsy" and "outdoorsy" are the feeble words usually used to describe a scent that is distinctly masculine. The main thing is to avoid the flowery perfumes which proclaim femininity, the "cheap" smell of the usual barber tonic, and the overpowering scent of too much of anything.

your nails

. . . should be clean, short and trim. In your *strictly private* parings, you might shape your nails a little—but not point or taper them. Rough hangnails and cuticle are unattractive, not to say uncomfortable, and if you can't keep up with them you ought to cultivate a manicurist. But don't let her put polish on your nails! A good buffing is healthy, and the gloss added by a buffing powder is clean looking, but any and all sorts of liquid polish are apt to give you a scare once you step out into the harsh world beyond the barber shop.

your chin

. . . won't fool anyone worth fooling if it is powdered instead of shaved.

your posture

. . . can do a lot of good or evil for your clothes. If you would put up a good front, remember the gentle advice of the drill sergeant: *SUCK IN THAT HORRIBLE GUT!*

THE ANATOMY OF ETIQUETTE

Here are the bare essentials of everyday etiquette in everyday social intercourse—the firm skeleton which remains after all the impractical embellishments of other days have been stripped away:

YOUR HEAD

Take off your hat (civilian, that is) whenever you are indoors, except in a synagogue and except in places which are akin to public streets: lobbies, corridors, street conveyances, crowded elevators of non-residential public buildings (department stores, office buildings). Apartment house elevators and halls are classed as indoors, and so are eating places!

Take it off *outdoors* whenever you stop to talk to a woman —and keep it off for the whole conversation, unless you walk and talk. Take it off whenever you pray or witness a religious ceremony, as at a burial, outdoor wedding, dedication. Take it off whenever the flag goes by. And fergodsakes take it off when you have your photograph taken for the place of honor on her dressing table—and take it off before you kiss her!

Lift it momentarily as accompaniment to courtesies when hello, goodbye, how do you do, thank you, excuse me or you're welcome are expressed or understood. The gesture is to grasp the front crown of a soft hat or the brim of a stiff one, thus to lift the hat slightly off and forward, and simultaneously to nod or bow your head as you say (or smile) your say.

Whenever you perform a service for a strange woman, or ask one—when, for example, you pick up something she has

232

dropped on the sidewalk, or ask her (indirectly) to get her bundles the hell off that vacant bus-seat—you tip your hat to acknowledge her thanks or to give yours. Whenever you greet in passing or fall into step with a woman you know (your wife included), you tip your hat. In fact, the tip of the hat is a must for all brief exchanges with women, known or unknown.

A man rates your hat-lift, too, when he has performed some service for the woman you're with—when he's given his bus seat to your wife, for instance (in which case you should give him a card to your psychiatrist, as well). And also when he has been greeted by your woman companion, you tip your hat whether or not you know him. If she stops and if she introduces you, your hat comes off—but this is because you are standing and talking with a woman.

Ordinarily, you don't lift your hat to and among men, when no women are present. It would be awkward to lift hat and shake hands, and men usually shake hands in greetings and goodbyes. A polite young man lifts his hat to an older man, however, and an abbreviated hat-tip (more like a loose salute) is always a friendly gesture from one man to another.

Check it, whenever there's a checkroom provided. Except at the theatre, when you know there's a hat-rack under your seat and you know even better that the checkroom will be in a jam after the show, it's better not to stand on your principles than to have to sit on your hat. This can get pretty expensive, to be sure, if you're making the rounds and will have to check your hat ten times in an evening—but what's $2.50, anyway, to a man with ten drinks in him?

YOUR BIG FEET

Hop to them whenever a woman enters a room where you are sitting, and stand on them until she sits or goes. An old-school gentleman never sits unless and until all women in the room are also sitting; and then, unless he is in his own house, he sits only on invitation. A modern man adds a layer of good sense to that layer of good manners. He sits down at crowded cocktail parties when the standing women and the standing hostess are in groups apart. He only half-stands when, pinned behind a restaurant table, a woman pauses to say hello to anyone in his group. (To stand all the way would be more comfortable for him but less comfortable for the woman, because she would have to apologize for causing a big table-moving fuss.) He doesn't hop up and down every time his wife passes through the room during a quiet evening at home. (But he does act the gentleman-in-good-standing when outsiders are present, or when he's trying to set an example for his sons, or when she makes her first entrance or greeting.) And he probably has a separate, lesser set of manners for strange women in public places: he keeps his seat on the subway except for an old or pregnant or obviously overburdened woman (but he doesn't knock even the youngest woman down in a race for the seat!) . . . he keeps his seat in public lobbies unless a woman greets him or speaks to him from on high . . . and he doesn't interrupt his work to stand for non-social exchanges with women (see page 4, Business Etiquette).

Stand up for men, too, for introductions, greetings, leave-takings. This "comes natural"; it's not comfortable to shake hands from a sitting position, so you stand whenever a handshake is imminent.

Stand up when someone, man or woman, is trying to pass in front of you in a row of theatre seats. Only a very small child can squeeze between your knees and the next row of seats in the usual theatre, no matter how tight you think you've drawn yourself up.

Step out of the elevator, and out of the way, when someone farther back in the car wants to get out and you are blocking the door. Elevator riding is not supposed to be among the contact sports.

Walk on the street-side of the sidewalk when you can do it gracefully. There are few run-away horses, these days, but there are still splashing puddles and other terrors of the street from which you can "protect" your woman companion. It is better, however, to walk on the inside than to convert a simple stroll into a ballet: don't cross back and forth behind her or be forever running around end just to get into position. The rule is supposed to be for her comfort and her safety; she finds nothing comfortable about talking to a whirling dervish, and nothing particularly safe about leading the way through traffic while you're running around her heels. Keep her on the inside and/or on your right if you can, but remember that it's better to have her on your left and on the outside than to shift positions every ten feet, as strict observance of the rule might sometimes require.

The same rules (or lack of them) apply whether you are walking with one woman or three: keep women on the inside or on your right, but only if you can do it without awkward shuffling.

Y O U R   H A N D S

Shake hands for all introductions and all goodbyes to men —but don't ever offer your hand to a woman unless she extends hers first. When she holds out her hand, you're supposed to do the shaking: two or three short up-and-down movements will do it—no pump, no crush and no lingering. Try to remember that she probably has rings on her finger —even your *junior* bear-trap grip can turn her smile into a wince. (Your fellow-men are not too pleased with bone-crushing contests, either.) Don't, of course, *kiss* a woman's hand unless you are a Continental, and a not-too-far removed one at that. For anyone else, hand-kissing is an affectation.

235

Besides, you might get it wrong and kiss a single-girl's hand when the treatment is supposed to be for married women only.

Remove your right glove before shaking hands with a woman, *if you can do it inconspicuously and without delay.* But if you are trapped into a gloved handshake, *don't* say "Excuse my glove." That one belongs with "After you, Alphonse," and there is no comfortable response to it.

Take your gloves off when you're indoors, unless you are a white-gloved usher at a formal wedding (in which case you do not remove them for handshaking). Leave your gloves with your hat.

Give your hand to a woman, palm up, as a kind of rest or ledge for *her* hand when you help her down from busses, out from cabs, down into boats, and so on. In these situations, you precede her so that you can be in a position to help and, naturally, you offer your hand first. But as soon as she has regained her balance, let go. Hand-holding comes later.

Put your hand under a woman's elbow almost never. Modern women do not like to be steered; they hate this bastard version of offering your arm, and they find it more hindrance than help in stepping off curbs and crossing streets. Fastidious women are annoyed on another account: they do not like to be touched meaninglessly. The only time you can properly cup your hand under a woman's elbow is when it is absolutely necessary to boost her upward —when she has begun an actual fall, for rare example. Caution: when the gesture seems most necessary, it will probably be most resented; the girl in the narrow skirt, trying to mount a high bus step, needs her hand for lifting the skirt—your unwelcome elbow-grip will *really* immobilize her!

The conventional form of offering your arm has just about gone out. You do it only at formal dinners (see page 391) or at the grand march for a costume ball. At such times, you offer your right arm, bent at the elbow and with forearm parallel to the floor. She links her arm loosely through yours and away you go. Once away from college campus or country beer party, you and your lady-fair seldom walk in public with arms linked.

Your hands are an important part of your dancing position. Your left or leading hand should hold hers lightly and naturally; contorted positions make bad manners as well as bad dancers. Your right or holding hand should be placed firmly yet loosely just above her waist—not grappling her neck, not sticking to her bare back and certainly not slid underneath her jacket. What you do with your hands when you're off the floor is something else again, but while you're dancing your manners matter—to onlookers and to your partner, if not to you.

Hands in repose belong in your lap at the dinner table, at your sides when walking or standing. It's all right to put your hands in your pockets or fold your arms or clasp hands behind back *sometimes,* but watch out for the unconscious hand mannerisms which could be offensive to others or unbecoming to you: the sloppy look of a man whose hands are *always* buried in his pockets . . . the pompous look of the man who *always* talks over pressed-together fingertips . . . the barbershop look of the man who *at any time in public* picks at his ears or buffs his nails or pats his hair or strokes his chin.

The helping hand, the basis of most etiquette situations between men and women, is not so simple as it once was—perhaps because women are not so simple as they once were (or once pretended to be). As often as not, the modern woman forgets to give you *time* for the correct or the courtly gesture: she opens the door because, preceding you, she reaches it first; she hops out of the car before you've had a chance to walk around and help her out; she slides into her coat before you know she's ready to go. At such times, with such women, your insistence on the letter of etiquette will squelch her spirit; she'll feel awkward, embarrassed at her own commendable casualness, if you make a Thing of your helping hand. But at other times, or with other women, hesitate and ye are lost. A nice sense of time and place is your greatest asset in this area. Here are the rules, but— caution: use only as expected:

1. *It's "ladies first,"* except when your going first is in form of service to her. Thus, when there's a waiter to lead you to a table or an usher to lead you to your seats, you fall back and let her precede you—but when there is no one else to perform the service involved, you go first in order to find the table or the seats. When the path is clear and unobstructed, ladies first; but when there's a mob to be elbowed or a puddle to be forded or a steep step to be navigated, gentleman first.

When you go first, however, be sure that the reason for it is apparent. You get off the bus first so you can help her down to the curb, not so you can be the first to reach the bar on the corner. You go first down the steep stadium steps so you can hand her down as you go, not so you can lose her in the crowd. If she's behind you, keep her close behind and make it clear that you are helping her. If there can be any doubt in her mind as to the reason for your going first, say something like, "These stairs are pretty dark; maybe I'd better lead the way."

2. *Hold all doors for her,* just as if she hadn't a muscle in her body. The classic maneuver requires some cooperation on her part, however. Because of "ladies first," she arrives at the door before you. She steps slightly to one side, so that you can reach the doorknob and so that the door can open toward her without knocking her down. You open, she passes through, you follow—and on to the next door. If she doesn't pause or step aside, if she grasps the doorknob herself, the best you can do is to pull further open the door which she

has begun to open. That much you should attempt—and you should never let her stand holding the door as *you* pass through!—but let her set the pace by her approach to the door. That is, don't knock her over to reach the door first, don't brush her hand off the knob, don't get into the "allow-me" type of conversational help, and, whatever the situation calls for, don't make a Thing of it. One more don't: don't expect her to be consistent. Just because she opened the last three doors, foiling all your efforts to play the gallant, don't be surprised if she waits expectantly before yon magic-eye door. Your job is to be ready and willing at every door, and to let her specific conduct be your guide at each one.

When the door pushes in, rather than opening out, you could correctly precede her through the door in order to hold it for her. More than likely, however, she will push ahead and you will have only to extend your arm over her head to take the door's weight from her as she passes through. Try not to get into that ungainly position of standing at the sill, trying to hold a push-door in front of you and forcing her to duck under your arm. This is not the minuet or London Bridge, after all, but just a helping hand. When the door is revolving, reach out and slow it down so that she can step in, then give a push on the piece in front of her, so she can walk through without effort. (If you push on the piece behind her, you might unwittingly knock her off her feet; if that's your aim, pick a better place than a revolving door.)

When the door, of whatever type, is in a public or crowded place, remember that your duty is to your woman, not to the public at large. Follow her through the door. If you exaggerate your etiquette into holding the door for the next woman behind you, and the next and the next, *your* gal will be standing alone and lonely in the lobby crowd. Look behind as you pass through, of course—you don't want to let the door fly in any face, male or female—but get on with it.

Car doors produce special problems, but only if you let them. When you are in the driver's seat and she beside you, you are supposed to get out on your side, walk around the car, open her door for her, and then—if the step is steep or the exit otherwise difficult—offer your hand to help her out. This convention presupposes country roads and front-door parking, however; edit it to suit the circumstances when you're in clogged traffic.

If you can't park there long enough to give the full treatment, it's all right to reach across her to open her door—explaining as you go. And if there's a doorman to open her door, or if she opens it herself without ceremony, relax.

When you're both passengers, and there's no doorman, you should get out first—even if she's closer to the door than you —so you can hold the door and help her to the curb. When the doorman is on the job, she goes first unless you're closer— in which case you step to the street and either help her down or stand attentively as the doorman helps her. Even if you're going on and are merely dropping her off, get out with your helping hand and your goodbyes. Unless you're driving, and it is obvious that you can't leave your car unattended in mid-traffic, you shouldn't sit at ease while she alights and takes flight.

3. *Hold all chairs for her,* when she sits and when she rises. The idea of holding a chair for a sitting duckie, by the way, is *not* to trip her off her feet by jabbing the chair edge into the back of her knees. Nor is it to contribute to her sense of insecurity by letting her sit into space. Just pull the chair back as she steps into place in front of it, then push it under her (without touching her with it) as she bends her knees to sit. In reverse order, the technique is the same when she rises; don't yank the chair back with her in it and don't push it back under the table until she has stepped out of range.

Again, the gesture is what counts with an independent dame. She slides into a chair before you've had time to hold it for her, but she may still take it amiss if you then slide into yours; your best bet is *always* to walk around behind her chair, to help her off with her coat if not to make one final adjustment of the chair's position. If you're not going to do that, do nothing. The common practice of reaching across the table—in the vague direction of the back of her chair, which you couldn't possibly reach—is ungainly and serves only to remind her of the larger gesture she might have let you make.

Needless to say, you don't "hold" sofas, built-in wall seats or anything which cannot be moved out for easier seating. All you do, then, is see that she is seated before you sit.

4. *Help her in and out of her coat.* Again, the extent of your help is up to her, but even for the most determinedly helpless frail you should *not* fluff her hair outside her collar as if you were her lady's maid, or reach under her coat and pull down her jacket as if you were a barbershop porter, or chase her flailing arms about with the coat as if you were roping a calf. *Just hold the coat.* Hold it right side up and in shape, so she doesn't have to be an acrobat to get into it; hold it a little lower than shoulder height, so she doesn't have to use a back stroke to reach the sleeves; pull it up onto her shoulders once her arms are started into the sleeves—but *let her get into it herself.* She doesn't want you to dress her—not right now, anyway—so content yourself with being a coat-rack, not a valet.

Incidentally, she'll be grateful if you help her take care of her furs. Unless she's wearing her old mink (or wants you to think so), she'd rather not sit on it: fold it over an empty chair at the table instead of simply dropping it back over her chair as you would a cloth coat. Do it automatically, without implying that she doesn't know where her next mink is coming from, and you'll get a few unspoken thanks.

5. *Light her cigarettes whenever you're close enough* and, be you ever so far across the room, whenever she is appar-

ently lightless. If she's sitting within reach of a lighter, and if she's not crippled, nobody expects you to walk a mile with a match. But if she's sitting with virgin cigarette in matchless surroundings, she ranks as a damsel in distress; she must be reached with dispatch, and with match, regardless of inconvenience to you. That's a nice point, there—another example of the fine line between exaggerated, unbecoming courtliness and natural, expected courtesy. If you and your lighter are forever stumbling across rooms, breaking off conversations, jousting with other men for the dubious honor of lighting cigarettes, you're a bore. If you and your lighter sit motionless while a woman sitting within arm's reach lights her own cigarette, you're a boor. Light somewhere in between.

If you're a smart Boy Scout, you'll be prepared—whether or not you smoke, yourself. Instead of grabbing her ready match-pack out of her hands to light her cigarette—a tactic which might very well make her feel as foolish as you look— carry your own matches so you can extend one, already lighted, without a lot of folderol. If you're wise, you'll hold the light high—she doesn't want to have to lean over it, singeing her eyelashes and smoking up her eyes. And if you're not in the movies (or very much alone with your love), you won't light her cigarette along with yours in your own mouth.

In the matter of which woman's cigarette to light first, let your conscience be your guide. If you and your wife are host and hostess, you will doubtless light your woman guest's cigarette first, just as you seat and de-coat the guest first. The hostess' first concern is supposed to be her guest's welfare, not her husband's motives. If you and your wife are guests, you will probably light your hostess' cigarette before your wife's, on the same general theory, reversed. But if this is not a host-guest relationship—if, for example, you're just a part of a large Dutch-treat group—your primary responsibility is to your "date," your wife. If your date is not your wife, she rates as your guest of honor, not your hostess, when you are the host; give her top billing, always, unless the other women are much older or have greater (mutually recognized) claim on your attentions. Your date will probably think you're "nice" if you light your mother's cigarette before hers—but she'll have less pleasant reactions if you put the visiting blonde before her.

6. *Man is a beast of burden,* but he got a break during the war when it was widely understood that a man in uniform did not carry packages. No longer must you snatch every odd package from every woman you walk so much as two steps with. Let her carry her own junk, if she's so graceless as to be toting on a date; she won't be as uncomfortable under her light burden as she will be if you insist on looking like a dray horse when she'd rather be seen with a man. Of course, you should still relieve her of *heavy* things—suitcases, briefcases, books and magazines which give her too many things to carry. If she's your wife, or if you'd be proud to have someone think so, you should carry the biggest bag of groceries and push the heavy baby carriage. If you think it's safe, you can still make the *gesture* toward odd parcels, coats, umbrellas and model's hat boxes. ("Is that too heavy for you?" is safer than "Here, let me carry that.") But if there's a chance she'll say "yes," rest in this peace: a man of good modern manners totes for milady only when his strength is needed, *not* when she could carry the stuff as effortlessly as he.

7. *It's the man who pays,* but not necessarily for expenses which come up during a *chance* encounter with a woman. You're not expected to pick up the check when you have only happened on to her at the drugstore lunch counter, nor to buy her train ticket if you find that you're both going out of the same station. It's not bad manners to make a move toward paying a small expense—her bus fare, say—but it is by no means necessary and, with modern women hipped on "in-

dependence," it can make them sorry they saw you. They will be embarrassed, as well, if you come up with money for the cleaner, the shoe-repair man or the butcher when you catch them at their errands; they might like to be "kept" women, but not on that small and public scale! In any case, don't protest if a woman says she has the money ready or otherwise indicates that she doesn't want you to pay. The Big Scene over the Small Sum is especially silly when it stems from this mistaken idea of gallantry.

YOUR EARS

The man who believes everything every woman ever tells him needs more than an etiquette book to straighten him out, but these are the times which try men's credulity. You *want* to take her at her word but it's good manners *not* to when she says:

"*Please don't get up*"—or, if you have already struggled to your feet, "*Please sit down.*" No matter what she says or how much she means it, you gotta stand while she stands (see page 233). If she really meant it she'd sit or leave, so you could relax.

"*Don't bother—I can manage.*" She probably can, but if you stand by while she does it all herself, and it is a struggle for her, you're going to look pretty silly to people who haven't heard her protests.

"*You go ahead; I'll be all right.*" This in all its variations is supposed to excuse your leaving her alone on the dance floor or letting her find her way home by herself or setting her free to free-lance in any situation where your firm duty is to take care of her. Nine times out of ten it doesn't excuse you even in her mind (to say nothing of her parents' or her friends'); she expects you to insist—in action, not words. The tenth time, when she really means it and it's really impossible for you to live up to your normal good manners, you'll know it's

244

all right to "go ahead." Even so, you'll follow up by telephone or otherwise check to make sure that she made it all right . . . even so, you'll try to make it up to her later . . . even so, you'll decide it would have been simpler all around to do your duty.

YOUR MOUTH

table manners

When feeding your face, the idea is to do it neatly, quietly and all but incidentally. If anything bothers you about table manners, put the question to those three tests. If the technique makes a mess or noise, or if it calls attention to the fact that you are determined to stuff yourself, it's bad manners.

For a man, a fourth general "don't" assumes equal importance: don't be prissy. Don't cock your little finger or pat-pat your pursed mouth daintily with your napkin.

The way you eat is a matter of habit. That's 99 44/100 per cent fortunate, because you'd probably starve to death if you had to think about every muscle and every move involved in the intricate process of propelling food from plate to mouth. But it's 56/100 per cent unfortunate, too: if your unconscious eating habits are unattractive, even your best friend won't tell you.

But *you* can tell; watch yourself for these signs of the four scourges of the dining table.

1. THE SLOB

ties his napkin around his neck or tucks it into his vest. The napkin belongs in your lap during a meal, loosely laid to the left of your place when you leave the table. Whether paper or damask, it should neither be folded for reuse nor blithely tossed into your plate.

245

Leaves a sample of every course on the rim of his drinking glass. He sins on two counts: he drinks when his mouth is not empty, and neglects to use his napkin before using the glass.

Makes every mouthful a full course meal in miniature (and not so miniature at that). Instead, of course, he should take small bites, chewing and swallowing each bite before he takes the next. And he should keep separate foods separate, if that's the way they were intended. Sauces and gravies may be poured directly onto the food for which they were intended, but jellies, condiments and all other accessories should be put on the plate in virgin state, only then to be spread on bread or forked onto meat in bite-size portions.

Forms a bridge from table to plate with his knife and fork when they are not in use—handles on cloth, working ends propped on plate. In his less virulent form he lays knife and fork on plate, as is correct, but so close to the edge that they fall off when the plate is removed.

Talks with his mouth full.

Cleans his teeth at the table—with toothpick or fingernail or by running his tongue around his teeth, with grimaces.

Spits out anything he doesn't like. (You don't have to eat the inedible of course, and if you *must* remove something from your mouth, first be sure that it bears no resemblance to regurgitated food, then grasp and remove it with your fingers—that's the quickest way. Correctly you could take it out on the same spoon or fork it went in on, but this maneuver is too acrobatic for grace in most instances, and it runs dangerously close to spitting. Actually, you can usually cut out bones and stones before they get into your mouth. And you can manfully swallow something that offends your palate.)

246

Breaks crackers into his soup. If they are meant to go into the soup, they are meant to go in whole. You spoon them directly into the soup if they are croutons; if they are oyster crackers you put them first on your butter plate or on the cloth, then drop them in *whole,* a few at a time.

Eats messy things with his fingers. The best way to decide when to pick food up in your fingers (if you're not content to follow your hostess' example) is to decide *in advance* whether you can do it neatly. Picnics are something else again of course, and some foods like lobster are messy whatever your *modus operandi,* but with neatness as your guide you can't go far wrong. The guide works both ways: it's neater to pick up an ear of corn than to watch it skitter across the plate as you try to cut it; it is neater to leave the hard stalk of asparagus if you can't cut and eat it with the fork as you did the tips. And if an approach by hand seems indicated, as with a sandwich or a piece of fresh fruit, it is neater to cut it into manageable sections before you pick it up.

Blows on his food, instead of waiting quietly for it to cool enough to eat.

Bites off the ends of a forkful of spaghetti, usually in mid-air. If he can't cut it on his plate, or twist it around his fork in a neat and manageable ball, he ought to order ravioli instead.

Gesticulates and points with his eating tools.

Puts soiled silver on the table. If there is no saucer under the cup (but there always will be) leave the spoon in the cup rather than placing it on the tablecloth. And never do the dishwashing or silver polishing at the table: if the implement is really not clean, ignore it as you would ignore a hair in your soup. (In a restaurant, of course, you may ask for another fork or send the soup back).

Puts his mouth into the food instead of the food into his mouth. You shouldn't meet your food even halfway. You bring it up to your erect head; you don't duck down to meet it coming up.

2. THE RACKET-EER

chews with his mouth open, making no attempt to muffle the noise (or conceal the sight) of his cement-mixer mastication.

Clanks silver on silver, or silver on plate. When he stirs his coffee he does it fiendishly, like a witch standing over a boiling cauldron, and every revolution of the spoon sets up a racket. When he puts his knife and fork down, you wonder that the force does not smash the plate. He winds up by scraping his plate with his fork. And if he's the "helpful" as well as the noisy type, his final sin against the eardrums is to stack his dishes, crashingly.

Slurps his soup. Suction is superfluous—just put the side of the spoon to your mouth and sip quietly.

Drums on the table, or cracks his knuckles, or chews on the ice from his water glass, or otherwise sounds off between noisy bites.

Pushes away from the table at dinner's end, with both hands shoving against the table edge and the chair screeching across the floor. Instead, you should reach down and lift the chair back as you rise slightly.

3. THE PIG

digs in the moment he's served. He knows he doesn't have to wait for the hostess, who will be served last, but he's apparently too hungry to remember that he should wait until two or three others at the table have also been served.

Pushes his plate away from him when he's finished, as if to say, "Well, *that* was good, *now* what do we eat?" Instead, he should sit quietly and without rearranging the table, without pushing or tilting his chair back, and without loosening his belt.

Uses a piece of bread, tightly gripped in his hand, to mop up every last drop of sauce, every last morsel of food. His plate then looks as if it had just come out of the dishwasher. If his favorite food is bread and gravy, he may break off a small piece of bread, drop it into the sauce, then eat the bread with his fork—but he shouldn't scrub or mop or use an unbroken slice of bread.

Spreads butter on his bread in mid-air and all at once, as if he intended to eat the whole piece in one bite. Except in the case of tiny, hot biscuits, bread should be broken and buttered only as needed—in quarters or bite sizes. It should be held against the rim of the butter plate during the spreading, not waved all over the place or held chest high.

Gnaws on bones, as if he's afraid to miss the tiniest morsel of meat.

Sucks his fingers, on the same sort of compulsion. If he is so messy as to get food on his fingers, he should use a finger bowl and/or the napkin, not his lips.

Cuts up his whole plateful of food at one time, as if he couldn't bear to stop eating once he had begun. Unless he is under ten years old, he should cut his food only as he eats it.

Tilts his soup bowl toward him. Properly, he would tip it away from him, just as—properly—he would spoon the soup away from him. But this is not the shortest distance between two points, and the pig is blatantly starving.

Elbows his way through the meal. When he cuts, his elbows are like flapping wings. When he eats, his spare arm serves as a prop, enabling him to eat much faster. Elbows on the table are "socially acceptable" when you're not eating, but the safest course is to keep your spare hand in your lap. While you're eating, your elbows should be as close to your body as in a good golf swing.

Squeezes the last drop of juice from his half grapefruit. If you can't get it out with a spoon it's out of bounds.

4. THE PRISS

purses his lips when he eats—in exaggerated "refinement." He couldn't look less pleased if he were eating cyanide or castor oil.

Leaves a little of everything on his plate, in terror of appearing greedy. What a waste! If he doesn't intend to eat it, he shouldn't take it.

Is always saying that he doesn't like or "can't eat" certain foods. If he is not blessed with a catholic taste, or a genuine enjoyment of all foods strange and familiar, he should *pretend* that he is. The very least he can do is keep quiet about his allergies and his prejudices.

Is a hesitant, obvious copy-cat, making everyone else as nervous as he over which fork to use. *It's not that important.* If you can do it unobtrusively, it's all very well to watch your hostess or more knowledgeable guests to see how they handle certain unfamiliar dishes. But if your concentration on the fine points of etiquette is going to make you an inattentive conversationalist, shrug off your worries. It might help you to know that silver is placed on the table in the order of its use, the fork farthest from your plate, on the outside, being meant for the first fork food, the one on the inside for the last. If you are served both fork and spoon for dessert you may use both (spoon for the ice cream, say, and fork for the meringue), or you may use the fork to hold the dessert steady while you cut and eat with the spoon, or you may simply use whichever seems more appropriate. The butter plate and glasses on your right are for you; your salad, unless served as a separate course, is on your left. (See page 392 for intricacies of formal service.) But no one worth knowing will care if you use a fork when a spoon was intended, and if you don't get flustered and apologetic, no one will even notice.

Is afraid to use a knife on his salad because he's heard it's not proper. If there is a salad knife at his place, he can be sure that it is not only proper but expected. And if he can't manage the salad neatly with his fork alone, it's better to use his dinner knife than to emulate a rabbit, with lettuce hanging out of his mouth.

Transfers his fork from left hand to right after he has cut his meat, even though it is more natural for him to eat with tines-down fork in his left hand. *Either* way of eating is "correct." So whether you learned to eat by the Continental or the criss-cross method, there's no point in changing your style to fit whatever the current fashion happens to be.

cigaretiquette

The business of putting cigarettes in your mouth is governed more by common sense than by formalized etiquette. Gone are the days when a gentleman had to ask permission to smoke in a lady's presence. Gone, too, are the days when it was considered effeminate to smoke cigarettes—today, cigars and pipes are more the exception than the rule.

Still there are a few warnings worth reviewing:

1. Don't smoke in full view of a three-foot sign saying "No Smoking." You may get away with it until the conductor comes through or the guard spots you, but a few quick drags will have raised eyebrows and noses in your immediate envi-

rons. And, if you have to be reprimanded, the scene could conceivably embarrass your companions.

Never smoke in a church. Nor should you smoke at weddings, funerals, dedications or other religious ceremonies outside the church. It is also best not to smoke in crowds—crowded elevators, parade crushes, pushing lines of people —but this of course is a matter of safety. There is no convincing way to say, "I'm sorry" as you watch your neighbor go up in smoke.

2. No less binding are the unwritten "no smoking" signs you occasionally encounter in private houses. Even non-smoking hostesses, unless they are violent objectors, usually offer cigarettes or at least provide ashtrays. But now and then you'll run into a place absolutely barren of smoking accessories. That's your tip-off—you'd better lay off the weed for the nonce.

If you are really dying for a cigarette, and if you're not really convinced that your hosts are as rabid as all that, you may say, "Do you mind if I smoke?" reaching vaguely toward your still-pocketed cigarette pack. The rabid objector will then say she wishes you would not and that's that, but if she hasn't the strength of her convictions she'll bring out a chipped china saucer as an ashtray. If she also opens all the windows in the middle of January, or stands poised to carry out the offensive ashes the moment you've finished your cigarette, you might as well give up as gracefully as you can. Be a good guest this time; next time you can stay home with your pipe and your slippers.

At the tables of gourmets or of conservative and formal hosts, you are not welcome to smoke during dinner. Let the table setting be your guide. If there are cigarettes and ashtrays at your place, feel free to light up whenever you like. If not, wait until cigarettes are passed or until the dinner is over. Even if the makings are in full view, think twice before smoking between courses among people who live to eat. It's a demonstrable fact that smoke dulls the palate, and the mere odor of your cigarette will interfere with others' enjoyment of the food.

3. Where smoking is clearly acceptable, you needn't bother about whether to smoke your host's or your own cigarettes. No one will be upset if you prefer your own brand, nor will anyone count up the pennies if you chain-smoke the brand provided.

4. But whether the cigarette is your host's or your own, it should be managed with respect for property. Ashes may indeed be "good for the rug" but let your hostess do her own spreading. Never put a cigarette down on the edge of a piece of furniture, even if you're positive you'll remember to pick it up before it scars the surface. And don't take it for granted that every candy dish and lamp base is intended as an ashtray, either. You may always ask for an ashtray if none is available, and you may always ask to be checked out on what is and is not an ashtray. You may be sure that food dishes, coasters, empty fireplaces, vases and growing plants are *not*.

5. Try to smoke attractively. Even if you are wearing a gray suit, there's no excuse for letting ashes sprinkle down your front. Almost any other mannerism which makes the cigarette an attached part of you is equally unbecoming: the cigarette dangling from your mouth while you talk or shake hands or tip your hat . . . the cloud of smoke which obscures you to the person who is talking to you . . . the odd bits of tobacco or paper which cling to your teeth or your chin . . . the prominent nicotine stain on your fingers.

6. Try to erase from your memory the awful Cigarette Shortage: break the wartime habit of furtively slipping one lone cigarette from a package hidden deep out of sight. Whenever you want a cigarette, take the package *out*. Offer cigarettes to everyone in your immediate circle and only *then* help yourself. This is particularly important to women:

be sure to offer your woman companion a cigarette *every* time you take one, unless she has said she does not smoke. (If she says, "No, thanks" to your first offer, that's not the same thing; it may be that she smokes but doesn't want one at that very moment.)

THE RUSH

HOW TO FALL ON YOUR FACE

The beautiful babe you met at a big cocktail party a couple of nights ago answers her phone, after about five rings, with a hoarse "Hello." Equal to any occasion, you say, "Hello, baby, guess who *this* is?" She's the polite type, so she restrains her impulse to hang up and go back to sleep. Ten minutes later, still talking, you come out with the big question, "What are you doing next Saturday night?" She's as patient as she is beautiful, and you're plain lucky, so she still doesn't hang up. You make a date to pick her up at eight next Saturday.

This is big stuff, so you arrive wearing white tie and carrying a large box of three orchids. You find her dressed in a simple wool suit, but it only takes her a couple of hours to change into an evening dress. She puts two of your orchids in her refrigerator, pleading a complicated allergy which allows her to wear only one at a time. Then she's ready.

You say, "Well, where would you like to go?" Refraining from telling you where she thinks *you* ought to go, she hems and haws around until you suggest some place specific. She says that will be fine, but when you get there you find that there will be an hour's wait for a table. So you go to another place, and then another, and then another; just your luck, the ropes are up in every damned one! About then she faints from hunger—a lucky thing, too, because you didn't know she expected to be taken to *dinner; you* always eat at seven o'clock and after all you made the date for *eight!* You buy her a hamburger at Joe's Diner (no reservations necessary); her evening dress and your orchid are a conspicuous success. When she's feeling better, you get a bright idea and take her down to the Village. The bars are crowded and the doohinky on her dress keeps getting caught in the traffic, but the jazz is terrific. She admits it, with only a few references to some guy named Smetana.

Even so, the smoke gives her a headache and she says she'd like to go. You've just picked up an interesting conversation with a couple of guys from New Orleans, so she insists that you stay on. You're an etiquette kid, if nothing else, so you give her a dollar for the cab-driver as she leaves.

When you try to call her the next day, to tell her what she missed, you find that her number has been changed. Information says it is now unlisted. Oh well, you may run into her at another cocktail party soon—probably wearing one of your leftover orchids, the gold digger!

Admittedly, that's a preposterous picture. It's preposterous to suppose that any girl would go out with you in the first place if you played "guess who" on the phone. Unless she knew you well enough to know you were a diamond in the rough (or unless she was desperate for a date), she'd plead parturition before she'd get involved in such an evening. She'd know that anyone who knew so little of the feminine mind as to ask, "What are you doing tonight?" would be sure to show up in unexpected clothes, carrying too many unplanned-for flowers, expecting the girl to arrange the entertainment and all but guaranteeing a miserable evening.

H O W   T O   M A K E   *H E R*   F A L L

This, then, is the way that beautiful baby would *like* to be handled—which is another way of saying:

In a woman's world, this is etiquette:

1. *She wants you to prepare her for hearing from you.* In the old days, you would have asked if you could "call" some afternoon when she and her mother were at home. Today, it's enough to register yourself on her consciousness when you meet, then get her permission to telephone her. "Permission" is a pretty tight word to use for a loose situation—you don't *have* to say, "May I call you for lunch some day soon?" —but you want to find out where and how you can reach her, and if there are any complications which would make an unanticipated phone call unwelcome or embarrassing to her. The where and how will probably come out in your conversation, but you'll have to give her a definite opening in order to learn the complications. They can be as complicated as a husband or as simple as a rule against personal phone calls at her office; she can't go around giving everyone she meets the ground rules, so if you intend to call her, let her know of your interest before you rush in.

2. *When you call her,* she wants to know, immediately, who you are and why you called. She hopes you're calling with a purpose greater than idle conversation—if she's a woman, not a teen-ager, she thinks of the telephone as an instrument for making arrangements, not for aimless chitchat. If you *are* calling just to pass the time of day, she hopes you'll say so at the outset, not keep her dangling on the ropes waiting for the invitation which is not to come. And even if she knows that you know that she knows your voice as well as she knows her own, she wants you to start with "This is George Davis" or, at the very least, "This is George." The implication that there might be other men in her life—even

other men named George—is flattering to the most devoted one-man woman in the world.

3. *She wants your invitation to be explicit.* "I have two tickets to the Merman show on Friday night. Would you like to go with me?", not "Have you seen the Merman show?" (which, for all she knows, may be a build-up to "Have you read any good books lately?"). If she wants to see you but not Merman, she'll say so. You can offer to change your tickets, make a date for another night or just say how sorry you are about the whole mish-mosh, but you're already in a good bargaining position.

The explicit invitation gives her a chance to invent a previous engagement if she doesn't like your idea, and thus spares you the double jeopardy of spending your money on the wrong thing. It also gives her a chance to pretend she hasn't a previous engagement, if your bait is irresistible and she is so unscrupulous as to break a date (in secret) for you. It protects both your egos, and your purse as well.

On the other hand, the Inquiring Reporter invitation ("Are you free Friday night?") might not be an invitation at all. It puts you both on a limb. She doesn't want to admit that she's "free" before she knows why you're asking; equally, you don't want her to agree to a date before you've made it clear that you mean to spend the evening watching her television set. If she accepts your specific invitation, you can be sure that the evening will be a success: she wants to go out with you, and she wants to do what you have planned.

The invitation does not, of course, have to be elaborate— only explicit. "Would you like to go for a row in the park on Sunday afternoon?" is just as good as "Would you like to go to the opening of Pinza's new show, and to a champagne party for him afterwards?" The idea is not so much to entice as to inform. In your definite words she finds counsel on what to say, what to wear, when to plan on getting home, *what to expect.*

P.S. She also wants the invitation to be positive. The negative approach— "You don't want to go to the fights, do you?" —leaves her in a conversational hole.

4. *Once she's accepted your invitational outline,* she doesn't mind being consulted on minor details—but she wants you to remember that she is consultant, not engineer. She likes it if you get her approval before you change the date into a double, with a couple of people she might not like. She likes it if you give her a choice between seven and eight, or between Henri's and Fred's, or between winding up at the club or the hotel; she doesn't like it if you say, "What time?" "What do you feel like eating?" or "Where shall we go next?" Vague questions tell her too little about what you're prepared to spend, for one thing, and, for another, they indicate that you haven't given much thought to this occasion. If you know her well enough to ask her where she'd like to go, you also know her well enough to *know* where she'd like to go. Plan according to her tastes . . . subject your plan to her either-or approval . . . but never force *her* to plan *your* evening. If you do, you will deserve exactly what you get.

5. *If you're sending her flowers to wear,* she wants you to send them ahead of your arrival. This is not a plot to prevent your plucking a second-hand gardenia off a drunken dowager you meet en route; it's insurance that your flowers will be a *pleasant* surprise. It gives her a chance to select a dress that will go with the flowers; it gives her a chance to rip off all the fern and ribbon junk the florist used to disguise the flower, or to pretend that only two gardenias arrived if she wouldn't be caught dead wearing three. And all without appearing to be an ingrate.

If the surprise would be that you *didn't* send flowers—if they were the customary offering for the spring dance, for instance—better to get the flowers to match the dress. Ask her in advance what she's going to wear, or if she prefers flowers for her hair to flowers for her shoulder strap.

6. *She wants to be called for and delivered.* Door-to-door service is a must—and curb-to-curb service, hand on horn, is a bust. The exceptions to this rule are for exceptional women or exceptional circumstances; even then, the suggestion must come from the woman. You must always assume that you are going to pick her up and take her home. If she lives with her parents, you had better insist on it, no matter how she protests and no matter how inconvenient it is for you. *She* may be "modern," but her parents are sure to be pretty conventional when it comes to their daughter. If she is not under judging eyes, if she is sure not to think the less of you for your abbreviated manners, and if she insists that she can "meet you there" —let her have her way. But with even so delightful a date you should always "see her home," and safely inside her door, any time after dark.

7. *She expects you to dress up to her—and to the occasion.* If you're going to deviate from your local standard of date clothes, there should be a reason for your casual dress—a reason so obvious that she too will trot out in skirt and sweater, leaving mink stole and high heels behind. She wants to match, and she wants to be far away when the major-domo tells you that you can't come in without tie or jacket. (Read clothes dope, pages 206 to 229.)

8. *She wants to have your first drink with you.* It's unforgivable to show up under the influence of liquor—and consider- ing your responsibilities as her protector it's best to stay out from under said influence all evening.

9. *Throughout the evening,* she wants to be treated like Someone, and preferably Lady Someone. The red carpet—not the red rope—greets her wherever you go. There are no scenes with bad waiters, no pick-up conversations with people who have not been presented at court. She has everything she

259

wants before she even knows she wants it; you anticipate her every whim. And all this, apparently, is free. You handle the finances without comment. She, of course, is allowed to pay for nothing—not even cigarettes, if she runs out or hasn't brought her own . . . not even tips to ladies' room attendants, if she lets you know she has forgotten her mad-money. You come up with dimes for the phone calls she makes and drinks for the piano-players she takes up—automatically, and without a doubt that everything's on you from door to door.

10. *At evening's end,* she's the one who says she has to be getting home. It's up to you to suggest going some place else —that is, she'll wait for you to indicate that dinner is over or that it's time to be getting on to the dance—but you can't be the one to call a halt to the festivities. The convention is that she can't suggest that you spend any more money or otherwise take the wheel, and you can't suggest that health, sleep, money or the morrow are more important than her everlasting company. If you're about to drop and she is obviously geared up for the dawn patrol, the only thing you can do (within convention) is to stall. You can't *initiate* the homeward trek. (But you can anticipate the problem by indicating in your invitation—point 3, above—that you are not without morning-after responsibilities.)

11. *At her door,* your technique is much more important but the etiquette is as follows: you thank her for the evening (even at these prices, *you* thank *her!*) . . . you try not to say anything so infuriatingly vague as "Let's do it again some time," unless you really have no desire to see her again; the complimentary thing is to ask for a specific date and let her be the vague one with her "call me" routine . . . you say good night . . . and that's all. It's up to her to invite you in, if she wants to, and it's up to you to say "no, thanks" if you know very well that her parents, her conscience or Mrs. Grundy would not approve.

260

Perhaps this is a question of technique more than etiquette, but whatever you do don't ever ask a woman if you may kiss her. There's only one thing she can say, but there are several things she can do. Make a move, or don't, but don't have a lot of conversation about it.

Beyond all that, of course, she expects you to be equal to, if not above, any situation you take her into. She may be a past master at handling headwaiters or hailing taxis or squelching mashers when she's alone—but when she's with you, etiquette renders her helpless. You're It. The primary idea is to avoid being conspicuous, for her sake. When in doubt about two courses of action—whether to smash a fresh stranger in the face or quietly gather up your girl and leave . . . whether to fight with a waiter or simply ask the captain to change your table—take the course of least fuss, even if the unobtrusive course sometimes seems unmanly. And when in doubt about feeling at *home* in a place, stay away— or at least make a dry run, first, to be sure you won't be given the freeze or the bus boys' table.

PUBLIC PROTOCOL

Everyday manners are all you need, in most cases, but here are some special routines involved when you take a woman to public places of entertainment.

at a restaurant

You check your hat and coat as she waits. You offer to check her things only if she's carrying bundles or umbrella or wearing a sopping raincoat; ordinarily she doesn't check her hat or coat. She goes ahead of you to the entrance to the dining room; you stand slightly behind her there until the head waiter comes up. You say, "Two, please," or you give your name and say that you have a reservation for two. The man leads the way to the table, your date on his heels and you bringing up the rear. He probably holds a chair for her, or pulls out a table so she can slide into the banquette; if not, *you* do, picking the best seat for her. After she is seated, you help her out of her coat, dropping it over the back of her chair—or you stand at your place while the waiter does this.

Thereafter, you are the intermediary between her and the restaurant's employees: you ask her what kind of cocktail she'd like, then you repeat her order, along with your own, to the waiter. This routine prevails through the whole meal, despite the fact that the waiter can easily hear her the first time: she cannot speak to the waiter directly—she can't even speak to you of what she'd like to order, until you've asked her—so she's in your power.

When she's had a chance to study the menu, you ask her what she'd like (or, better, you say something first to calm her fears about the prices. Not "I'm loaded; skip the vegetable plate," but something like "The lobster is very good here, or you might like to try their breast of guinea hen."). Once she's told you her choice of a main dish, you ask, "What would you like first—oysters? shrimp?" If this is an à la carte menu and you fervently hope she'll skip the preliminaries, you may phrase the suggestion differently— "Would you like something to start?"—but you must make the offer. It's not necessary to go through the entire menu this way—appetizer, main dish, dessert and beverage are enough, or, if she declines a first course, main dish, salad, dessert and beverage —but remember that she is hamstrung if you do not make the initial suggestion.

If you think she's watching the right-hand column too carefully, you can lead her more forcefully. "Let's have a salad, shall we?" or "I think I'll have a salad—would you like one?" You almost have to do this in the drink department.

"Would you like another drink?" sounds somehow accusing, where "Let's have another drink" sounds convivial.*

When, in speaking to the waiter, you must refer to your date, call her "the lady" "Blue points for the lady," not "*She* will have blue points" or "Those are for honey-pie, there."

When it's time to go, you ask the waiter to bring the check. It's perfectly all right to look at the tab and, if you've been overcharged, to summon the waiter and say something like "I think there's been a mistake; we settled our bill at the bar before we came in." But it's *not* all right—because presumably it is embarrassing to her—to get out your adding machine, to launch into a sarcastic discussion of the "entertainment" for which you are being charged a back-breaking twenty per cent tax or to mutter over your calculations of the tip. (See Tipping Chart, page 413.)

When the necessary evil of paying up is attended to, you stand, walk around to help her with coat and chair, then let her precede you to the checkroom. You buy back your hat and coat, without flirtatious banter with the hat-check girl. You walk manfully past the fluffy dogs the cigarette girl is trying to sell your date. You ask the doorman to get you a cab—and you're off.

at the theatre

She waits in the lobby while you stand in line (if you must). She goes first through the outer doors, but you go first, then, until an usher takes over, when you again drop behind. Yours is the seat on or nearest the aisle.

---

* Strictly speaking, you should eschew the words "another" and "more." "Will you have a cup of coffee," even if its her sixth, not "another cup?" or "more coffee?" This gets a little silly when she's sitting behind a half-drunk martini and might answer, "Will you have a drink?" with, "I *have* a drink." When you're inquiring about a second drink in order to advise the waiter to delay the food, you can safely say, "We're going to have another drink, aren't we?" But it's nicer to order "two martinis" rather than "two **more** martinis."

If your date can't see because another woman's hat is blocking her view, you may ask the other woman if she will please take off the guilty bonnet. Your date may take this matter into her own hands but here, as everywhere, you are supposed to anticipate her needs and wishes—and your primary duty is to your date as against another woman.

At intermission time, she goes with you for a cigarette. If you must leave her to go to the john, you should take her to your seats, first, rather than leave her to stand alone in the lobby. If *she* goes on such a sortie, wait for her so she doesn't have to find her seat alone.

If the play or movie is painfully bad, you're the one to suggest walking out. As your guest, she has to pretend pleasure until you relieve her of the responsibility. If you say, "This is terrible—let's read about it instead of sticking it out," she can say no, she likes it, or heave a sigh of relief and adjourn. But the first move is yours.

dancing

You should have the first and last dance with her and, in between, see that she does not get stuck or stranded, either on the floor or at your group's table.

THE BRUSH

Since there *are* a few women who can resist your charms, and since you can resist a few females yourself, there comes a time when it is necessary to know the etiquette of the brush. Without etiquette, a simple little decision to call the whole thing off can be troublesome or humiliating, boring or embarrassing, depending on which end of The End you're

264

holding. But with etiquette, you can take or administer the brush with grace—that is, without histrionics.

It is possible, of course, that what looks like the brush is in fact a come-on: many a wife got that way by "calling off" a previous, less permanent arrangement with her husband. Only the man on the spot can tell the difference between threat and promise, but when in doubt, duck. If you've misread the handwriting on the wall, she'll let you know soon enough.

H O W   T O   T A K E   I T

In brief, then, here are the guideposts:

1. *If she's "busy"* three times in a row, when you ask her for a date, let *her* make the move for the fourth try. You can't tell much by the effusiveness of her regrets—if anything, she'll be more desolated when her previous engagement is imaginary than when it's real. If she's really that busy, and if she really wishes she could go out with you, she'll be at some pains to prove that she has not been giving you the quick brush: she'll call *you,* or she'll invite *you* somewhere. Your previous misses have let her know that such forwardness on her part will not be considered pursuit, so sit back and wait. If she doesn't make the move, boy, you've had it.

Incidentally, it's best not to take the three strikes in one turn at bat. If she "can't make it" for the first event you suggest, it's all right to name a second occasion then and there —but don't make a third try, and don't invite her to a Christmas dance in July. Such persistence may persuade her to drop etiquette and take up rudeness, to your sorrow. You don't want her to take a direct aim at your ego, so quit while there's still some area of doubt.

2. *If she breaks more than one date* with you, with less than a life-or-death excuse, don't give her another chance.

You don't make a scene or conduct a cross-examination when she breaks the date, of course—you pretend to believe her reason, if she gives one, and you let her think she has gotten away with it—but you don't go back for more punishment, either. The only time an ethical damsel breaks one date to accept another is when she wants the discarded suitor to cross her off his list. The broken date is a form of shorthand for "get lost"; don't give her a chance to say it in longhand.

3. *If she is forced to be more positive,* less subtle, in administering the brush—that is, if she has your ring or you have the key to her apartment and explanations are necessary —your pride will prod you in the right direction. Be understanding, not accusing, and cut the scene as short as you can. There will be further complications if this has been a formal engagement: her parents will have to send an announcement to the press or recall wedding invitations; she will have to return to you the ring and any valuable present you've given her; she'll have to return the wedding presents. But the whole thing can be less traumatic if you don't press for explanations.

In such serious instances, your public role is a quiet one. The decision to call it off is supposed to be mutual, and it's nobody's business which of you spoke up first. It is not ungentlemanly to let it appear that she has cast you off (even if the reverse is true), but it is boring to your friends to hear about it, and to have to look at your broken heart. Keep your tears or your relief to yourself, and expect her to do the same.

HOW TO GIVE IT

The above three points work both ways. You too can be busy or always late; you too can forget a date or have to work late. But the whole operation is a lot simpler when it's the man who wants out. In the early stages, all he has to do is nothing. Don't call; stop asking her out; that's all there is to it. If she is so dull as to call *you,* or to ask you why she hasn't heard from you, be indirect. The idea is to conduct your retreat so quietly that, in retrospect, it will seem to have been an unsuccessful attack rather than a run for cover. She'll always be fond of you if she thinks *she* made the break. If she forces you to declare your lack of interest in so many words, however, you'll be a heel for life. It's all too true that hell hath no fury like a woman scorned. See if you can keep it a secret that she's scorned and you'll come out a lot better.

In the later stages, where you really have some obligation to the girl, you may have to come right out and say that you're through. Make that a last resort, however. With only the slightest application, you can bring her to say, "You can't fire me; I quit." If that doesn't work, and if you simply can't escape explanations, try to make your reasons impersonal. This may be difficult, if you have been lying awake nights thinking about her incredibly annoying faults, but you'll be glad if you avoid the truth in favor of a few thin lies about finances, or invalided mothers, or impending doom. In short, get out of it without saying that you don't love her. The perfect exit, you see, is one in which *she* opens the door and you depart sadly.

A note for the very young: no man can afford to be known as a Don Juan or a heel, but, at the same time, no man can afford to be trapped by every woman who thinks she has a claim on him. It is dishonest, of course, to use the promise of marriage as a weapon (or to allow feminine conclusion-jumping in that direction). But it is also dishonest to marry the girl when you don't *want* to. A true moralist would say that an honest man owes it to the girl *not* to marry her solely under pressure of conscience. Sometimes, as Shakespeare said, you must be cruel only to be kind.

IN EARNEST

Seduction has no etiquette, except the stricture against "kiss and tell." By definition, it rules out force—and likker is a heel's kind of force—but otherwise it's a matter of man over manners.

Courtship is something else again. If your ultimate intentions are matrimonial, you are circumscribed by etiquette. Take, for instance, the matter of

PRESENTS

Books, candy, flowers and an engagement ring were all the old-fashioned girl could accept from her "intended." Today, the safe list includes almost anything so long as it is not personal, not expensive and not "maintenance." You can give her an addition to her hobby or sports equipment: a $15 light meter, but not a $200 camera; a $30 tennis racket, but not a 39 cent pair of tennis socks; an antique demi-tasse cup for her collection but not a thing for her boudoir. A less cautious list would also include certain "personal" things: compacts, cigarette lighters, writing papers, even scarves, handbags, costume jewelry and other incidental accessories for *outer wear*. But never underclothes (stockings included), and never major components of an outer costume (sweaters as much as mink coats).

If it would not be a presumption on your part (and consider this carefully), you could also give her things obviously meant for your enjoyment as well as hers. Not the bottle of brandy under-arm when you arrive for dinner—that suggests that you feared her own provisions for you—but perhaps a lap robe to prevent her freezing beside you in the stadium this season, as she did last.

But the safest present, always, is the impersonal and the

268

unwearable. Don't, by the way, be so impersonal as to give her a gift certificate. This is objectionable on two counts—on technique as well as etiquette. A gift certificate puts a $ sign on your present and a vacant sign on your cranium. It could also be considered money—that is, "maintenance."

Once the date has been set, you may give her things which are much more expensive and a bit more personal, but you must still be careful of presents which would be considered "maintenance." You're supposed to "keep" her after the wedding, but not before. This explains why the bride's family pays for the wedding and the trousseau, no matter how much easier it would be for the groom's family to do so. (See weddings, page 278.)

If you are going to furnish an apartment or buy a house before the wedding, the purchases and deeds are in your name, however much the selection is in her hands. These are not presents. If such appurtenances of marriage are to be "hers," transfer title after the ceremony.

She will be following much the same pattern of thought in her presents to you, if any. They will almost certainly be things you don't want, but that's another subject. She buys your wedding ring, if you agree to a double-ring ceremony. She may properly—but not necessarily—give you a hunk of platinum as an engagement present. But on the whole her presents to you will be fewer and less consequential than yours to her. Woman being woman, she is embarrassed if she gives you a present and you don't give her one, but she is not embarrassed if you give her a present and she has not thought to get one for you. You get the message: when in doubt, do.

PARENTS

When your status is that of a "date," everyday manners will get you past the pitfalls of dealing with her parents. The difficulty, of course, is to remember that they exist. Concentrate, and you won't forget to greet them when you arrive, say goodbye to them when you leave, exchange a pleasantry or two (or at least state your name) when one of them answers your phone call to Her. Send her mother a bunch of posies once in a while if she's fed you, take a house-present for a week-end and be generally considerate. Remember that they (not their daughter) are your hosts whenever you are in their house; remember that they are your seniors; show them the agreeable deference due them on both those counts, and you'll come out all right.

There's a danger, often augmented by the girl herself, in making yourself too much at home. You are not expected to return her parents' hospitality in kind—presumably they'd be as bored as you if you asked them to make it a foursome at dinner—but try to remember that they pay the bills. If you have too many one-for-the-roads and too many nightcaps from their liquor locker, they may develop an unconscious grudge that will work against you in the long run. Never mind that *she* pressed the drinks on you, or that a nightcap now and then is small enough return on your entertainment of her. Play it safe and think up an excuse to send the old man a bottle of his favorite Scotch now and then.

They will probably call you by your first name but you should call them "Mr." and "Mrs." until insistently directed to do otherwise. And if they insist that you call them "Ma" and "Pa," buy a bulletproof vest.

When you've decided to marry the girl, your obligations are a little more precise. There are still a few shreds of the "speak to her father" convention to bind you. You no longer ask her father for her hand, of course—she's the only one who can say "yes"—but you do ask him for his approval. As soon as she has said the fateful word—the morning after, or then and there, if her father is immediately available—you ask for an appointment to see him alone, making it clear that you both know what you're going to talk about, and that you are at his disposal. He suggests a time and place; you brace yourself, preferably without benefit of alcohol; you appear. You tell him what he already knows, in color, from his daughter: that love is in bloom and a wedding is in view. You are then supposed to tell him all there is to know about your finances, to prove that you can support a wife, and to answer any questions he may have.

More than likely, however, he already knows all about you, and you already know if he is for you or agin you, so the only etiquette involved is the bid for his approval. If he refuses it, or if he asks you to wait until you are earning more (or until the draft law is repealed or until the cows come home), your course thereafter is determined by the girl. She will not thank you if you make promises binding on her (and she will probably be furious if you seem too amenable to reason in the face of supposedly mad passion), so the complementary close to such a negative interview with her father is your renewed avowal of devotion, your expression of regret at his disapproval and your promise to discuss it further with your love. You may never see the old boy again—whether or not he becomes an in-law—so be as pleasant as possible.

Suppose he gives his approval. Your next move is to see that your parents call on her parents. Unless both families live in the world of formal calls (see page 400), this will probably be managed by your mother telephoning her mother and, after the obvious gush-eries, saying that she and your father would like to come to see your in-laws-to-be at such and such a time, if that is convenient. Or perhaps your parents invite her parents to dinner. The only certain

271

"form" is that *your* parents make the move. Similarly, after the engagement is announced, all your immediate relatives are supposed to call on the girl and her family.

If you and the girl are in a different city from either or both sets of parents, all this can be managed by mail. You write her father instead of talking to him; on receipt of his reply, you write another letter, this time to both her parents. Your parents write to her and her family instead of calling on them. The tone of all such letters, except your original supplication, is one of ain't-love-grand.

If it can be managed, personal meetings ought to follow the letters. Certainly her parents should meet you, and yours should meet her, before the wedding. But it is better to write immediately than silently to wait out a geographic delay in meetings. Your letters may seem hard to write—you may think that, after all, they have the news from the girl, and you have their reaction from her, so what's it all about? Struggle through it, though; it's important not only to ephemeral etiquette but also to your lifelong relationship with her family.

Divorce sometimes complicates marriage, in more ways than the obvious. Who is "her father," in terms of asking for his approval, if her father and mother are divorced and both remarried? Consider as "her father" the head of the house where she makes her home; whether this person is a stepfather or a guardian or an older brother or her widowed mother or a maiden aunt, the required treatment is the same. But if her real father is living, however estranged, write him, too, if only to give him the news. Your fiancée will be the best assessor of such subtle relationships—consult her—but don't think you're going to get out of this duty simply because it's complicated!

FRIENDS

Long before anyone ever heard of a "Dear John" letter, newly engaged couples, individually, were writing letters which began, "I want you to be the first to know . . ."

The idea is simply to spare your intimate friends the possibly-wounding shock of hearing of your engagement second-hand. Before the announcement party, or before the engagement is officially announced in the press, let your other lady-loves down lightly. Presumably, you won't be seeing them again; a carefully composed letter now may save you a lot of trouble later. Even where your friendly news-letter is not necessary, it's nice: your fond ex-nurse, no less than your rich aunt, will appreciate hearing from you.

MRS. GRUNDY

Once you two are engaged, and it is thus a matter of public information that your relationship is not Platonic, you have to be on guard against gossip. 'Tis a time to be conventional, even if there *isn't* anything to hide. This means trying to avoid such tongue-clackers as:

1. *The Disappearing Act.* If you two are very, very long in getting from one party to the next, if you sit out one dance and come back to find the scrubwomen at work, if you are generally unreliable as to time, some busybody is going to figure out what you're doing instead of being on time.

2. *The Compromising Situation.* These rules apply to women in general, but for your fiancée you had better observe them. A wooin' man and unmarried woman are not supposed to remain alone in an apartment, his or hers, after the dinner hour. You may have a cocktail there before going out for the evening, and if you are discreet about it you may step inside for brief good nights, but if you are really toeing

the line there will be attending servants or sleeping room-mates in calling distance even then.

You should make it a point to leave her apartment with the other guests (or perhaps a kiss later, while the others wait outside). You should not entertain her in your apartment without benefit of chaperone (a married or antique woman, to suit Mrs. Grundy; also deaf and dumb, to suit you). If she lives in a switchboard-apartment house or hotel, you should announce your arrival by telephone from the lobby, leaving it to her to say, "Come on up" or "I'll be right down."

And if you violate these rules, you should be careful not to be seen doing same—that is, do not wake the neighbors with Tarzan calls as you depart from her dark house at dawn, do not answer her telephone at any time, and do not let her use your apartment as her mailing address.

The irony of it is that an engagement requires you to be much more careful of appearances than you were before you promised to make an honest woman of her. Before Engagement, you two may have made long trips together as boss and secretary, or as week-end guests of mutual friends, or as fellow-patrons of a resort popular with your group. In some cases this would not have been strictly Emily Post, but it would not have set the town on fire, either: the mission was more interesting than your relationship. Now, however, an overnight trip "alone together" is very much taboo. Mrs. Grundy no longer gives you the benefit of the doubt.

The point is the usual one of protecting her reputation, particularly vulnerable during an engagement, but there is a subtler reason for being circumspect. She will be working up a case of bridal qualms. When the malady hits, it will be better for your cause if she has no reason to think that you have cut off her avenues of retreat (or that you have "had your way" and might prefer to pass the permanent ceremony). It would be cynical to suggest that you, too, might

like to be able to retreat without fear of rice shot from guns;
if such were a possibility, however, you'd be glad you hadn't
fed Mrs. Grundy's mill.

THE DIE IS CAST

THE RING

It may be more romantic to pluck a diamond solitaire out of
your back pocket the moment she says "yes," but it is more
customary to let her have a say in the selection of her own
ring. She may think diamonds are trite, or prefer a big birth-
stone to a little sparkler. She may even want to skip the engagement ring (it's not a legal necessity) in order to have a
more elaborate wedding ring. In any event, it's safer to consult her.

The usual procedure is to make a date to go ring-
shopping. In advance of the date, the man cases the shop,
making it clear to the jeweler that he is not made of money.
The jeweler then sets aside a group of rings or stones and
settings within the prescribed price, and when the bride-
to-be makes her entrance she doesn't get so much as a peak
at the Kohinoor, or the price tags. Even if she is already perfectly acquainted with your budget, and even if you and she
have already discussed ring prices with complete frankness,
she will appreciate the absence of a lot of "how much? too
much!" conversation over the counter.

It is perfectly proper to pick out (and try on) the wedding ring at the same time, particularly if you want the two
rings to complement each other. The jeweler will hold the
wedding ring for later delivery, have the engagement ring
delivered to you so you can put it on her finger in private at
a suitable time—the day of the announcement party, if any,
or the day your engagement becomes public information.

Incidentally, money is *really* incidental in this department; men are unnecessarily embarrassed if they can't afford the biggest solitaire and the chunkiest diamond wedding band in town. You can count on your gal to be more sentimental than mercenary, just this once: she may *prefer* your grandmother's opal to an emerald-cut diamond; she may *want* a plain gold wedding band. Don't think you have to protest too much, or put yourself in hock.

THE ANNOUNCEMENT

This job falls to the girl's parents. They send a note to the newspapers and/or they give a party. They do *not* send out engraved announcements. If there is a party, you and your bride-to-be are the guests of honor; you may receive with her parents, and you may stay on until the other guests have left, but you are supposed not to play the host, merely to be pleasant and to receive the congratulations of the guests as gracefully as you can. If the assembled company drinks a toast to you, as is the custom, you ignore your sudden, overwhelming thirst and refrain from drinking to yourself. If only the girl is toasted, of course, you rise and drink to her with fond pride.

If you are called upon to make a speech, you have only to thank your friends for their good wishes and indicate that you consider yourself quite a lucky guy. This is not the place to practice your public-speaking lessons; you are *expected* to be engagingly flustered.

If you are caught up in the toasting spirit yourself, the appropriate person for you to toast is your hostess, your gal's ma.

PRENUPTIAL PARTIES

Your parents may give a party to introduce your choice to their friends; your friends may give parties for you both, sometimes just for fun and sometimes to "shower" you with household items; and during the wedding-week there will be one event after another. At all but one of these, you are a guest, with no responsibilities other than those of a display-piece. But at one, the bachelor dinner, you are the host.

The bachelor dinner is a crumbling institution. It is by no means necessary, and it is often supplanted by an evening on the town staged for you by your attendants, or by an impromptu, Dutch-treat pub crawl—but if you want it and if you can afford it you might as well do it right. Here's how:

Make it two or three days before the wedding, first checking with the wedding engineers to make sure that evening is free on the schedule. (You'll feel bad enough, on your wedding day, without a hangover cultivated at a last-night bachelor dinner.) Traditionally, you invite only the male members of the wedding party (fathers included), but if there is room it's pleasant to ask husbands of the bride's attendants, as well. In any case, your mother or other would-be-hostess should not be allowed to put in an appearance. This is a party for men only.

Your best man makes the arrangements—usually as simple as reserving a private dining room in hotel or club, then turning a professional caterer loose on the matter of food and drink—but you pay the bills. You get there first, not only to act as host but also to put your presents to ushers and best man at the places at the table. You sit at the head of the table and then, when festivities are under way, you propose the first standing toast to the bride. After the toast is drunk—unless you'd like to edit custom and spare the cost of glassware—you smash your glass against the wall and the others follow suit. After that you can settle down to some serious drinking and forget all about lesser traditions!

THE WEDDING

Your bride and her mother will be running this show, so all you have to know is how to say, "Tell me what I'm supposed to do and I'll do it." They'll tell you—and they won't think any the less of you if you behave as if the whole thing is out of your experience and over your head. Better that you know how to soothe distraught females than how to arrange a bridal table . . . so stop worrying.

They'll tell you all this, too, but here are your responsibilities:

1. *To make all arrangements involved in getting the marriage license,* in plenty of time to allow for your state's waiting period or health tests. You pay for the license, of course, but you don't offer to pay your bride's doctor bill if she chooses to skirt the Public Health Department for her premarital exam.

2. *To submit, with your parents, a list of guests* to be invited to the wedding and/or reception. The bride's mother will tell your mother how many are feasible; all you have to do is think of the names and find the addresses of your particular friends. Unless it is a very large wedding and you know for sure that your in-laws-to-be are doing the same, don't include strictly-business acquaintances. Your wedding is a social event, and it's on the bride's father, so resist the temptation to make business capital of it.

3. *To choose a best man.* He is usually your brother or your best friend, bachelor or benedict; he can be your father. But whoever he is be sure you can *count* on him. He it is who must:

Arrange for your bachelor dinner, if any.

278

See that the ushers are properly dressed, clearly instructed on their duties and on hand at the church at least an hour before the ceremony.

Take complete charge of your luggage and your bride's, stowing it in your get-away car, expressing it ahead to your honeymoon spot or taking it to your first-night hotel well in advance of your need for it. (If he's wise to the witlessness of bridegrooms, he also *packs* for you!)

See that the clothes you will wear away from the reception are complete and ready for you at the place appointed for your quick change.

Help you dress for the ceremony—which means that he him-self must be dressed well ahead of time.

See to it that you have the marriage license.

Get from you and present to the clergyman, in a plain en-velope, the fee for performing the ceremony.

Get you to the church half an hour before the ceremony, then try to think of bolstering words while you both wait in the vestry.

Carry the ring in his waistcoat pocket, ready to hand you at the appointed moment in the ceremony.

Relieve you of your gloves as you wait for the bride at the chancel steps. (If he anticipates any fumbling with the ring on his own part, he may also remove his own gloves and hand both pairs on to another attendant.)

Offer the first toast to the bride and groom at the reception, on signal from the wedding consultant or whenever every-one has been served. ("To the bride and groom" is enough, if the Muse doesn't move him to more extensive wishes for your future happiness. He has only to stand, get the attention of the guests and hold his glass on high.)

Make sure that your going-away car is in going-away condi-tion, and in readiness, then help you and your bride dash into it.

Send a thank-you-for-the-lovely-wedding-and-bride telegram
to your new in-laws, in your name, so you may be free
to think of other things.

Collapse—but not before he has so nobly served as valet,
confessor, nurse and manager.

4. *To choose your ushers.* Their number will be determined by the size of the wedding—there should be one usher
for every fifty guests. They should be special friends of
yours, but if they are numerous they should include one relative or special friend of the bride's, as well. (Similarly, she
will ask you if there is a girl you'd like to have as one of her
bridesmaids. Old flames need not be nominated.)

5. *To appoint one of the ushers as head usher.* His duties
then are to take both mothers up the aisle, to walk first in
the procession and to see that the other ushers know what
they are to do.

6. *To house your best man and ushers*—their wives, too, if
any—if they come from out of town. They pay for their own
transportation to and from your city, but once they are there
they are your guests. You put them up in hotel or club, at
your expense, or arrange for them to stay with local friends.
(The bride does the same for her attendants, and the wedding expenses include transportation from church to reception for all the party.)

7. *To send your attendants* identical ties and gloves and to
have identical boutonnieres waiting for them at the church
on the big day. They wear their own clothes, of the type you
have prescribed, otherwise—not identical except by coinci-
dence.

8. *To give each of your attendants a present* at the bachelor dinner or, if there is to be no such affair, sometime before
the ceremony. (The bridal dinner affords a good opportunity.) You give identical presents to the ushers, something
a little better but of the same sort to your best man. The
usual things are tie clips, watch chains, cigarette cases or

lighters, cuff-links, studs or stud boxes, wallets or money clips. They can be expensive or not, monogrammed or not, engraved with the date or not, but they ought to be *lasting* mementoes of the occasion.

9. *To give your bride a wedding present, something for her personal adornment.* Jewelry is the best—the real stuff if you can afford it—and it can be anything from the traditional, prized string of pearls to an important piece of costume jewelry. Give it to her before the ceremony so she can wear it for the I do's. (She may give you a present, too, but it is not a must as is your present to her.)

10. *To arrange all details* and of course pay all expenses entailed in your honeymoon. And to keep your plans secret from prank-minded friends.

11. *To provide the wedding ring* (see page 275). See that your best man has it: he's to hand it to you at the altar. In a double-ring ceremony, the bride pays for the groom's ring and the maid of honor carries it to the altar.

12. *To pay the clergyman who performs the ceremony.* The amount can be as little as $10 or as much as you can afford; try to scale it to the size and swankiness of the wedding. The money is usually in cash, a new bill enclosed in a plain envelope and presented to the clergyman immediately before or after the ceremony by the best man. (The money is ostensibly for him and his services, not for the church, so it is not tax-deductible; but if you want to use a check instead of folding money, anyway, make it payable to him.)

13. *To send the bride flowers* to wear with her "going-away" costume. Usually the groom is financially responsible for the flowers the bride carries at the wedding, and for corsages for the mothers and grandmothers, but these are selected by the bride or her wedding consultant as part of "The Grand Plan" for the wedding; the groom has little to do with choosing them. "They'll tell you" about that, but don't forget the going-away posies.

14. *To be the first man to kiss the bride,* and to be as genial as you can when every Tom kisses her at the reception. That first kiss may happen not at the altar but on the church steps or in the car to the reception—the custom varies from church to church—but you'll be instructed on whether or not you may kiss her before you lead her down the aisle as your wife.

15. *To receive with your bride* and her attendants at the reception, introducing to her any friends of yours she may not know and saying "thank you" to congratulations and good wishes. Guests up on their manners will not start long conversations at this juncture; help them by not asking otherwise-conventional questions which might lead them into dissertations.

16. *When the guests have all arrived* and been greeted, to take your bride to the bridal table for the wedding breakfast or whatever food has been planned. To stand with her on your right, your hand over hers on the knife, when she cuts the wedding cake. To stand and say "thank you" after the best man has proposed and the bridal table has drunk a toast to you and your bride. To lead off the dancing, after the breakfast, by circling the floor once with your wife. And then, when you have been cut in upon by her father, to dance with the bride's mother, your own mother, the maid of honor and each of the bridesmaids before reclaiming your partner-for-keeps.

17. *To say goodbye to your parents upstairs,* before the last-minute gay dash to car and wedding trip. To wait at the landing upstairs so that you and your wife can come down and take off together; no matter how long it takes her to dress, she doesn't want to have to rout you out of the bar when she's ready. And to shake hands with all your attendants before you leave.

18. *To know that, from here out, the expenses are all yours!*

THE HONEYMOON

Whether it is a one-night stand or a three months' cruise, the idea is supposed to be aloneness . . . but aloneness *together*. You're off to a bad start if you take your dog, your mother or your secretary on your wedding trip; your bride is due for doubts if you let her shift for herself while you play golf or make business calls. And as desperate as you may *both* be for new faces after a few days, you are both obliged to pretend otherwise—at least, the bridegroom is not supposed to drum up parties of friends and is more or less expected to protect his honeymoon against such worldliness.

This is the sort of play-acting which led someone to describe the honeymoon as a period punctuated by "Excuse me" and "If *you* want to . . ." It's the sort of tradition which leads you both to admit, on your tenth wedding anniversary, that your honeymoon made you both think that marriage was going to be pretty confining. But that's the way it is: unless you've picked an eminently sensible girl, mature enough to distinguish between love and romantic symbolism, you'd better play the game. It won't last forever, and marriage will be the fun you expected it to be after you get it back in context.

In the meantime, allow for supreme touchiness, inconsistent modesty, uncomfortable deference and at least one burst of unexplainable tears. She'll be making similar allowances for you, and so long as neither of you suspects that the other is making allowances you'll be all right.

None of the following matters in the least, unless you think it does or she thinks it does, but here are some pointers you won't find in that other book you bought for the occasion:

1. *How to sign a hotel register:* "Mr. and Mrs. John Yourname," not "John Yourname and wife."

2. *How to be sure that flowers from you* are in your hotel

suite when you arrive: *take* them there, before the wedding. If you can manage this side-trip, you will at the same time be able to check over the accommodations, be *sure* that there are no old lipsticks or unmade beds to spoil her first impression. If it is unthinkably complicated to see where you're taking her, and to see that the flowers are there as you ordered, then take the hotel's room clerk into your confidence (and into your wallet)—commission him to handle this for you.

You might also register and get the key, so that you can spare her the possible embarrassment of standing around in the lobby thinking she looks like a newlywed.

3. *How to be sure that you are not disturbed* once you close the door behind you: order the champagne and the dinner in advance. The extra value of this will be to give your wedding-wrought gal the impression that you have not been an idle stick all these weeks, after all.

4. *How to* . . . oh, that's the *other* book.

AND EVER AFTER

The basis of marriage etiquette is, of course, something you can't get out of a book—mutual consideration, prompted by love and respect—but sometimes the little things, foreign to the male mind, loom large. The trick is to stop trying to *understand* why your wife is annoyed by inconsequential things: just accept the fact and fall in with it. What if she *does* use your toothbrush when the toddler has made off with hers? That doesn't mean she'll be any less irked if you use her comb or her towel. What if she *does* leave the butter out of the refrigerator overnight? That's no sign she is melting on the matter of the ice-trays you leave for her to refill and replace. What if she does ask people over for bridge without consulting you? Her crime doesn't condone your bringing home unexpected guests.

She will take a dim view of a lot of strange things. She probably won't like it if you holler to her from afar instead of coming to find her when you want to speak to her. She'll doubtless bristle if you fall into the habit of asking her to wait on you "while she's up." She'll screech—and rightly so —if you call her "the little woman," "the missus," "the ball and chain" or "mother." Some days she'll resent it if you don't ask her what she did while you were downtown; other days she'll think your questions are prying invasions of her privacy. She may play the martyr if you expect her to walk around the golf course with you—or if you expect her to stay happily at home.

Instead of looking for reason, look for her particular peeves; adjust yourself to the little things, and perhaps you can adjust her to the big ones.

There will be some "little things," by her definition, which are big things to you. If yours is a good relationship, there is no earthly (and no etiquette-ly) reason why you cannot simply state your whim and ask that she indulge you in it. Regardless of the reconnoitering she does to test the extent of your mastery, she expects you to be the head of the house. She *wants* to defer to your wishes—or, at least, she wants your wishes to be hers. She doesn't want to "wear the pants" or "take the wheel"; if she does so, it is by default. All this is to say that a husband is supposed to be positive, firm, the master—when it counts. If you are a doormat, out of a mistaken concept of chivalry or etiquette (or, for that matter, of *marriage*), your wife is at least as disappointed as you.

The key words in that paragraph, of course, are "if yours is a good relationship." If it is, instinct will instruct you on the front you and your wife present as a couple in public. If it is not, and if you want to cultivate a surface veneer of social-acceptability, mind the following manners when any third person is present:

1. *Observe the ordinary politenesses for your wife at least as much as for other women.* Tip your hat, hold her chair, light her cigarette, order her dinner—all as if, twenty minutes before, you hadn't seen her with cold cream on her face and blood in her eye.

2. *Observe one extraordinary politeness, too: listen* to her. Okay, so you've heard the story before, or she's getting it wrong, or you didn't think it was funny the first time, or you're just plain tired of hearing her talk. Okay, but don't let any of these reactions show in your face. Don't yawn or correct or interrupt or anticipate or start a side conversation or try to shut her up, any more than you would if the story-teller were your boss' wife instead of your own. This does not mean that you have to go around oh-ing and ah-ing at every thrice-told tale—everyone will know, from the nature of the story (or from the nature of marriage) that this is not news to you. It means only that you should complement, not contradict, augment, not diminish, your wife in others' eyes.

Complementing her, if nicely done, can be less passive than mere polite listening. You can back her up, show her off, take pains to let it be seen that she is a person in her own right and not merely your chattel. But if there is any danger of overdoing this—(husbands and wives who act as claques for each other are apt to be as boring as husbands and wives who heckle each other are embarrassing)—settle for ordinary kindness. Don't belittle her; don't criticize her; don't think it's your responsibility to shut her up with some deflationary remark like "These people don't want to hear about that." (It may be true, but "these people" would rather be bored by your wife than embarrassed by your public rudeness to her.)

3. *Say "our house,"* even if the deed is in your name; it's hers, too. Say "our children," not "my children" . . . "we

decided," not "I decided" . . . "when we were in Paris," not "when I was in Paris." In short, speak as part of a team. This can be carried too far, of course. Wives, no less than other people, like to preserve their own personalities. They don't want to be spoken for when they are able to speak for themselves. But neither do they want to be apparently ignored by your grating use of the first-person singular when you are speaking of joint possessions, mutual experiences or things which involve the whole family.

Y O U R   L I T T L E   M O N S T E R S

Your wife will doubtless worry more about your children's manners than you, and take more of the direct responsibility for teaching them their please-and-thank-yous, but your own role is important on several fronts:

1. *If you expect your little savages to acquire a veneer of civilization,* you will have to set something of an example. For reasons known only to psychologists, you are their Model in all things. Until the day when they discover your feet of clay, they learn best by imitation; "Do as I say, not as I do" is a hard lesson for anyone to learn. Thus, even if your wife quite agrees that home is a place to relax in, you had better start holding her chair and standing when she enters during the period when you're trying to beat such manners into your little boys.

The family table is perhaps the best place to teach, by in direction, a great many of the social graces: the give and take of conversation, the art of being pleasant. Treat your children at home as you would treat adults at a dinner party and you'll be getting a little good practice, yourself.

2. *Your children's telephone manners can have business implications*—as you'll know the first time your six-year-old forgets to tell you that your boss called—so you might want to lay down some special rules in this department. Teach

your children to identify themselves when they answer the phone, so your caller will know he's in the hands of a child and speak accordingly. Teach them to ask the caller to call back rather than leave a sure-to-be-garbled message.

Teen-aged telephonophiles are quite another problem. Have you considered giving them a separate wire, or restricting their phone calls during certain hours when you might be expecting a call?

3. *When you are not alone, you and your family,* your conduct toward and with your children should be adapted to the comfort of those others who are present. Usually this kind of conduct is best for the kids, too, but that's another subject. Put yourself in the guest's place and proceed accordingly: does he *want* to hear an enforced recitation of "Mary Had a Little Lamb," however precocious (what can he say when it's over?) . . . does he *want* to witness a spanking or an obvious correction of any kind? (how must he feel, especially if your correction is on *his* account?) . . . does he want you to save him a dime by telling him Johnny is not allowed to accept the money he has offered, or would he rather you saved his face? . . . does he want to be called by his first name, even if he says so? (the rule is "Mr." and "Mrs." except by special dispensation from "Mr." and "Mrs.")

When you get right down to it, wouldn't he rather say hello, followed very soon by goodbye? And wouldn't your children prefer the same brevity of meeting?

LET YOUR WIFE DO IT

As even a misogynist would admit, there is a great social advantage in being a husband. The moment you are married, you are relieved of all obligation to extend or respond to invitations; etiquette says that your social life as a couple is your wife's job. In practical terms, this means that you are not bound by the rule requiring you to give your answer on the spot when you are invited verbally; the reverse is true. People should phone or write invitations to your wife in the first place, but if they make the mistake of speaking to *you,* instead, you have only to say, "I don't know what Mary has planned—call her, won't you?" Or, if you think that sounds like a lecture in etiquette, say something like, "Mary doesn't trust me on these arrangements. I've got the world's worst memory for dates. Call her and give her a chance to write in her new engagement book, will you?"

Apart from catering to your wife's wishes (she will balk at going to the Jones' on your say-so alone), this device has the nice advantage of giving you a firm protection against dull evenings. Warn your wife that the Smiths are brewing up an evening of boredom, and she'll have time to invent a previous engagement before Mrs. Smith calls her.

Conversely, you should not extend invitations in your wife's name. It is her job to speak to the other wives, so none of this man-to-man arranging for social engagements! The other man doesn't know but what your invitation will be news to your wife; the other man's wife is doubly worried about the twice-removed bid; this can develop into a real mess.

If you run into Smith, and only *then* think how nice it would be to have the Smiths over to dinner, you can pave the way by saying that your wife has been going to call his. You can then follow through by seeing that she *does* call, but you can't make the deal yourself.

When the invitation concerned is strictly business, and does not include wives, that's another matter—see page ooo— but if it's useful, you can still pretend you have to check your wife's social plans before accepting a possibly-conflicting business invitation.

The point is that your social life is *expected* to be in the hands of your wife. You are not being "weak" or "hen-pecked" if you make a point of deferring to her engagement book.

DIVORCE

Etiquette dictates that she divorce you, no matter what, and, no matter what, that you don't talk about it. The rest of it is a matter for lawyers and bankers, but there is a convention that the wedding presents (like the trousseau linen) belong to the woman.

Once the divorce is final, she substitutes her maiden name for your first name—Mrs. John Jones, née Mary Smith, becomes Mrs. Smith Jones. Your children keep your name until legally changed, with your consent. *Your* name is probably mud.

Your previous marriage has no effect on the etiquette of any future wedding you may step into. Unlike the divorcée, you don't have to dress differently or behave differently when next you are married, as a penalty for having been through it before. Your previous marriage has some effect on the etiquette of your next one, of course—you will know enough to avoid comparisons; you'll know better than to try to kindle a friendship between your first and second wives; you'll be wise enough to forewarn old friends so that you don't have to explain the divorce in front of your new wife.

Something you might not know: if there has been any unpleasantness about the divorce, your new wife may run into trouble at department stores and banks and such places where your former wife did business. They know "Mrs. John Jones" only as a name. Take the trouble to write brief, business-like notes, to re-open old charge accounts in the name of the new Mrs. Jones, and you'll spare her the trouble of explaining in person.

When you and your ex-wife happen to meet in public, your conduct should be designed to avoid embarrassing others. Old-school-tie chumminess can sometimes be as embarrassing to onlookers as evidence of dislike. Impersonal politeness, if it's possible, is always safe.

the things you say

GOSSIP

Not all cats are female, but it sometimes seems that the female of the species gets all the cream. When a woman carries tales or talks behind another's back—even when she scratches pretty hard—she has the common view of her nature on her side. She is forgivable, if not lovable. But when a man gossips he courts a double penalty: he throws suspicion on his manhood as well as on his manners. Unless you would be known as an "old woman," let the people involved report their own news, in their own way, to confidantes of their own selection. That goes for good news as well as bad.

A good rule to follow is a variation of the old Army rule: "Never volunteer"—information. If you never volunteer information about other people (and if you're as noncommittal as possible in answering questions about them), you'll avoid most of the pitfalls of gossip. No one will ever misquote you, if you haven't said anything to quote. No one will ever wonder if perhaps you are betraying a confidence, or put you down as someone it's best not to confide in. No one will put your little scrap of news to his wider knowledge of the principals to reach a conclusion you hadn't anticipated. No one will use you as a catalyst in a situation outside your control. And no one (including yourself) will have reason to fear your innocent running-off-at-the-mouth.

Those are negative advantages, but there is a positive advantage, too. In the gossip world, the rule is an "I heard" for an "I heard." If you speak no evil, pretty soon you'll hear no evil; with no tales to carry, you'll be spared even the *temptation* to gossip. For in this realm, ignorance *is* bliss.

If "don't" is a good rule for tale-bearing, it's even better for back-biting. As the Talmud puts it: "Thy friend has a friend, and thy friend's friend has a friend, so be discreet."

Some seem to think that a prefatory remark like "I'd tell him this to his face" is excuse enough for criticizing another behind his back. It is not. Your friend may be close enough to you to take face-to-face criticism with grace, but he is never so close as to welcome public discussion of his foibles —particularly when he is not there to defend them. Nor is it excuse if the person you are criticizing says the same thing about himself. *Let* him.

Quite apart from your defenseless friend's interests, consider the impression you make on your listener. How can he help wondering, "What does he say about *me* when *I'm* not around?"

The question of talk becomes subtler when you are on the receiving end. Ideally, you should not even *listen* to malicious remarks—silence is a form of assent—but practically, you have to decide when a good defense of your absent friend is going to be a bad offense to your gossiping friend. If, as Francis Bacon said, good behavior is to retain your own dignity without intruding upon the liberty of others, your course is fairly clear. Try to strike a comfortable medium between stooping and towering.

In no case, of course, should you carry the story back to its subject.

All this leaves a wide margin for individual variation, but there is one rule which is unbreakable: a gentleman does *NOT* talk in personal terms about the women he knows. There has been a relaxation (not to say collapse) of the old rule that gentlemen did not discuss women even in the abstract; these days, unless your remarks can be interpreted to refer to a particular woman, you can be as witty as you like about the genre. But under no circumstances can you talk about *a* woman. Even a would-be complimentary remark about a woman you know socially is open to misinterpretation and is a breach of etiquette. That includes the long, low whistle when a name is mentioned. If the woman is your wife, of course, you have a perfect right to seem knowledgeable about her, but you have less right to bore others with extensive recitations.

Probably only college boys need to be warned against boasting of their "conquests," real or imagined, but otherwise mature men continue to deal in innuendo. Knighthood may be in seed, but every man is still a self-appointed protector of every woman's frailest possession—her "good name." The more tenuous her hold on the good name, the more tenacious the protector must be.

Oscar Wilde said, "Talk to every woman as if you loved her." Etiquette says, "Talk *of* every woman as if you'd never met her."

CONVERSATION

There used to be a great many more "don'ts" about conversation. (Maybe that's why it was called an art; it took an artist to find a safe topic for talk.) But today, when you can talk about almost anything so long as you do it interestingly, these "do's" will be more useful:

1. *Suit the subject to your listener.* Well applied, this primary rule will keep you from being either boor or bore. It means that once-verboten subjects of conversation—sex, servants, sinuses—are now acceptable if they will interest and will not embarrass any one of your listeners. (Remember, though: the woman who loves to talk sex to you alone may pretend Puritanism in the presence of other women.) . . . It means that you *can* tell "dirty" jokes—to men who like them. (You had still better watch your language and your humor with strangers, with women of unknown background and whenever you're in doubt.) . . . It means that you *can* argue politics or religion, if the others obviously want to; many moderns think that a good argument makes good conversation. (A "good" argument, however, is still impersonal and unemotional.) . . . It means that you *can* talk shop, if everyone within earshot is shop-minded, or if you can make it general enough to interest the uninitiated. . . . It means that you *can* talk about yourself if you are of compelling interest to your listener. (With anyone but your mother or your lover, however, you'd better question that "compelling interest." They say a bore is one who talks about himself when you want to talk about yourself, so see that your "I" has overtones of "you.")

It also means that the "nicest," most traditional of topics is bad if it is over your listeners' heads or under anyone's mood. Don't talk ethics at an average woman, or ethnics at an average cocktail party. Remember, too, that it is as impolite to leave one of your group out of the conversation as it is to whisper to one in front of another. That's probably why philosophers claim you can't have a decent conversation with more than one person; the talk necessarily seeks the lowest level.

Needless to say, you can't *ask*, "Am I boring you?" or "Does this embarrass you?" Your listener will be too polite to say "yes"; your question itself will be boring, and embarrassing. Instead, *watch*. Even the professional good listener gets a glazed eye, or fails to ask interested, intelligent questions to encourage you. And whenever you're in doubt, follow, don't lead, the conversation.

2. *Take your turn*. This means, of course, no monologues. If ever you find that you have talked for three minutes straight, without question or comment from your listeners, you can be pretty sure that you are talking on a subject of interest only to yourself—hark to the drone in your voice! If the others have nothing to contribute, it's a speech, not a conversation.

Taking your turn also means not interrupting when others are talking. There are two kinds of interruptions. The obvious one, interrupting the speaker in mid-sentence, is easy to avoid: just wait until the other has stopped talking before you start. (And don't ever say, "Have you finished?" You might as well say right out that he's a windy numskull and you thought he'd never run down.) The other kind of interruption, equally culpable, is often prefaced by "That reminds me . . ." or "By the way." Such phrases usually signal a digression or an irrelevancy. When you interrupt another's train of thought, or send a discussion off into a tangent, you indicate that you are either stupid or rude, either unable or unwilling to stick to the speaker's point.

Even if everyone else observed these rules, telephones, doorbells and new arrivals would always conspire to interrupt you in mid-point. When you are interrupted, the politest thing to do is the hardest thing: shut up. Don't go back and finish a story—don't excavate a buried point—unless you are asked to do so. If a new listener has come up in mid-story, a polite someone else will brief him on the subject and ask you to go on; the polite newcomer will second the nomination; only then, with the briefest possible synopsis of what you said before, can you go on. If you are not given these cues, it may be because your story is not appropriate for the newcomer's ears, or because the situation gets beyond control; it's not *always* because your audience was bored. So, if you get a chance to make your point later on, don't air your annoyance with a petulant, "As I was trying to say a little earlier . . ."

3. *Think before you talk, and think beyond the subject at hand.* That's the secret of tact. The object is to avoid making anyone uncomfortable, unhappy or simply self-conscious —accidentally. Tact's opposite is not, contrary to popular opinion, truth. The opposite of tact is just plain thoughtlessness. *Think* before you tell a psychiatrist joke to someone who has just begun psychoanalysis; where one's emotions are involved, a joke is not always a joke. *Think* before you fascinate the widow with your war stories; she might be a war widow. *Think* before you talk the gourmet to your plain-cook hostess.

"Don't limp before the lame," Rabelais said. The tough part, in modern social intercourse, is to remember who is "lame," and where, before you speak. You can't know everybody's sensitive spots, but you can guard against touching most of them if you cultivate the art of temporizing. Try not to be positive on subjects involving taste or opinion. "It seems to me . . ." and "There's a school of thought that says . . ." will get you into less trouble than "This is the way it *is*."

Indicate, and believe, that other viewpoints, other tastes are as valid as your own. Try not to be funny about subjects others might, for personal reasons, consider very serious. Then you'll be fairly safe.

When you do blunder into an awkward situation, you can only say, "I'm sorry" or "I didn't know" and *go on* to another subject. Overlong apologies or involved explanations only prolong the mutual embarrassment.

4. *Respect others' privacy—and reserve a little for your-self.* The American habit of "interviewing" every new ac-quaintance is appalling to Continentals; sometimes the ques-tions are dismaying even to the fellow-Americans they are designed to "draw out." You have to place people, a lit-tle, before you can know what conversational topic will interest them. But do it, if you can, by exchange of informa-tion, not by questions which might appear prying.

There's seldom any danger in a question like, "Do you play golf?" but more personal questions court a conversa-tional turn which may embarrass you, if not your inter-viewee. What if you say, "Are you married?" and she says, "Not very"? What if you ask, "Have you any children?" and she launches into an agonized account of why not? "Where did you go to school?" or "What do you do?" can be embar-rassing in totally unexpected ways.

All such questions might have been safe in the bad old days, when "society" was stratified and people were more apt to be what they seemed, but then, of course, the ques-tions were also unnecessary. Today, if you want to know all those things about your new acquaintance, volunteer the same information about yourself—not as a recitation, of course, but as a part of a story or statement. Nine times out of ten the new person will match your information with his own, but the option is *his*. If he thinks it's none of your busi-ness, or if he'd rather not be reminded that he never finished high school, he can pass—and much more gracefully than if you have asked the question outright.

With old acquaintances, similar restraint in question-asking is desirable. When you know a person well, the more reason to suppose that he'll *tell* you anything he wants you to know; so even your fishing should be relatively guarded, particu-larly on questions of money.

As to your own privacy, suit yourself within these two boundaries of taste:

Don't burden casual acquaintances with your troubles.
(what *is* there about cocktail parties that curries confessions?)

Remember that everything you say can be used against you.

More policy than etiquette, but worth bearing in mind:
the person who is said to "wear well" is usually one who
saves something of himself for his intimates.

5. *Be natural.* You've often heard that what you say
and how you say it is a first impression give-away to your
character and your background—but there's a sleeper in
that bromide: It's a bigger give-away to pretend to be something you are not than to be what you are without apology.
In short, affectation will out.

No matter what the lady-books say about "cultivated
speech," a man's speech had best not be cultivated; it ought
first of all to be natural. If it's not natural for you to talk like
a Boston scholar, why try? Equally, if slang sits uneasy on
your tongue and your "a" is just naturally broad, why try
to sound like a drummer from hunger?

This is not to discount the value of grammatical, articulate
speech, nor to imply that you *must* say "boid" for "bird"
just because that's the way you foist loined the woid. It's
only to warn that a natural "ain't I?" is better than an uncomfortable, inconsistent "am I not?"—and vice versa. It's
only to point out that a genuine, regional accent is more
help than hindrance to a man.

It is true that, like the best manners, the best speech is
the least noticeable speech—but you can count on this: an
honest, unself-conscious way of speaking, be it ever so different from your listeners' way, is always less noticeable than an affected "correct" way. Improve your grammar,
your diction, your English usage if you can—but improve
along the lines of your true self. Don't ape the fashionable
phonies who speak as "they" speak.

And what is this advice doing in a book of etiquette? Just this: because most of the niceties of etiquette have been recorded (if not created) by women, an ordinary man wanting to say the right thing has been in no little danger of sounding precious. The pretty politenesses of speech you find in the girls' books are not for you, sir. If you mean "Sorry," *say* "Sorry"—not "I'm *so* sorry," not "I *beg* your pardon." If you mean that the dinner was damned good say so; don't mince around with uneasy words like "exquisite" or "lovely." Leave the "my dears" to the aged, and *"do comes"* to the feminine gender. And forget all about the supposedly gallant phrases like "Allow me" and "After you."

It is not etiquette to say things the long way or the fancy way. Be yourself. Be a man. Even in the china shop of a woman's world.

P. S.

EIGHT RULES

1. *Don't correct another's grammar or pronunciation, not even indirectly.*   It's as much a correction to say the word properly, later in the conversation, as to stop him in midmangle of the language. This doesn't mean you have to go around saying "between you and I" for "between you and me" or "program" for "program"; it just means that, in this delicate situation, synonyms and paraphrases are a man's best friend. As Oscar Wilde said in another context, "It is always a silly thing to give advice, but to give good advice is absolutely fatal."

2. *Don't say, "Stop me if you've heard this . . ."   because no one ever* will *stop you.*   Even practiced boors wait until you've finished a story before they let you know that

it's a twice-told tale (tedious, by definition). Considerate people, wanting you not to be embarrassed at having repeated a familiar story, will let you think it's new to them. So what's to be gained by the delaying preamble?

3. *Be careful of compliments.* Give them in private, wherever possible. To compliment one person in front of another may be taken to mean that there is nothing to compliment the other about.

Receive them with grace, however it kills you. Nothing embarrasses a sincere and well-meaning acquaintance so much as to have his compliment disparaged, denied or argued. Women are the greater offenders, with their "oh-this-old-rag" type of false modesty, but men are often the more genuinely embarrassed by compliments.

Except from an intimate, a compliment properly refers to an accomplishment or an obvious major possession—to the way you handled the staff meeting, not to the way your hair lies down in back; to your new house, not to your button-down shirt. Such compliments lead into conversation—about the people who helped make the meeting a success, about the enjoyment you and your family have had from the house. For the more personal and usually more embarrassing compliments, a simple "thanks" is all you need say in acknowledgment. Protest will only be interpreted as a kind of fishing for further compliments, so let it go at that.

Needless to say, all common sense *and* etiquette bars are down when it comes to compliments and women. The only acknowledgment to a compliment *from* a woman is a much more lavish compliment *to* her. The only limit to compliments to a woman is your imagination—and the only improper compliment to a woman is an absolutely incredible one. But your imagination will run out long before her credulity does.

4. *Don't say, "Huh?" or "What?" when you mean, "What did you say?" or "Sorry—I didn't hear what you said."*

5. *Don't use a lot of foreign words and phrases*—unless your pronunciation and usage are impeccable, and unless your listener would use the same expression himself. The plain old Anglo-Saxon word is almost sure to be better, in any case, so don't strain for the "elegant" word. Even if it just slides off your tongue naturally, because you speak French as easily as English, the tendency toward sprinkling your speech with French is worth trying to curb.

The caution against elegance of speech applies to English words as well: if the word on the tip of your tongue is "refined," try to substitute a simpler source. Why "my employer" instead of "my boss"? Why "wealthy" instead of "rich"? Why "home" when you mean "house"? And why "darn" and "my goodness"? Anyone who would be shocked by "damn" and "God" won't accept your polite substitute, either. Etiquette is agin cussing in mixed company, but if you *must,* do it like a *man.*

6. *Don't give second-hand opinions or ideas without crediting their source.* Sooner or later the idea thief is always caught in the act. No one cares if an interesting thought or witty observation is not original with you—unless you try to pass it off as original.

7. *Call her Miss or Mrs. Lastname—until she invites you to use her first name.* If she doesn't come right out with the request that you call her by her first name, she lets you know by using *your* first name. In any case, it's *her* privilege, not yours, so don't say, "Call me Johnny," or "May I call you Mary?" The exception would be if you are a celebrity, a man much older than she, or in some sort of position (boss, professional adviser, official) where she would hesitate to exercise her feminine prerogative to start the first names rolling.

The point might seem academic—particularly in worlds where strangers call each other "darling" until they know each other well enough to use the less formal "baby"—but there remain a few women who like either correctness or preliminaries. And the rule on first names is: Ladies First.

8. *In public the best manners are the quietest.* Try not to attract attention to yourself or to your friends. You wouldn't commit the high school offense of loud talk and laughter in public, or the housewife offense of talking across strangers as across back fences. But you might, in all good will and with no wish to attract attention, holler to a friend across the street. Don't! Catch up with him before you greet him. If you *must* call out, don't use his full name; he doesn't want to be a public spectacle, and if you make him one he'd rather be anonymous.

Similarly, you should not use others' names in places where they can be overheard. Strict adherence to this rule will have you talking in riddles—"the man we were talking about" rather than "Jones"—or, better, not talking at all in the hearing of strangers. There is a reason, you see, for conversations left in mid-air as the silent, crowded elevator descends.

ON THE TELEPHONE

When an ill-mannered person is at the other end, the telephone is a real instrument of torture. And if *you* are that ill-mannered person, you may go to your social death wrapped in telephone wire. You can avoid most travesties against telephone etiquette by stopping to consider the good old Golden Rule. Chances are that you, too, would be annoyed if you were on the receiving end of these telephone terrors.*

1. *"Mr. Webb speaking."* That might be an acceptable greeting over a *business* telephone, but the only correct way to answer a home phone is "Hello." Your maid should say, "Mr. Webb's apartment" (or "telephone," or "resi-

* See page 254 for how *not* to call up a girl and see page 29 for the telephone etiquette of business.

dence," or "house" or whatever best describes the telephone's environs).

Quite apart from that, you should never call yourself "Mr." to social acquaintances. Though you be on the most formal of Mr. terms with the person you're speaking to, don't give yourself airs. You are "James Webb" whenever you introduce yourself, except to tradespeople and servants. And even then, your "Mr." carries a note of superiority; it's "correct," but it sticks in a lot of nice guys' craws.

2. *"Who's calling?"* This one's no better when dressed up into "May I ask who's calling, please?" And it's very little worse when blurted out as "Who wants him?" There would be no need for it at all, on the receiving end, if your callers would mind their manners and identify themselves immediately upon hearing "Hello." Your caller should say, "This is Joe—is that you, Jim?" or "This is William Carr—may I speak to Mr. Webb, please?" But if he is not so polite, that doesn't excuse your rudeness in asking who he is *before* you say whether or not you are available to talk to him. You should either say *"This* is James Webb," and take your chances, or you should bring out your Swedish accent and pretend that Mr. Webb is out. If you are your own Swedish servant, you might then say, "May I ask him to call you?" But if your mystery man at the other end of the line lets *that* one drop, you may *never* find out who he was. It's better for you to be in doubt about his identity, however, than for him to be in doubt about your manners. If you say, "Who's calling, please?" and *then* say you're out, he'll wonder if you're out only to *him.* If you say, "Who's calling?" and then say you're *you,* what have you gained— except a one-minute jump on the name he was going to give you eventually anyway? The same principle applies even, or perhaps especially, when an employee is answering the phone for you. Unless you're the type who really *is* in to some and out to others (or unless you want to seem so), see

that your butler (or your cleaning lady) does not say anything resembling "Who's calling?" until it's time to take a
message.

3. *"What number is this?"* If you've drawn a wrong number, what difference does it make *what* wrong number
you've got? Say, instead, "Is this Lincoln 4-6000?" And if it
isn't, say you're sorry; it might not be your fault, but it's
certainly not the wrong number's fault, either.

Reverse this considerate conduct when you're on the *receiving* end of a slip in the night. Say, "I'm afraid you have
the wrong number; this is Lincoln 6-4000"—and then *don't*
slam the phone down. Cuss, if you must, as you drip back
into your shower, but don't take it out on your fellow-victim
of the electronic age.

4. *"Who is this?"* When you've placed the call, say who
you are and ask for the person you want to speak to. The
middle man will probably volunteer his name if it matters;
if he doesn't and you *must* know, you can take a guess: "Is
this Johnny?" But if you spit out, "Who is this?", you deserve an answer like, "What's it *to* ya?"

5. *"Yackity, yackity, yackity, yack."* If you're settled down
for a long conversation, ask *first* if this is a convenient time
for your friend to talk. Your call may have taken him
from bath or booze or blonde, or his maiden aunt's ears may
be flapping at phone-side. He has every right to break in
with something like "We were just going in to dinner; may I
call you back in a couple of hours?"; he really *ought* to if
catering to you means neglecting his guests. But give him a
chance.

6. *"Hang on a second, will you, please?"* If it *is* only a
second, okay—but if it's going to be a longer interruption
give your caller an option: "Someone's at the door (or whatever)—may I call you back?" It is particularly rude to keep
the other waiting if *you* are the caller.

7. *"Not you—I was talking to somebody else."* A pox on

side conversations! If the house catches fire or the dog starts chewing your favorite hat, of course you can't stand on ceremony—but you *can* explain and apologize after the crisis is over. Lesser interruptions should be ignored or handled by sign language or at least screened from transmission by your tight hand over the mouthpiece.

8. *"Okay" or "See you" or just plain old "click" instead of a definite "goodbye."* You wouldn't deliberately hang up on anyone; take care you don't do it accidentally by hanging up before you signal the end of the conversation and exchange conclusive goodbyes. (Incidentally, the person who placed the call is usually the one to end the conversation; he's the one who knows whether he's completed his mission or not.)

Besides all that, of course, it is not endearing to shout or mutter. And you'll have little further chance to do either if you don't return calls when a message is left for you.

INTRODUCTIONS

THE HOW

Someday, if you are very lucky, you will get the chance to make introductions between the President of the United States and the King of Tasmania, a young priest and an elderly countess, a foreign ambassador and your wife. Then, like the first-year French student who finally worked *"la plume de ma tante"* into the conversation, you will probably be so overjoyed that you will forget everything you know. So never mind about the technicalities of introductions. Forget the exceptions (royalty, the presidency, church-rank and extreme age); just remember that:

A man is always presented *to* a woman, not a woman to a man.

The honored one's name is said first; the name of the person being presented follows.

Don't bother, either, with anything except the names. No need to hesitate on the brink of "May I present?" or "May I introduce?" or "I have the honor to present." They're all correct, but they're a bit stiff for modern usage. A plain and simple, "Mrs. Whistle, Mr. Wolf" is enough—or, if you like, "Mrs. Whistle, this is Mr. Wolf." In addition to being easy to remember, this brief form will keep you clear of the bad forms: "Shake hands with," "Make the acquaintance of," "Meet," "Say how-de-do to" and the rest.

"Mrs. Whistle, Mr. Wolf" . . . that's all you have to say. You shouldn't then reverse gear with "Mr. Wolf, Mrs. Whistle"—they both heard you the first time. And you needn't go on to give each a biography of the other; those "conversational leads" can be deadly, if not dangerous, so unless it's perfectly natural and logical to explain people to each other, let them find out for themselves that they "have *so* much in common."

"Woman'sname, this is Man'sname"—what could be simpler? There are subtleties, to be sure, but if you think they'll confuse you just skip the next paragraphs:

If you're in a first-name kind of world and you're introducing one first-name friend to another, you may correctly dispense with the titles: "Nellie Whistle, John Wolf," or "Nellie, this is John Wolf—Nellie Whistle." When you are on first-name terms with only one of the pair, however, it's best to be consistent; rather than presuming to use the remote person's first name, use their titles for both: "Mrs. Whistle, Mr. Wolf," not "Nellie Whistle, Mr. Wolf."

The exception to *that* one (and there's always an exception) comes when your first-name relationship with the one is obvious and to be expected. When you are introducing a member of your own family, whose last name is the same as yours, it sounds less pompous if you omit the last name in favor of the relationship: "Mary, this is Mr. Boss . . . my wife." * Or "Mrs. Bosswife, my son John." Or "Mother, this is George Guest."

If the relative's name is different from yours, tack it on later to avoid confusion: "Mother, this is George Guest . . . Mrs. Stepfather." Or "Betty, this is Mr. Boss—my sister, Mrs. Marriedname."

When introducing a man to a man, or a woman to a woman, your best bet is simply to say the names in the same tone of voice, giving no more importance to one than to the other. By the rules, you should present the young to the old, the lesser to the greater, but when you thus appraise the age of women or the importance of men you are courting trouble. So forget the fine points—just introduce 'em. If there is an obvious, mutually acknowledged honor due one or the other—as when you introduce your fiancée to your grandmother or your roommate to your professor or your brother to your boss—your instinct will tell you to mention the more important name first. But if you're using the short form, nobody will notice or care if you miss.

When more than two people are involved in your introduction, the situation only *seems* more complicated; it's really much simpler. Convenience and dispatch are more important than "form," so if there are more than four people involved, forget about rank and sex (for the moment). Mention the newcomer's name, then the names of the others in the order in which they happen to be sitting or standing at the time.

If the group is really large or inattentive, a general in-

* Under no social circumstances do you ever refer to your wife as "Mrs. Yourname." She's "Mary" to people who know who "Mary" is, "my wife" to people who don't know her first name.

troduction is not necessary. Introduce the newcomer into a handy cluster of people and let it go at that.

THE WHEN

An etiquette book of 1834 said, "Never introduce people to each other without a previous understanding that it will be agreeable to both," and, "An adherence to Etiquette will relieve you from the awkwardness of being acquainted with people of whom you might at times be ashamed, or be obliged under many circumstances to cut."

The very formal, the very conservative and the very snobbish might still endorse that view, but for most moderns the problem of introductions is not so much a matter of the obligation involved in acquaintance as it is a matter of convenience. If you make introductions right and left, on the slightest encounter, you can be criticized for delaying the world but seldom for having bad manners. The only time when it is definitely bad form to "do the honors" is in another man's house.

On the whole, it's safer to err on the side of commission, but these are times when wholesale introductions are *not* necessary:

At large informal parties in your own house (see page 344). Your roof is introduction enough for your friends, and it is a nuisance to everyone to take each new guest on an introduction-tour of the room.

In public places when the meeting is to be brief. When you run into one friend on the street while walking with another, you will doubtless exchange only how-are-yous; an introduction will only obstruct traffic further. The person you were walking with should walk on a few steps and wait until you rejoin him, thus making an introduction unnecessary. If he doesn't walk on, and if the conversation shows signs of stretching out, everyone will be more comfortable if you do the honors; otherwise, skip them. Table-hoppers are best not introduced (they ought to be traduced, instead); if the hopper is going to insist on saying more than just hello, either ask him to sit down or lead him a slight distance away from the table so the others at your table can get back to their food or talk.

Anywhere, where there's no point in the introduction—that is, where the how-do-you-dos are not to be followed by conversation. There's no point in introducing the departing guest to the arriving one as they meet at your door. There's no point in introducing your companion to your friend the florist when you've only dashed in to pick up a box. And, by the way, what's the point when either of the persons could be embarrassed by the introduction, or when it is necessary to explain one's presence to the other? Why introduce Mrs. Grundy to your best friend's wife, say, when Mrs. G. drops in on your tête-à-tête to borrow a drop of vermouth; give her the vermouth and the door—her gossip will do less damage if she doesn't know the lady's name. Similar strategy will be the best manners, in the long run, when you and your wife "run into" your boss and his secretary, any attractive business woman who might address you a little too gaily for the occasion, or anyone who might say anything like "Oh, is *this* your wife? I thought . . ."

You get the idea! Size up your own "no introductions necessary" situations.

In addition, there are times when introductions are seemingly not necessary but they're *nice:*

When you think (or know) that the people have met before, but you can't be sure that they remember each other's names. Better than asking one if he knows the other—putting them both on the spot if one remembers and the other has forgotten the previous encounter—is this device: "Miss Jones, Mr. Smith—I think you may have met at our Christmas party" . . . or . . . "You know each other, don't you? Miss Jones? Mr. Smith?" That way they can both say "how do you do," with or without reference to the previous meeting, as they choose; no feelings will be hurt.

This nice, neutral, *safe* approach will also endear you to people who know each other very well (but very privately). Though they are nursing a joint hangover, Miss Jones and Mr. Smith may *want* to be introduced when Mrs. Smith is present; let *them* be the ones to acknowledge their acquaintance.

Incidentally, when you are introduced to a woman you have met before, let her be the one to say, "We've met." Elaborate exposition of how you couldn't possibly have forgotten how beautiful she looked at the Winfield party may seem very gallant and may indeed be true, but save it for a private talk. For all you know, she wants the others to think she was sick in bed the night of the Winfield's party.

Whenever you *greet an acquaintance "out of context"*— that is, in surroundings or circumstances different from those in which you first met. Introduce *yourself*. Your "Hello, Mr. Green"—if not immediately interrupted by Mr. Green's use of *your* name—should be followed up right away with "I'm John Jones; we met at the Smiths' anniversary party." Mr. Green will of course say, "Of course," and make you think he knew you all the time, but he'll be grateful for your reminder. If you say nothing, he'll probably say, "Hello, there!" ("there" being as common a name as Jones, these days), and as soon as you've gone he'll say, "Now who the hell was *that?*" If you say, "Don't you remember me?", without giving your name, you'll deserve the unprintable things he's think-

311

ing about you. So even though you are the most unforget-table character anyone ever met, *give your name.**

W H E N   Y O U   A R E   I N T R O D U C E D

. . . you stand, whether being introduced to a man or a woman, and say, "How do you do?" With informal contem-poraries, "Hello" is all right. "How are you?" is not so good. No one ever says how he does in response to "how do you do?", but "How are you?" is apt to surprise someone into saying, "Fine"—then the ritual of "How do you do," "How do you do," would be ruint!

You may add the newly-met person's name if you like, but you ought not to acknowledge the introduction with the name alone. "How do you do, Mrs. Jones," not just the curt, "Mrs. Jones."

To Mrs. Jones, you give a simultaneous nod, modern ver-sion of the bow. You do not offer your hand to her unless she first offers hers. To Mr. Jones, you cross the room or go to almost any lengths in order to shake his hand; he'll meet you halfway. (If your host is attempting a mass introduc-tion, and hand-shaking will snarl him up by slowing him down, the modern manner settles for a nod. It takes two to break a rule, however, and if Mr. Jones starts a broken-field run to shake your hand, he dooms you to equal athletics for him and for every other man you are introduced to in that particular exchange.)

Only after this routine can you say anything faintly re-sembling "pleasedtameetcha." Expression of honest pleas-

---

*Not a bad idea, either, whenever anyone falters at introducing you. It's a simple thing to say, "John Jones" as you stick out your hand, thereby fore-stalling any embarrassment your friend might feel at losing your name in the fluster of a mob introduction. It takes nice timing, to be sure—you don't want to take the play away from him unless he needs help, and yet you want to step in before the Big Silence. But even a delayed rescue is better than having to be *asked* your name.

ure at meeting someone you've long heard about is not to be censored just because etiquette bans flowery forms like "Happy to make your acquaintance." But save it for your conversation; don't use it in place of "how do you do."

the things you write

The business of social correspondence is not nearly so complicated as you may have been led to fear. All you need is a supply of visiting cards, some good paper, a pen, a typewriter and a little good will. If you have a wife, you don't even need those: she will do the letter-honors for you.

ON CARDS

First, about the cards. They can spare you a lot of letter-writing and telephoning, so even though you expect never to make a formal "visit," get yourself some visiting cards. They should be white or off-white, cardboard or parchment, glazed or unglazed, but without raised border. Some highly glazed boards and parchment don't take ink very well: try writing on one before you buy. Their shape should be narrow, rather than squarish like a woman's card. The size can range from 1 $\frac{7}{16}$" to 1 $\frac{3}{4}$" deep by 2 $\frac{7}{8}$" to 3 $\frac{1}{2}$" long, so choose the size that best accommodates your name. If you choose the smallest size, there may be precious little room on the card for messages. In that case get a fold-over card, called an "informal," in addition, or instead. A standard size is 2 $\frac{1}{4}$" by 3 $\frac{7}{8}$".

The cards should be engraved in black and carry no color elsewhere. The lettering can be Roman or script, shaded or not, but watch out for too big or too fancy lettering.

All this fuss will seem a little foolish, considering that you will be crossing out your name on most of the cards you use, but study the effect to see that your card looks masculine, unaffected and conservative.

Order envelopes to match and, for those cards which will go through the mail, extra, larger envelopes to mail the small ones in.

On the card should be engraved:

1. *Your title:* This is "Mr." (abbreviated) unless you are a doctor, an officer on active duty, a minister or a high public official, in which case the appropriate title (preferably spelled out) precedes your name. Take care that the "appropriate title" does not appear to take honors best bestowed by others. Although you are called "Colonel," engrave your

card "Lieutenant Colonel" . . . although you are addressed as "The Honorable," engrave your card "Senator" or "Judge" . . . although you are called "Professor" or "Doctor" (Ph.D. variety), use "Mr." on your card.

The bare, untitled name is seldom used socially except by diplomats (whose posts are engraved beneath their names in lieu of title) and by minors: you *may* use "Mr." as soon as you have entered college; you *must* use it as soon as you are twenty-one.

2. *Your name:* Spell it out, using no initials, if this is not unwieldy or unnatural. "Mr. Algernon Joseph Smith" is preferred to "Mr. A. Joseph Smith" or "Mr. Algernon J. Smith." Strictly speaking, "Mr. A. J. Smith" is permissible only on a business card. If "Algernon" is a deep, dark secret between you and your parents, why don't you drop the "A." altogether? Men who part their names on the side are sometimes suspected of putting on airs. And if everybody calls you "Shorty," don't be embarrassed to see yourself as "Joseph"; there's no place for nicknames on visiting cards. Even tough Bills must be sweet Williams on copper-plate.

3. *Your address:* This is not necessary but it's helpful if you travel a lot, or if you live in a large city or in the remote country with a forgettable post-office address. Your address is your home if you live with your parents or your wife, your club if you live here-and-there. Never use both home and club on one card, and never use a business address on a social card. A club address is engraved in the lower left-hand corner of the card; a home address is in the lower right-hand corner. Telephone numbers do not usually appear on visiting cards.

Avoid abbreviations of streets and states if you can do it without crowding the card; but don't be afraid to use numbers. Trust your eye.

It is not necessary to include city and state if the cards are to be used locally or if the street address speaks for itself. Thus "New York City" scarcely ever appears on a visiting card, but suburban towns do.

4. *Your caboose:* Sometimes a suffix is part of your name and therefore must appear on your card—"Jr." or "junior," for instance, to distinguish you from your old man.* If you use such a suffix, insert a comma to set it off from your name. And if you are in *doubt* about using a suffix—M.D. or D.D.S. or Ph.D. or whatnot—then it can't be an indispensable part of your real name. Skip it, lest someone think you are advertising your own honors. ("Esquire," by the way, is redundant with "Mr." and, unlike its namesake, it's old hat.)

HOW TO USE THE CARDS

Okay, so you've ordered a hundred cards and instructed the engraver to hold your plate, pending a re-order. Now are you to go up and down the streets saying "my card" as you peel off these little replicas of you? Not quite, but you'll unload them almost that fast.

As invitations: For an informal party, you can simply write the occasion, the date and the time across the top of your cards and mail them out. If you want an answer, put RSVP (or R.S.V.P. or R.s.v.p.) in the lower left corner. Or, if your party is to be at an address different from that engraved on your card, write the party-address in the available corner and put "RSVP to" over your mail address. Usually you strike out the Mr. before your name, and if you are going to sign the message "Joe," you cross out the whole name. You may abbreviate at will—you almost have to, to get it all on—so these make painless invitation forms. The only time they are not good is for very formal or very small

---

*You should drop the "junior" from your name when your father dies. If this makes a mix-up between your mother and your wife, both Mrs. John Smiths, your mother may add "Sr." or "senior" to her cards. Your wife's card should always read the same as yours, so she does not hang on to "junior."

affairs—the former because the visiting card invitation is casual, the latter because it implies a crowd, or at least a party.

As replies to invitations: Instead of a note (if you have trouble with them) and instead of a phone call (if you hate them), you may send your visiting card in answer to any informal invitation. Write "Thanks—I'll be there" or "Accept with pleasure" or whatever you like across the top of your card, along with the date and time for which you are accepting. If you cannot accept the invitation, it is not necessary to state the hour—only the date; the rules say you must give a reason, however, and the sparse space for writing on a visiting card may persuade you to break out some note paper instead. Or perhaps you'll welcome the cramped space—it allows you to say simply, "Sorry—will be in Mexico the 18th," without a long explanation or an attempt to be clever about why you're going to Mexico. Again, it's best to cross out your name and write an informal signature when addressing first-name friends, and it's best to cross out the "Mr." in any case.

Here are a few samples of visiting card invitations and replies:

To toast Mary and Jim —
Saturday Feb. 15
5 to 8
~~MRS. GENIAL HOSTESS~~
Laura

RSVP   One Fifth Park Avenue

I'll be there Saturday the 15th,
at five — thanks

~~MR. JOSEPH BACHELOR~~

great about M & J, isn't it?

Joe

150 East 72nd Street

Sorry, but involved in a
country weekend over the
15th — Thanks anyway —

~~MR. JOSEPH BACHELOR~~

and my best to M & J —
Joe.

150 East 72nd Street

Cocktails, WED., Jan. 18
J - 7

MR. JOSEPH BACHELOR

at the Madison

R.S.V.P. to

150 East 72nd Street

or, a note saying something like "Gosh, I'm sorry, but I had already made plans to go to the country over the week-end of the fifteenth, and I'd be leaving three ardent golfers in

319

> *We'll be at the Madison at 5 on the 18th! Thanks!*
>
> ~~MR. AND MRS. HONORED GUEST~~
>
> *Joe & Marie*
>
> 488 Madison Avenue

the lurch if I fouled out now. Please tell Mary and Jim how much I shall miss seeing them, but I hope to see you as well as the bride and groom at the wedding next month. Sincerely, Joe"

> *Breakfast for the Cassidys — after the Queen lands*
>
> MR. JOSEPH BACHELOR
>
> *WED, Oct. 18, about noon*
>
> *R.S.V.P to:*
>
> The Yale Club   *at the Plaza*

> *Will you come to a stand-up supper on Saturday, the 18th, about seven?*
>
> ~~MR. JOSEPH BACHELOR~~
>
> *Joe*
>
> *R.S.V.P.*   One Fifth Avenue

320

To wait out the reviews
of John's new play —
Wed., Oct. 15 — 12 M to ?

~~MR.~~ JOSEPH BACHELOR

there'll be supper!

Please reply   One Fifth Avenue

As "letters" of introduction: When you send one friend to meet another, in a distant city, you may use your visiting card like this:

Introducing Clarence Culpepper

MR. JOSEPH BACHELOR

The Club

You still have to write the distant friend to prepare him for Culpepper's presentation of your card (and please see page 335 before you jump into these complications), but your visiting card introduction saves you the chore of writing a separate letter for Culpepper to present.

As vehicles for short messages: To notify your friends of a change of address you may simply mail out some of your new cards showing the new address. To say goodbye when you leave town, you may write "P.P.C." in the lower left corner and mail the cards to your acquaintances. "P.P.C."

321

stands for "pour prendre congé," which means "to take leave."

There are some other French abbreviations: P.C. for *pour condoler* (to condole), P.F. for *pour féliciter* (to send best wishes), P.R. for *pour remercier* (to thank). All are correct, but unless you are showering cards on Gallic readers of etiquette books they are apt to be bewildering, if not amusing—precious, if not pompous. Our advice is: say it in American. (R.S.V.P. is an exception; everybody knows that it means *"répondez, s'il vous plaît"* and its Frenchiness is forgiven. "Please reply" is no less correct, but RSVP is still more commonly used.)

Write across the top of your card whatever message is appropriate—"I'm off; see you in the fall," or "Don't forget: you're going to look me up on your trip West," or "Just heard the news: congratulations!" or "With deepest sympathy," or "Thanks for making my stay so pleasant" or whatever. Strike out your name and sign it "Joe," or strike out the "Mr." and let your engraved name stand. And, if you can possibly afford it, and if you really *mean* "thanks" or "sorry" or "best wishes," send the card with flowers instead of with a three cent stamp.

Which brings us to the main and never-ending use of visiting cards:

As cards: Enclose your card with all presents and flowers. Except at Christmas time, when colorful tags are more appropriate, your card is always handsomer (and more impressive) than standard greeting cards. Cross out your name or only the "Mr."; write in a brief message. Your card will save you many an hour of wondering what in hell to write on the big white blank the florist gives you. Somehow, a simple "Love, Joe" written on a blank card looks impoverished, but on an engraved visiting card it takes on quite a different character.

ON PAPER

Next, about your writing paper. You will need: 1) something on which to reply to formal invitations (this can be used as well for all hand-written notes, or you can lay in a supply of less expensive paper for such purposes if you'd rather); 2) something for personal letters, longer than notes; 3) something for personal-business letters (this can be your personal stationery but it's more economical to have a separate supply for orders to stores, letters to suppliers, etc.).

A man's paper should look like a man's paper—that is, it should look like the last thing that cute blonde next door would think of ordering. Leave the pink papers, the subtle (and unsubtle) scents, the deckle-edges and the odd shapes to her. Leave the dinky sizes to the boys with dinky handwriting. And run a mile when the stationer tells you that this is "the latest thing"; your paper ought to be conservative, inconspicuous, *masculine*.

You can't go wrong if you stick to white, cream or gray paper—plain and simple, not duked up with borders or obvious grain or complicated folds. Dark blue is acceptable, but why take the risk of getting an electric blue or a baby blue?

Have the engraving (or printing) done in black, gray, dark blue or dark red. Avoid envelope linings except when necessary, as for airmail papers, and then see that they match the paper or hit a dark shade far, far away from pastels. Write in blue or black or blue-black; write in blood, if necessary, before you use green or purple or brown ink. Resist the temptation to use sealing wax, and think twice before you exhume a family crest (even if you have a perfect right to it).

And if you spend a fortune in order to get the best possible job, don't let it show. Obvious extravagance is conspicuous and ostentatious. Give your letter a good, quiet setting that speaks well of you, but don't let the setting steal the show.

You could get along very nicely with the following "wardrobe":

1. *A box of plain note paper,* about 5¾" by 7¾", or 5" x 7⅞", to use for answering wedding invitations and other formal summonses. This paper usually has a side fold. The "how" is simple—you just follow the form of the invitation. For example:

This invitation:

Mr. and Mrs. Happy Day
request the honour of your presence
at the marriage of their daughter
Mary Jane
to
Mr. Lucky Man
on Saturday, the sixteenth of June
at half after four o'clock
Saint James Church
and afterwards at the reception
488 Madison Avenue
New York

R.s.v.p.

is accepted like this:

> Joseph Bachelor
> accepts with pleasure
> the kind invitation of
> Mr. and Mrs. Clay
> to the marriage of their daughter
> Mary Jane.
> to
> Mr. Lucky Man.
> on Saturday, the sixteenth of June
> at half after four o'clock
> Saint James Church
> and afterwards at the reception
> 488 Madison Avenue.

or "regretted" like this:

> Joseph Bachelor
> regrets that
> owing to an absence from the city
> (or a previous engagement, or whatever)
> he is unable to accept the kind invitation of
> Mr. and Mrs. Day
> to the marriage of their daughter
> Mary Jane
> to
> Mr. Lucky Man
> on Saturday, the sixteenth of June
> and to the reception afterwards

As you notice, you repeat the time and place when you accept (so that everyone knows that you know when and where to appear) but you repeat only the date when you regret (since it wouldn't matter if you didn't go to the wrong place at the wrong time). Notice, too, that you have not referred to yourself as "Mr."; if your wife were replying for you both, however, she would say "Mr. and Mrs."

An invitation to the church ceremony alone requires no reply, but an invitation to a breakfast or reception, whether included with the church invitation or sent separately, demands a prompt reply. If the invitation is complicated by any of the things which can complicate it—the bride's name being different from her parents', the groom being in military service, the reception taking place at an address different from the reply address, etc.—that's no worry of yours: just copy off the invitation, as above, in drafting your reply.

The same note paper can also be used for your own invitations (when they are formal, or when your informal instructions are too complicated to relay by visiting card) . . . for thank-you notes (when the relationship is too distant for a friendly typewritten letter) . . . and for other short, faintly formal correspondence.

If you have enough use for such paper, you might have it personalized. A monogram is too precious for a man, but block, unadorned initials are safe; they may be engraved or printed, in the upper left corner or in the center. Your full name is also acceptable, except in strictest circles, but it is less versatile; when you're signing the note "Loveboat" it seems a bit stiff to have your whole name at the top, and when you're writing a third person reply to a formal invitation the name forms a redundancy. Therefore, initials are the most utilitarian form of personalization—and in the long run you may be happiest with plain, unpersonalized paper (so long as it is of good quality, suggesting a man's writing desk rather than a drugstore's clearance sale).

2. *A box of letter paper,* for longer, personal correspondence. And now hear this: the typewriter is not only acceptable but, from the poor reader's point of view, preferable. There may be a stray female who will think darkly that hard print is not fitting for soft sentiments: you may have hairshirt days when you'd *prefer* pen to portable; but if you know how to operate a typewriter we suggest that you select a paper large enough to take typing. The standard size for typewritten social correspondence, as distinguished from the regulation business size of 8½" x 11", is 7¼" by 10 3/4"—but if your letters are long, your type is pica and your handwriting large, you may be able to find some 8½" by 11" that is not too business-like in appearance.

This paper can be initialed, but it will be more generally useful if it includes your address. Best bet is what is called "house paper"—engraved with your address and (optional) your telephone number, but not with your name. This is usually centered on the first sheet; second and third pages are unmarked, but the same paper. If you live at Mrs. Clancy's boarding house, rather than at a permanent address that

327

will look good in dark-blue engraving, you might use your club as the "address," or use initials, or use unmarked paper. Don't ever use just your first name, in the manner of young girls who engrave their nicknames on their paper; almost as unsuitable, because of the self-conscious stiffness which contradicts the personal nature of the letter, is your full name.

Envelopes for this paper should be marked with a return address, usually on the flap. An apartment number or other such specific "return" for the post office is better than your name; consider your correspondents, who might not want everyone in the world to know that the letter is from *you*.

3. *A box of paper for personal-business correspondence.* If cost is no object, this can be the same paper as #2, but more than likely you will want to use printing rather than engraving. For this purpose only, your full name and address may be printed on the paper—but since, presumably, you will be signing your full name to such letters anyway, your mailing address is sufficient.

LETTER-WRITING

When it comes to putting words to all this fine paper, you should use a few rules and a lot of common sense. Remember, mostly, that your letter represents you in your absence; you are not there, when your letter arrives, to explain that you didn't mean what you seemed to mean, or that this was supposed to be funny and that was supposed to be tossed immediately into the fire rather than saved for a public reading from the witness stand.

There's a good old rule that says, "Never write a letter in anger"—write it, if you will, but don't mail it until you've cooled off. For a man, a corollary rule might be, "Never write a letter you wouldn't want published on the front page of tomorrow's paper"—say it, look it, act it but don't put it in writing unless you're sure you're sure.

But instinct will instruct you on touchy letters, and genuine feeling will inspire you on really personal letters, so let's restrict ourselves here to the conventions of formal and relatively impersonal correspondence.

The forms are these:

The personal-business letter follows the rules of business correspondence (see page 61): inside address, colon or three dots after the salutation, formal close, full-name signature. The main point here is to use your personal-business paper, not your company letterhead, for such correspondence.

Social letters do not include an inside address; they start right off with the salutation, flush with the left margin. The conventional salutation is "Dear Name." More formal is "My dear Name"; more intimate is "Name, dear," and on down the line of "darlings" and "my owns."

The salutation is followed by a comma, rather than the colon of business usage, and then the letter begins.

Ideally, it does not begin with an apology, or with any opening which suggests that letter-writing is a hateful chore which you put off as long as possible (if not longer). Perfectly, it suggests friendly thought of the addressee.

As it goes to the point of its mission, be that a friendly communication of personal news, a thank you, an invitation or whatever, it plays down the overbearing "I" in favor of a "you" approach. You needn't write all around the "I," or be rendered wordless by the rhetoric teacher's impossible stricture against beginning a sentence with "I." But try to report your thoughts or reactions or letter-writing purpose in terms of the letter's recipient. "I went to the animal fair; the birds and the beasts were there" might better be followed by

"They all spoke of you" or "You'd have chortled at the big baboon"—something which draws your reader into the scene and into your thoughts. For even more obvious reasons, you should also comment on the news or views of the letter you are answering.

When the letter has accomplished its purpose, it comes to an end. Often there is a last line in which the writer asks to be remembered to another of the family, or looks forward to a meeting, or otherwise tapers off in modern substitute for the old, long-winded "beg to remain" form of close. Or it can simply *end*.

Then comes the close, at the lower right-hand corner of the letter. Like the salutation, the close covers a range of formality. The conventional social close, faintly formal, is "Sincerely yours." This is comparable to the business close of "Yours truly." Next in line come "Sincerely," . . . "Affectionately," . . . "As ever," . . . "Yours," . . . "Love," . . . and the Promptings of Pashion. For intimate letters, almost anything goes—but your girl will resent the vagueness of "As ever," much preferring an uncliché-ed variation of "Yours with love" . . . everyone will resent the faint condescension of "Cordially" and other forms used in business . . . and most of your social correspondents will be made mildly uneasy by flowery phrases like "Faithfully," or "Respectfully." Perhaps "Sincerely" is the best all-purpose close to use in letters to acquaintances, and any *natural* close (like "Goodbye for now" or "All yours") for more personal correspondence.

Comes then the signature. This must always be in ink and must never include "Mr." To friends who will know which John you are, just "John." To others, "John Jones."

The date on a social letter may be in the upper right or the lower left corner. It may be simply the day of the week, or the complete date, but it shouldn't be a set of numbers (9/19/53) and ideally it will not abbreviate the month.

Here, then, is a "dummy":

Your engraved address or your initials or nothing

June 16th*

or

June 16, 1954*

or

Wednesday*

Salutation,

The letter. If you're typing it, you may use single or double spacing, block or indented-paragraph form. If you're writing by hand, use indented paragraphs.

The close,

The signature

* (or date here)

There are a few letters you *must* write.

1. *Bread-and-butter letters.* Whenever you have spent a night as a guest in someone's house, you must write a thank you to your hostess. Your card, inscribed with an appropriate form of "Thanks" and enclosed with a lot of flowers can get you out of this chore; otherwise, make it unchorelike by following something of this form:

Date—preferably within one day and certainly not more than a week after your departure

Salutation to your hostess. (Only in the case of a bachelor who has played host-and-hostess-in-one would you address this letter to a man. The hostess is your host's wife, mother, sister, daughter or *some* female relative in residence)

The letter:

a. Thanks for whatever-it-was.

b. Some comment about why you enjoyed it so much. This could be anything from "You've no idea what a treat it was for me just to relax, with never a word about investment problems" to "It may take me a year to catch up on my sleep, but these bags under my eyes hold memories of the nicest blur I've ever been in." Anything, so long as it is pertinent to the hospitality you have just received.

c. A kind of news paragraph, usually reporting on your adventures after leaving the house, and often turned to point up the contrast between the pleasure of your stay and the displeasure of your return to reality.

d. A looking-forward to meeting again—either a specific invitation, or a vague kind of thing like, "When you are back in town, I hope you will come up for a drink—maybe I'll have learned to match your martinis by then."

e. A "thanks again" and a request to be remembered to the other members of the family.

The close,
Your signature

(or date here)

2. *Other thank-you letters.* It's good manners to write thank yous for any presents or expressions of good will which have also taken to the mails. When someone writes to congratulate you on an honor, or to wish you well in your marriage, or to offer his sympathies on your bereavement or the like—write back. Your thanks *can* be delivered orally, except in the case of thanks for letters of condolence, but when someone else has taken the trouble to write instead of simply telephoning or speaking to you, it makes sense to return the favor in kind.

Such thank-you letters can be very short; you needn't struggle to convert them into news letters. Express your appreciation in a personal, unstylized way, if you can; if not, settle for a simple thing like this: "Thank you very much for whatever-it-was. Your whatever-it-was did much to whatever-it-intended. Thanks again." Comment directly upon the present or the letter, so the recipient cannot suspect that you are copying a cold form.

The only real rule: Never use a printed (or engraved) thank-you card. If you are incapacitated, dictate your thanks or delegate them. If you are swamped with congratulations, send identical telegrams of thanks. But don't use a form except in business (or politics-business); even then, the personal touch would be better business.

We admit that this rule is being circumvented, and that even the toniest stationers now sell engraved thank-you cards, but for once it seems that an old rule of form makes more good sense than its new short cut. When someone has taken the trouble to write you a personal message of condolence—just about the most difficult kind of letter to write, in everyone's book—he cannot but feel slapped if your thank you is impersonal. Who can blame him if he wishes he had sent a greeting card from the drugstore, complete with weeping willow and inside verse, instead of struggling to express his sincere sympathies? For you, it will be very little more trouble to write a line of thanks on plain notepaper than to address a boxful of expensive and meaningless form-cards. And remember that both jobs can be delegated, if not to the relative who has relieved you of other unhappy "arrangements," then to one of the close friends who asks how he may help.

3. *Letters of reference.* If you are called upon to give a former employee a reference, in general—a letter he or she will show "to whom it may concern"—begin it without salutation. Don't use "to whom it may concern" unless you are not concerned about whom. Sign it with your name only— no complimentary close is necessary.

Like the Army fitness report, in which "satisfactory" is a blight on the record, your letter is expected to be enthusiastic. If it is reserved, or if it leaves out any important qualities, it is taken to be a poor reference. This, then, is the minimum form:

"So and so was in my employ, as such and such, from date to date. His duties were thus and so. He discharged them to my complete satisfaction; he was (enumerate traits, remembering that future employers will want most to be assured about reliability, efficiency, cooperative attitude, sobriety). He is leaving for such and such reasons. I will be glad to answer any further questions."

4. *Letters of nomination or recommendation.* When you are proposing or seconding a new member to your club, the main portion of the letter is your personal recommendation. That is, it is assumed by the other members that you would not propose (and hence sponsor) someone who was not qualified under the various membership requirements, so you have only to state your relationship to the nominee, give identifying facts as necessary, then say that you recommend him.

Such letters are formal in tone. They are usually addressed to a membership committee or board of governors or similar body, so they begin "Dear Sirs," and close "Yours very truly"—regardless of how clubby you are with the individuals involved.

Usually these letters don't end with their mailing. As the potential member's sponsor, you must see to it that another member writes a seconding letter (or however many seconds are required); you must then see that your candidate meets the club officials, presenting him in person in whatever manner is customary in your club; once he is accepted, you must introduce him around and see that he gets off to a good start; and, ever after, you are in the books as responsible for him. So think twice before writing such a letter—and remember that none but an intimate friend should ask you to do so; the initiative is yours. When and if, here's how:

Date

The Proper Committee
The Club
The Address

Dear Sirs,

I should like to propose for membership in The Club Mr. Name Name, who I think would be a welcome and valuable addition to the club. I have known him for X years, first at Blank College where we were fellow-members of the class of XX. He has recently been transferred here from the City office of his firm, Clackety and Clack. In City, he was a member of the Comparable Club.

Yours very truly,

Your name (with no Mr.)

5. *Letters of introduction.* When an intimate friend of yours is going to visit a far-away city where another of your intimate friends lives, and when you are quite sure that the two will enjoy each other, you give the traveler a letter of introduction to present to the far-away resident. You give it to him unsealed, but correctly he seals it (without reading it) in your presence. He then goes his way, while you write a fuller explanation and a be-prepared letter to your distant friend. On arrival in the strange city, your home-friend sends your letter to your out-of-town friend. On his visiting card or hotel notepaper, he writes a message of anticipation, encloses this with your letter of introduction, and mails the whole works. (His purpose is to avoid a face-to-face meeting until after your letter has been read and digested.)

Regardless of the form of the package, the message is clear: your distant friend must entertain your visiting friend, no matter how much he'd like to avoid it. You have forced a match which only serious illness can prevent. Thus, when your distant friend reads your letter, he immediately telephones or writes an invitation to your visiting friend. Then they both write you to report on the meeting—how much they enjoyed or appreciated your match-making—and you write to say another thank you to the friend on whom you have imposed your other friend.

Still want to get into all this? Remember, a letter of introduction involves a social obligation, at the other end.

Much simpler, and much much safer, is the indirect introduction. You tell Traveling Pal that you have some good friends in San Francisco and, if he has time, you wish he'd call them up and say hello for you. (He does, or he doesn't, depending on how he feels about this particular form of fishing for an invitation. See page 431). You write your San Francisco friends, telling them that Trav is such and such a guy who will be in their town at such and such a time for such and such a purpose. You say you'll appreciate anything they can do to make his stay more pleasant, or you leave this between the lines. You ask them to stand by for a call, or you tell them how to reach Trav. And the rest is up to the individuals. If your distant friends knock themselves out for your traveling friend, they do it for him or for you, not for etiquette—and every one involved is more comfortable.

manners for the host

It is commonly supposed that the genuine, warm spirit of hospitality is the major ingredient of good hostmanship, and that, without it, all the trappings of form are empty and chilling. There's no black and white about this delicate business, to be sure, but—iconoclasts that we are—we bet on the other side.

The famous "genuine, warm spirit of hospitality," it seems to us, can go further astray than form. It may drive you to urge your guest to make himself at home—a pretty terrible thing to do to him, since he can't and he won't and if he does you'll wish he hadn't. It may drive you to urge him to eat and drink and amuse himself, to the point where he has no appetite for anything. In your wish to give him the most of the best, it may urge you to deprecate your less-than-perfect offerings, or to apologize for unavoidable inconvenience—and this will wear him out reassuring you that things aren't so bad as all that. And in a wider sense, it may lead you to entertain people whose tastes and habits are completely different from yours, or to try to be something you are not, in earnest effort to make your guests comfortable.

Thus it seems to us that the main requirements for a good host are self-confidence, self-respect and a clear idea of his responsibilities to his guests. If he also likes to entertain, so much the better.

THE HOST AT HOME

The first and foremost thing to be said about the perfect host is—he doesn't exist.

The perfect host makes every guest feel like a guest-of-honor, but he fusses over no one, exploits no one, spends no more time with one than another.

He makes even the dullest guest feel witty, a shining light among pleasant and appreciative companions, but he does not *appear* to draw anyone out. He is a witty fellow himself, but not so anyone can notice his wit as such; his wit is catalytic, somehow, making everyone else feel good.

He provides good food, good drink, good company—but he makes no point of any of them. The next drink materializes at the very moment when his guest notices that his glass is empty (not before, ostentatiously; not after, apologetically). The next conversational group moves onto the horizon at the very moment when the guests have begun to run down on their current topic (not in mid-discussion, frustratingly; not in the final stages of boredom, desperately).

He anticipates his guest's every need and wish, but not obtrusively; he makes it seem that he is prompted by his *own* desires. He is alert, but he appears relaxed.

All these things are engineered, but so subtly, so naturally, that no one ever thinks "What a good host," only "What a good time I had."

The perfect host, you see, is a wraith; no man is that perfect. And, ironically, the man who tries hardest misses by the biggest margin. He urges, he pounces, he interrupts, he is a host on horseback. He also *worries,* and his nervousness is catching. Even the too-casual host, scourge that *he* is, is apt to be better off than the E-for-Effort host. He forces each guest to be his own host; he relaxes so much that he folds up onto the bed in the back room; but one person, at least, has a good time at his party: *he* does.

The struggle for perfection, then, contains the seeds of its own failure. And real (rather than apparent) relaxation is a failure at the outset. With a little attention to detail, and a little practice, you can land somewhere in between. You will have a maximum of good moments, a minimum of bad ones.

GUEST LISTS

To begin with, give yourself an even break on the company: invite people who will get along together. For a small party, where the guests will have no escape from each other, it is vital that they have interests and sympathies in common (and their common acquaintance with you is not enough). Ideally, they should each have something to give the other —and something the other *wants*. They should not be *too* alike—they want stimulation, not mere affirmation—but they should complement each other, not antagonize or compete with each other. Your job is to figure out both ends of the exchange and be satisfied that they will be satisfied before you bring your friends together.

At a large party, where presumably a guest can pick and choose his talk-mates, you can take a little less care with the invitation list if you are prepared to take a little more care with on-the-spot matchings. That is, you can invite both the dogmatic Republican and the emotional leftist —*if* you see to it that they steer clear of each other. Still, you should be sure that there are two or three people whom each of them will enjoy—a fellow-fisherman who won't mind if Mr. GOP issues a few political edicts, an interrogative liberal who might want to find out how the left half thinks, a few attractive women who can be relied upon to bring the subject around to *their* specialty if the atmosphere gets charged.

A good rule to follow is to be sure that everyone you have

invited knows (and likes) at least two other guests: you don't want anyone to walk into a roomful of strangers, and you don't want to leave anyone without an escape hatch should the strangers prove stultifying.

In addition, you're stacking the cards your way if every guest has at least one talkable interest in common with every other guest.

Obviously, this precludes a party to "pay back everybody at once"; unless you want to neutralize your debt permanently, don't invite all your social creditors to one hodgepodge cocktail party. As you go over the list, and realize beyond doubt that the Joneses are bores, the Sterns teetotallers, the Smiths argumentative and the Cartwrights much too formal for your environment, this is as good a time as any to decide you will have a good party and let your social IOU's fall where they may. (In future, don't accept invitations from people who will be inconveniently difficult to entertain in return.)

INVITATIONS

After constructing a good invitation list, your next best preventive against embarrassing moments is to issue *specific* invitations. Whether you invite people by telephone, by note, by visiting card or in person (all correct, for all but the formal affair), be sure to make the following crystal clear:

The place

The date

The hour or span of hours

The kind of party (people want to know particularly if you are going to feed them, or if they should make other plans for the meal which might conceivably fall into these hours)

And, unless this can safely be taken for granted, the appropriate dress.

There are a few subtleties involved here. A potential guest is not allowed to ask who else is coming, and a host is not supposed to seem to brag that he is having a big party, or to use other guests as bait. *Correctly,* you would say (or write): "Will you come to cocktails on the fifth, from six to eight?" More helpfully (and thus, we think, more hostfully), you'd add, "There'll be a cold buffet, so don't take that eight o'clock closing any more seriously than you have to" . . . or . . . "There'll be quite a gang, but maybe when things thin out we can get up a Dutch-treat supper group and go out on the town" . . . or . . . "Just you and Molly and Pete, but I thought it was time we got together without a mob around."

You would not, in false modesty, say, "Come take pot luck," when you knew very well you were going to have a dressy crowd and a caterer. Nor would you lead your friends to get all duked up if you knew that you were going to be tieless and your other guests were coming straight from the golf course. Ignorance is not bliss, particularly for women, so give your guests a straight steer with your invitation.

Much of the necessary information is contained in the word you use to describe the affair and the hour you set for it. For some reason or other, "cocktails" implies a party, where "come in for a drink" suggests an impromptu and small gathering; for the party you expect your guests to be late and to overstay the closing hour —for the small gathering they will be interfering with dinner plans if they do either. With "supper" you suggest a buffet, probably large and late, where "dinner" means a sit-down meal at a prescribed hour. "Tea" means what it says, and guests are adequately warned . . . In very formal circles "We're not dressing" means quite the opposite, to the normal mind: it means black tie instead of white. There's no code word for blue jeans, so give a direct clue and live up to it yourself.

Although it is done every day (to the tune of wifely wails), you should *not* issue your invitation to the male half of a married couple. A visiting card or form invitation may be addressed to "Mr. and Mrs.", but if you are writing a note you address it "Mrs." and ask, "Will you and John come . . ." If you are telephoning, you call *her,* or leave a message of invitation with the servant who answers *her* telephone. If you see John every day and scarcely know his wife, you may tell John that you have written his wife, or ask him to tell her who you are, so that when you call she won't think you're a radio quiz program announcer. But you *must* have direct communication with John's wife; you must not use John as intermediary.

Needless to say, if *you* have a wife, you do no inviting at all; *she* does it. Society is instructed to ignore invitations from husbands; relax and enjoy this delicious form of discrimination. Also, if you are very young and your mother is hostess—*in absentia* or not—she should confirm your invitations by communication with the mothers of your guests. (Mothers are chary of parties which they suspect might be surprise parties on other mothers.)

Your invitations should be out at least a week before the event—two weeks if you expect replies. Three weeks is not too far in advance for large parties or busy seasons. But, except for a wedding, four weeks' notice has all the visemarks of a bear trap.

Two final points about invitations: 1) Don't invite A within the hearing of B. If you are not also inviting B, all three of you are embarrassed. If you have already invited B, A cannot be expected to know that, and B cannot be sure that A knows it, so again everybody is embarrassed. You *could* say, "B has heard all this before, and I hope he'll be there too, but could you come to, etc." But then a supersensitive A might think you have thus made him a second fiddle. Better to make your invitations individual, and private.*

And 2) Don't make like a social climber by inviting your friends' friends without inviting your friends. If you want to know better the Smiths, whom you met at the Browns' last soirée, you must invite both the Browns and the Smiths. This rule does not apply to romance—you can of course date up the blonde the Browns introduced you to, without including the Browns—but it does apply to Mr. and Mrs. teams, and to that hostess' delight, the "extra man."

SCENE-SETTING

To round out your insurance against bad moments, organize the mechanics of your party well in advance. You'll have plenty to do without having to decide, on the spot, where guests will put their coats or dry their hands or snuff their cigarettes. Plan the food and drink to stay well within the limits of your ability to serve them; better to offer a choice of a few drinks which can be produced promptly than to delay over the infinite variations on "What'll you have?" Better to have a simple dinner you know is going to be good and ready than a would-be impressive fare which overstretches the service.

MINIMUM HOSTING

When the appointed hour arrives, you should have nothing to do but *host*. This much is required routine for all informal affairs (see page 389 for formal entertaining):

1. *Greet each guest warmly and individually.* You open the door for each guest. You shake hands with the woman if

---

* Bear all this in mind when you're on the guest-end, too: don't refer to an entertainment, past or future, in front of someone who for all you know was not invited and thinks he ought to have been.

she offers to, then with the man, meanwhile saying something pleasant and welcoming. It can be as simple as "Good to see you—come in!" It should start you all off on the right foot as, obviously, "Thanks for coming" or "You're late" or "Oh, it's only you" would not. You take their coats (ladies first) or usher them to the rooms you have designated as powder room for the women guests, coatroom for the men. Then you stand by to take them in to the party.

If you have a servant who can handle the door chore, instruct him or her on what to say. The wording is not important (this side of "Hiya, bub—gents room down that way"), but the manner is: it should be cordial but not familiar. In a formal and "correct" household, where the guests could not possibly think that you were putting on airs at hourly rates, the servant would address your guests in the third person: "Will Madam leave her wraps in the room on the left, please?" or "Will the gentleman take his coat to the room on the right, please?" You might feel easier about something like, "Good evening. Mr. Host is waiting for you in the living room. Would you care to drop your things in the far bedroom on the right—and you, sir, on the left—before you go in?"

If it's a big shambles of a cocktail party, and servant (if any) is busy mixing drinks, it's perfectly acceptable—if not etiquette-book correct—to leave the door open and put up arrowed signs indicating coat-rooms, or simply to trust to your friends' intelligence to find their way.

The important thing is the warm, personal greeting as your guests enter the party room. (Everybody appreciates that this is your job, by the way, so no present guest is affronted if you break off in mid-sentence with "Excuse me, I see the Lees have arrived.")

2. *Introduce each person into the group.* As explained on page 308, this need not be a general introduction, in which you stifle the roar of a going party to mouth meaningless

names around the room. But it should be enough to get the new arrivals into the whirl. Either lead the new guest to a group where he already knows someone, or introduce him into a nearby group. See that the conversation gets started, see that a drink comes the new man's way as soon as possible, then on to the next arrival.

3. *Protect your guests from each other, and from circumstances.* The perfect host takes it upon himself to protect his guests from boredom, from loneliness, from left-out-ness. By a kind of musical chairs, he shuffles his assembled guests into new conversational groups whenever it seems necessary.*

The average host, afraid that all such mix-matching will be obvious and transparent, simply injects himself into a lack-lustre group, or changes a dangerous subject, or fills in embarrassed pauses with tactful remarks of his own.

All this takes a kind of social sensitivity and dexterity not within every man's ken (and not within the ken of every hostess who *thinks* it is, either). If you aren't the type, never mind about it: choose your guests carefully enough and you'll have very little trouble-shooting to do.

But the larger aspect of a host's protection of his guests cannot be ignored, even by the extremely casual. As host, you are responsible for whatever happens under your roof: you cannot stand by and let one of your guests be ridiculed by another any more than you can stand by while one guest beats up another. The perfect guest is obliged to fall in with whatever comes along, to pretend delight with the fellow-guests and so on, so he is helpless to defend himself. It is you as host who must extricate him if he is being worked over by an insurance salesman or pulled in over his head by a card sharp or insulted by a drunk. Your rescue

---

* It is necessary when you spy guests studying your indifferent pictures, reading your dusty Encyclopedia, fixing your split-second-perfect clock, or placing coast-to-coast phone calls.

can usually be accomplished without offending the offender —but sometimes, for the good of the group and the reputation of your house, it is necessary to be rude to one in order to rescue the others. This would be an extreme case—where you were sure that some one was cheating at cards or contributing to the delinquency of a young girl or doing something else so far out of line that the other guests would condone your forcefulness. The idea is simply that hospitality is not meant to be taken advantage of. A host is a man, not a mouse.

(The second time such a thing happens, of course, it's your own fault: you shouldn't expose your friends to guests you *know* to be unreliable.)

4. *Spend a little time with each guest.* Many a harried host, without meaning to, says nothing between hello and goodbye to many of his guests. Make a point of having at least a brief conversation with everyone.

5. *Be tireless.* Etiquette throws you on the mercy of the overstaying guest, for so long as he is under your roof you must appear to be delighted with his company and regretful when *he* decides he must tear himself away.

Etiquette, if your guests are aware of it, gives you a compensatory protection: most functions have a more-or-less understood closing hour (see below, and page 394 for formal affairs). Your specific invitations have also suggested that there are limits to your hospitality: you have said, "Come Friday night and stay through lunch on Sunday," not "Come for the week-end" . . . or "Will you come for the month of July?", not "Will you come and spend your declining years with us?"

Still, you will run into modified versions of the man who came to dinner. You just have to make the best of it. You will develop an obscure technique for speeding the parting guest—oblique reference to your morning meeting, perhaps, or a gourmet discussion of breakfast menus—but you must resist the temptation to use such devices as the standstill bar service, the pointed preparation of black coffee or the elaborately stifled yawn.

6. *Say an individual good night to each guest.* This will involve a stylized exchange in which he tells you what a good time he had and you tell him what a pleasure it was to see him or how glad you are he enjoyed it. It should not involve a long doorway discussion, but it is the guest's responsibility to go so the best you can do is to avoid *starting* a story.

In apartment buildings, the conscientious host sees his guests into the elevator, standing with apartment door ajar until the elevator arrives and the guests depart. If he has thoughtfully tipped the building doorman in advance, he tells his guests as much, indirectly, by saying something like "Richie will see that you get a cab."

In suburbs or country, the host sees his guests to their cars and stands looking after them as they drive off his property; in bad weather he perhaps produces an umbrella.

In either city or country, he sees that no woman has to go home alone, however she may insist that she is not afraid of the dark. He has either arranged in advance that another person or couple drop her off at her address, or he has asked her to stay so that he can see her home (leaving *with,* not after, the last guests). In the rare instance where neither of these is possible, he at least sees her into a cab himself, and telephones her later to make sure she got home all right.

7. *When the party's over, he does not repeat anything which happened to the discredit of any of his guests.*

PARTY GUIDE

Those seven standards apply whether or not you are blessed with a knowing hostess. The following may serve as practical guide for the host alone—the man who has no etiquette-expert wife to take the brunt of the arrangements for his parties:

the cocktail party

The usual hours are from five to seven, or six to eight. The usual crowd is large enough so everybody stands, or small enough so everybody sits; an in-between number is awkward. The usual drinks are two kinds of cocktails, one or two long drinks for mixed-drinkophobes, plus sherry for ingénues and a soft drink or fruit juice for eccentrics. The usual accompaniments are canapés, of the elaborate or the potato-chip-and-peanut variety, but there is an increased trend toward providing more substantial fare (a cold buffet) for those who have come a long way or cannot be expected to have made dinner plans. This is usually available throughout the evening, on a self-service basis.

A waiter, if any, wears a club-steward's white coat, with colored braid on lapels to distinguish him from a corner bartender. He wears no cap. A waitress wears a gray or black uniform with white apron, no cap. Drinks are better proffered on trays, rather than by hand; by the classic rule, no servant ever *hands* anything to employer or guest.

open house

This is usually a cocktail party in disguise, often on Sundays or holidays when cocktail parties would not usually be given. The usual hours are earlier, and with a three- or four-hour span rather than two hours, because people are expected to come and go more loosely: three to six, four to seven or three to seven are about par. A punch bowl is often the featured drink (or a seasonal variation, like Tom and Jerries or eggnogs). Instead of out-and-out canapés, the food often consists of small "party" sandwiches, little cakes, mints, etc. The open house can have overtones of a "tea," if that's the way you want it, but the routine closely resembles that of a cocktail party. One caution: if you call it a "house warming," your guests may think they have to bring presents for your new diggings.

the buffet supper

The food is generally laid out and the company invited to help themselves at a prescribed hour, as distinguished from the cocktail-party supper where the food is constantly available. The menu usually includes a choice of dishes, with a minimum of one hot, one cold, one salad, one bread, one beverage, fruit and/or cheese and/or dessert. Nothing served should require a knife, impossible to manipulate on knee-balanced plate. Guests eat off knees or floor or trays or small tables set up for the purpose, as you like. They help themselves, with or without carving assistance and suggestions from their host. They sit with whomever they choose; the host does not designate supper partners. The host watches for refill prospects and either leads an expedition to second helpings or does a little auxiliary serving himself. Coffee and dessert are usually brought to the guests where they sit, the supper dishes having been cleared away beforehand. The party then moves into brandy or long drinks.

The usual hours for serving are seven or eight P.M., for an all-evening party, or midnight, for an after-the-theatre party. Usually guests are invited an hour or two beforehand, for a cocktail period—but long drinks rather than cocktails precede a midnight supper, of course: cocktails are never served after dinner.

the dinner party

The formal dinner involves a tight ritual of its own (see page 389). You'll know better than to attempt it without a lot of prior practice as a guest. So let's confine ourselves to the informal, friendly dinner you give for a few friends.

The dinner hour is whatever you and your guests are used to—eight or seven, say, with guests invited to come in time for cocktails at seven or six. If you have a servant to wait at table, the following might be your procedure: the servant catches your eye when dinner is ready, you stand and invite your guests to go in to dinner. You lead the way, shepherding before you or guiding alongside the woman you are going to seat on your right. You seat her as the others file in, then, standing at your place at the head of the table, you tell the others where you'd like them to sit. You should not put men together or women together if you can help it, and you should separate husbands and wives. Your mental seating chart might look something like this:

		YOU			YOU	
YOUR DATE		MRS. Z	MRS. X			MRS. Y
MR. X		MR. Y	OR	MR. Y		MR. X
MRS. Y		MRS. X			YOUR DATE	
	MR. Z					

As soon as the women are seated, you and the other men sit. The table is set however you like, place mats to damask cloth; all the silver needed for the meal is at each place, in order of use working from the outside in. The first course, if any, is already at the places. You all fall to. When the last guest has put down his soup spoon or oyster fork or whatever, your servant removes these dishes, then sets before you the main dish and a stack of hot plates on which you are to serve. He may also put the vegetable serving dishes near you. As you fill each plate, the servant picks it up and takes it to the person you designate—first the woman on your right, then counterclockwise around the table. Or if you'd rather the servant passed the vegetables, etc., while you concentrated on the main dish only, you hand the plates down the table as you fill them, sending the first to the woman farthest from you. The servant then offers the vegetables to her, at her left, and so on around the table. (Notice that a lady is served first and that you are served last, but you do not hop-skip around the table in order to serve all the women before serving any of the men.)

When everyone has been thus served, the wine is poured —a little in your glass first, then for the woman on your right, counterclockwise around the table, and you last. (No need to taste your sample, which is just a guest-protection against cork, before the rest is poured; if you were really in doubt about the wine you'd have tasted it before your guests arrived.)

When the time is ripe for second helpings, the plates are passed back to you in the same manner you distributed them, prompted by a request from you ("May I give you some beef, John?"). You ring for a second passing of the other dishes. The servant keeps tabs on water and wine shortages, or if he is slow on the ball you ring and say, "Wine for Mrs. X, please."

When everyone has had enough, you ring and the servant clears the table—first the plates (from the right; one at a time if you're strict and patient; one in each hand, if you prefer speed; but no stacking on the spot), then the serving dishes, finally the salt and pepper and other impedimenta. He then brings in the dessert, which may be individually dished in the kitchen or brought to you with a stack of plates for serving in the same manner as the main course. Cookies or mints may be passed from hand to hand or by the servant.

After dessert, coffee may be served at the table or in the living room, as you like. If at the table, the dessert things are first cleared away. Then the coffee, cups, sugar and cream can be brought to you for service to your guests, or the servant can go from guest to guest pouring as each person instructs, or filled cups can be put at each person's right and then sugar and cream passed. If in the living room, small cups are usually used and the coffee is usually served black. Either place, liqueurs then follow—usually a choice of two or three, offered in like manner to the coffee. Later, tumblers of ice water may be offered; still later, long drinks. Both can be on a self-service basis, the servant merely setting the makings on a side table.

There are almost infinite variations on this service, from the Continental style, where all carving is done in the kitchen and platters passed to each guest for individual service, with nary a serving dish ever put on the table . . . to the cafeteria style where guests fill their plates from serving dishes on a sideboard before sitting down at the table. The servantless host may do his cooking at the table, in chafing dishes.

The classic rules tell you that actual dishing of main courses and accompaniments should not be done in the kitchen, except for those foods which are cooked in individual serving dishes. Common sense tells you that long delays in service will reduce hot and cold foods to an unpalatable tepid temperature . . . that the host's constant busy-ness will reduce guests to embarrassed discomfort . . . and that the clatter of plates and clutter of soiled utensils will reduce the enjoyment of the food.

Your knowledge of your guests will tell you when it's proper to be improper—that is, if you know they are in the habit of drinking coffee with their meals, why withhold the brew until the "proper" time after dinner? In short, any system you devise will be appreciated by friends so long as it puts your best food forward with the least fuss.

Although the formal dinner runs a predictable schedule, the informal dinner often puts before you a jelling mixture of guests and a long evening. If after-dinner conversation lags, you may suggest cards or games or dancing or whatever seems appropriate—but try not to railroad your guests into activity if they might prefer just to sit. That is, if you've provided for bridge, provide an alternate for those who don't or won't play. If you're determined on The Game, make it clear at the outset that there's a ping-pong table on the porch, or a bunch of old records in the basement, for those who stick their noses up at charades under *any* name. And if the evening's activity is not general, you had better keep yourself free to circulate among the different groups; it's hard to play bridge and look out for non-playing guests at the same time.

the luncheon

Even a guy who doesn't know what time it is can tell the difference between luncheon and dinner. The menu is lighter. There are no candles on the table. Place mats or colored cloths are used in place of the conventional dinner damask. If soup is served it is in cups rather than the rimmed plates peculiar to dinner. Coffee is more apt to appear in large cups and liqueurs are probably among the missing. Otherwise the procedure is the same as for an informal dinner. The hour is usually one o'clock.

the breakfast

Unless you know a few rare specimens who can manage to be sociable before they have been fed, your breakfast will probably be a second breakfast, served at ten or eleven or even later. It can therefore be as far removed as you like from the eye-opener of orange juice, toast and coffee. It can be preceded by cocktails (flips or frappés or mild punches, usually) and served like the informal dinner above, or it can be the hunt-breakfast kind of buffet, with self-service (and sometimes self-cooking) at the sideboard.

THE WEEK-END HOST

The week-end, incorporating as it does almost all other varieties of entertaining, presents a special problem to the host—a problem of endurance. If the forty-hour week is never whittled down to allow an extra day off, it will doubtless be because of the secret, undercover resistance of disgruntled hosts and disappointed guests. Unless they're in love, almost any two people can have too much of each other before three nights and two days of constant association have drawn to a drawn-out close. And when the two people become two families, complete with children and dogs and edited etiquette, the saturation point is sure to be reached long before the Sunday night farewells. Unless . . .

Unless the perfect host happens to be matched up with the perfect guest. Then nothing is too much trouble, and nothing appears to be trouble at all, and the week-end is a rewarding, pleasurable social experience.

You can't do much about the perfect guest, except make it easy for him to practice his art, but here are some of the marks of a perfect week-end host.

no surprises

It's all very well for your guests to have more fun than they thought they were going to have, thanks to your provisions for their comfort and entertainment, but not if they're unprepared as to clothes, equipment and frame of mind. Let them know what's up before they leave home—better, before they say "yes" to your invitation.

Pointers on specific invitations, page 340, will stand you in good stead, but the week-end invitation is tougher, and wordier, because it covers more ground. Just see that the ground is covered, one way or another, else you'll spend the whole time (and a large part of your temper) hunting up things your guests would have brought if they'd known. If there's golf or tennis in the offing, say so—the perfect guest won't *bring* sports equipment without being asked to, lest he appear to be expecting more than you expect him to provide. If there's a chance you might go sailing, say so—and, if your guest is a landlubber, add something like "so bring along some rubber-soled shoes." If you're all going to the country club dance Saturday night, say whether it calls for formal dress or not. And if your main enticement is a hammock and a very long straw, with only occasional glimpses of you and your relentless power-mower, say so (and live down to your promise; don't cross him up later by taking him and his dungarees to a fancy garden party).

You don't have to sound like a train-caller, rattling off certain and possible entertainments. You don't want to sound like a braggart, advertising your hostly provisions or exaggerating your "picnic life." But still you must protect your self and your guests against the mechanical failure of the week-end for which guests bring the wrong clothes, and the psychological failure of the week-end for which they bring the wrong expectations. Just tell the truth, and tell the whole truth. Then your guests' equipment will fit your plans and vice versa.

few disguises

Your physical set-up for week-end entertaining has certain limitations; let them be known. Unless you can do it effortlessly (an impossible feat in normal households), don't try to live beyond your usual style for the benefit of your week-end guests. They will be much more dismayed if your wife makes the beds than if she says, "We all make our own beds around here." The mistake would be to hope they'll make their own beds without your giving them the cue. They may not expect a private bath, but they expect to be warned that Junior might get into their shaving supplies if left within reach in the common bath. They don't want to knock themselves out helping with the dishes if, in truth, you hate to have people standing over you while you commune with your cookbook. In short, they want to know the ground rules. It is much easier for them to conform to known standards than to guess what they are.

Many of the more painful transgressions of guests are committed in ignorance—they are thus the host's fault. How is your guest to know, unless you tell him, that you want him to sleep late Sunday if he can, so you can get your chores done, or, conversely, that you want him to have breakfast with the family so the kitchen won't be cluttered up all day? How's he to know that there's a limit to your hot-water supply, unless you tell him *before* he takes that long and delicious shower while you're trying to do the dishes? And how can he know that you're dying for sleep unless you suggest that it's time to go to bed? It's the host(ess)'s role to end the evening when house guests are involved. A guest can sometimes ask if you mind if he turns in before the rest of your group breaks up, and a host can sometimes urge his guests to stay up beyond his own unreasonably early bed-time, but usually the guest awaits the host's cue—and everyone gives up at once.

You should never apologize for the limitations in your "service"—and of course you should not add to them, as by starting a rough-house with the children *immediately* outside the guest's door—but if you would avoid mutual disappointments you should make them reasonably clear.

All this has little to do with the breakfast-in-bed circuit, where guests never lift a finger and neither do hosts (see page 385). But the principle is the same: do what you can to make your guests comfortable, but remember that nothing is quite so uncomfortable as the unknown.

Some discomforts are avoidable, even on the least pretentious scale. You don't have to put on airs to eliminate these from your week-end offerings:

1. *The Spartan Bed, or the rock-studded one.* Sleep on your guest-bed yourself, to make sure you can't be accused of creating business for the local chiropractor. See that the sheets fit tight and stay tight. And provide, if you can, a choice of pillows—one thin and one soft.

2. *The Big Freeze.* There is always a need for another blanket, along about 3 A.M., and the slippery bedspread is no substitute. See that your guest has access to an extra blanket, even when you're also supplying him with a fan in mid-August.

3. *The Big Thirst.* If there is no adjoining private bath, put a glass of water and/or thermos pitcher on his bedside table.

4. *The Seed Catalogue.* You can do better on reading matter for your guest. Even if he's blind when he goes to bed he may wake up sleepless and ready to read. He will be defeated if there is nothing newer than your dentist's discarded copy of *Hygeia*, and nothing more inviting than your high school textbooks stored on the "spare room" shelf. In addition to a varied selection of books and magazines, give him a good reading light—one that he can turn on and off without getting out of bed.

5. *The Big Blank.* It's nice to have a room and bath set aside for guests, who thus are not forced to squeeze in with the family's hobby equipment and excess storage, but the bare, spare room can be as frustrating as the junk room. The guest room and bath should include supplies which he may have forgotten, and may not have known he had forgotten when you asked, "Is there anything you need?" Toothbrush, toothpaste, soap, razor blades and shaving cream, needle and thread, safety pins, cigarettes and accompaniments, a

357

silent clock, a whisk broom, facial tissue—all in addition to the towels and hangers which no guest would expect to bring for himself.

a loose plan

The only thing worse than the week-end where guests are herded from one activity to the next, regardless of their secret yen to sit down and do nothing, is the Big Question Mark week-end. The host has planned nothing, except to keep asking his guests what they'd like to do. The happy medium (and it works better if you *are* a medium, able to read minds) is to present your guests with a choice of activities, and then do whatever they seem to prefer.

When the perfect host defers to his guest's wishes . . . and the perfect guest defers to his host's wishes . . . the imperfect result is apt to be a lot of backing and filling. A little direction is called for, and it's up to the host to supply it— not so much that the guest feels like a member of a conducted tour, but not so little that everyone rides off in all directions, either.

The least you can plan is the meals—and try not to make every one a "party." Ideally, Friday dinner will be quiet and at home; your guests are probably travel-weary by the time they reach you, and they don't want to be bustled off immediately. Ideally, breakfasts will be flexible, allowing for late sleepers who miss the family breakfast and insomniacs who look for coffee-makings at six in the morning. You might have other people in for Saturday dinner, go out for Sunday lunch, or simply have meals at home for your guests the whole time, but your hospitable reputation suffers if you go out for every meal, if you allow your guests to take *you* out to dinner, or if you don't center the week-end around the place to which you've invited your friends.

Between meals, you ought to throw out a few ideas to nibble on—and you ought to be quite definite about the areas in which you have no choice, yourself. That is, if you must go to the village on a few errands Saturday morning, let that be understood Friday night: your guests may come along, if they like, but they might better sleep or lounge in the sun or set up the badminton net. If you're bound to cut the grass Sunday morning, again have it clearly understood, the night before, that your A.M. activity is neither criticism nor challenge.

Where pleasure, not duty, is the conditioner, you can again make your own preferences known without forcing them on your guests. "I thought we might play some golf tomorrow, but the pool would tempt me almost as much. Which appeals to you?" Not, "I've signed us up for doubles tomorrow morning. You *do* play tennis, don't you?" (The good host can go ahead and play golf, even if some of his guests choose the pool, so long as he *sees* to it that the pool-guests will be provided for in his absence. He oughtn't to play if *all* his guests vote against golf.)

One caution: if your guests, having been given a fair choice, elect to stay home and do nothing, let them. Don't keep worrying because you're not entertaining them . . . don't keep asking if they're *sure* they don't want to go swimming . . . and don't think you have to sit and talk to them constantly. You can read or nap or garden or do whatever you like once the particular "do nothing" period has been established. Now and then you will find yourself saddled with a guest who claims to want to read but really doesn't know how; there's nothing you can do about him, unless he says, "Gee, is it too late to change my mind?" Mostly, however, the people who do not snap up your proposals for activity *really* want quiet, peace and freedom from persistent hostmanship.

In the end, if you have pulled it off cleverly, your guests will ride off into the setting sun filled with good food, good talk and good impressions. They'll think you have a nice place, because you didn't *push* it at them, leading them out to the compost heap before they'd had a chance to unwind, and because you didn't make them keep it up for you in return for room and board. They'll think you have nice children because they didn't see too much of them; you left them alone when you had to take care of the kids, and they were free to join the children's hour or not, without censure either way. They'll think you have nice friends, because the ones you invited over during the week-end were carefully chosen to match. They'll think you have a nice life, whatever its hazards, and that you were nice to open it to them.

They may not say all that in their bread-and-butter letter, but you'll know it's true. The week-end will have been pleasant for you, too.

THE HOST AWAY FROM HOME

AT A RESTAURANT

At a Restaurant, your role as host to a group of friends is pretty much the same as your role on a date (see page 261). If your guests are to meet you there, it's better to wait until all have arrived before going in to the table. But if there's no comfortable waiting room, or if unreasonable tardiness of one is inconvenient to the others, you may go in, seat and drink the punctual ones and return to the door to greet the late ones.

As host to a group of six or eight or more, you should precede your guests—that way you can tell them where to sit as soon as they reach the table, instead of keeping them huddled in the aisles waiting for you. The seating is usually handled like that for a dinner at home (page 350), but where there is a choice between built-in sofa seats and less comfortable chairs opposite, it is customary to seat the women on the sofa, with the men facing them.

When there are more than four guests, you may want to order the meal ahead of time. As Henri Soulé, America's foremost restaurateur, has so often observed at his *Le Pavillon,* guests are flattered by the mere fact of a host's advance preparations. Also, service is bound to be smoother —and guests are spared the chilling sight of prices on the menu card!

Otherwise, the ritual gets complicated: you ask your guests' preferences and you order for them. For a table d'hôte menu, however (where the whole dinner comes at a fixed price), you may correctly suggest that each person order for himself.

The best way to handle the bill, if other men are present and they might conceivably squirm or struggle, is to excuse yourself from the table and have the check brought to you in private. (A charge account, or payment in advance, would be even better, of course.)

AT THE THEATRE

At the Theatre, the host sits on or nearest the aisle. He (or the hostess, if any) tells his guests how they are to sit before they go in, so they will go in that order and save a lot of thrashing about in the aisle. As is usual at other "company" affairs, he separates husbands and wives. Being on the aisle, he gets up first when the group is leaving, but he walks out with or behind the woman guest who sat next to him instead of waiting to bring up the rear of the whole gang. He pays for the cabs, to and from the theatre, and he usually entertains either at dinner before or supper after the show. It's a mistake to invite people to the theatre and then shift your weight from one foot to the other waiting for one of your guests to suggest an extension of the evening: you're the host, unless this is one of those trade-off double dates akin to a Dutch treat, so you should be explicit in your invitation and definite in your leadership of the evening.

AT YOUR CLUB

At Your Club, the ritual is much like that of entertaining at home. Greet the guest at the door, or at least alert the doorman to watch out for your guest and lead him to the appointed room. Remember that the guest can't buy anything, so be on the watch for a shortage of cigarettes, etc. Sign the check as unobtrusively as possible. And if you think your guest might not know the ropes, tip him off to the club's peculiar rules *before* he tries to tip a club employee or smoke in the dining room or whatever.

ON YOUR CAMPUS

At College: When a man dates a fellow-student at a co-educational college or university, a date is a date is a date: it's governed by his age-and-income's variation on date etiquette (see page 254). But when he *imports* a girl, as he does almost every time the week turns around at a men's college, a date is a Week-End is a Thing: it's worthy of the attention of a Clausewitz, or an Esky. If you can't tell the etiquette from the strategy in the following, that's as it should be: here's the word on how to be happy though hosting on campus.

the bid

First, of course, you have to invite the girl. (If she's so stupid as to invite herself, with one of those "I'm coming up to The Game with Mummy and Daddy" maneuvers, she's just asking to be told that you're tied up in term papers.)

You invite her by mail, usually, because the ring of a telephone has such an eager sound and, anyway, you'd rather not listen to her breathless nonchalance at long distance rates. Your letter is a study in casualness, in the "I'm not too interested but why don't you come" kind of vein, so you probably don't send it more than two or three week-ends ahead of time—maybe four, if it's the big game of the year or if she's stuck in one of those institutions which limit her week-ends or require specific parental permissions.*

This is not the first letter you've ever written her, though, so if it has been necessary to lay the groundwork with one chitchat exchange signifying nothing, you will have had to get an earlier start than meets her skimming eye.

This is not the last letter you're going to write her about this particular week-end, either, unless she writes you a "Dear John" declining the honor of your company, so you can save most of the vital statistics for your follow-up. But your letter of invitation, infuriating to her though it may be on other counts, must be specific in these two particulars: The Occasion (what game or party? what week-end?) and The Duration (what day of the week do you expect her to arrive, and how long do you want her to stay?).

So she says she'd love to. She's pretty casual, too, in the reverse-English effusive way that goes with being a girl, so she not only buries this acceptance on the last page of her letter but she also keeps you waiting a good week before she writes back. You're more than equal to this feeble strategy, however: you made all the necessary arrangements and reservations before you asked her, knowing full well that you could always ask someone else if *she* fouled out on you. (Your second and third choices will never know, of

---

* Let *her* handle the job of getting her parents' permission. The surest way to queer the deal would be to deal the parents in yourself. No one is more self-conscious about cramping a girl's style than her parents, so they would be at least as embarrassed as you and the girl if you were to write them direct.

course; they'll only think it's just like a man to wait until the last minute to ask for a date.)

the briefing

Next comes the letter of information, a delicate piece of writing which tells her exactly what clothes and pose to bring but without appearing to doubt her sophistication. This may be her first week-end at your college or anywhere, but she'd rather die than think you think so. *You'd* rather die than have her turn up in blue jeans or sequins, or bring every piece of luggage she owns to be on the safe side, so it's for your mutual benefit that you tell her the following:

NECESSARY
How to get there, and when

You may leave it to her to look up the trains and let you know her ETA, but it's safer to tell her what train to take out of what station at what time arriving where when.

How to find you when she arrives

If you're not going to meet her (as you should, at all but the Service academies), be explicit about where she's to go, how, from the station, and then what you're going to do about catching up with her when.

NICE
What other girls she can come with

Particularly if you know she's not a veteran prom-trotter, it's nice to find out which of your friends might have invited which of her college-mates. Even if she doesn't know Rosemary, your room-mate's girl, she can look her up and tuck herself under Rosemary's wing if she feels like it. Thus she can get some feminine advice on what to expect as well as some time-killing company en route.

What rr car to sit in, if she can, so you'll know precisely where to look for her on the platform and thus spare her the frightened, frozen-faced interval of wondering if she's going to be the very last to find her date in the melee

If you want to be really smooth, meet her at the stop just before the end of the line and ride in *with* her. This technique is more effective if it's a surprise: it gives you a chance to start the week-end off right with a kiss-greeting instead of the stiff-arm, two-hands shake she's practiced.

364

What you two will do as soon as she arrives

This information tells her what she should wear for the trip. If you're going immediately to a cocktail party, without so much as a stop-off at her camping spot, she'll dress differently than if you're going to walk her around the campus until time to change for the dinner-dance. One walk with High Heels, or one cocktail party with Moccasins, will convince you of the importance of being explicit.

Where she will stay

The suave move is to billet her in the outstanding place, but since there is probably only one good hotel and it was booked solid for this week-end when you were still in prep school, chances are you have to put her in a boarding house. Or maybe this is the week-end that the men turn their fraternity or club houses over to their dates. Be precise not only about the name, address and telephone number of the spot (emergency information) but also about the kind of place it is. Whether it's an adjoining-bath or a cold-dormitory type of stopover spot makes a remarkable difference in her packing. Don't, of course, *apologize* for anything less than the best, but tell *all*.

And then what, blow by blow

You don't have to spell this out quite as carefully as you've planned it out, but take pains with these key words: "and then go on to . . ." versus "and then change for." The whole idea is to coach her on what to wear where. You can and should be direct about the big events— *tell* her if the dance is formal or the picnic calls for blue jeans. The rest of the dope can be deduced, but the more explicit you are, the better dressed she will be.

Who will be staying with her

If you and your group take over an entire boarding house, you will have made an asset out of quarters that might otherwise be a liability. Your girl will feel more at home, and there will be less danger of her sitting around alone during your necessary wardrobe changes, if she's billeted with a flock of other girls who are doing the same things at the same time as she.

P.S. A weather report

Spare yourself the sight of blue lips or the plight of hunting up an extra raincoat by telling her what the weather's like in your loop of the ivy.

365

All this may seem like a lot of nonsense and trouble, but you'll find it's as important to you in the long run as it is to her in the first place. You've asked her for the prime purpose of showing her off—that wholesome-looking girl you really *like* rates only the opening game. So, let her show. If you don't tell her what she has to know, she'll play it safe in a little "basic black" which she can "dress up or down" when she sees what's up. But if you *tell* her: well, you might find out what a red dress in a sea of "little black" look-alikes can do for a man's ego.

There is one further advantage to giving her this careful précis: she will see that you have booked her time *solid,* and that suggestions from her are out of order. This may save you from her urge to "run over and see Old Joe," the cousin or the boy from home or the big wheel you "really *should* get to know." If it doesn't, and if you haven't anticipated her urge enough to have arranged the meeting she'll ask for, you can only stall or lock her up somewhere. Anything—so long as you don't let yourself get trapped into one of those embarrassing side trips.

the busy-ness

You have indeed planned the time down to the last second—and you've planned en masse, so that you and she will never be surrounded by fewer than fifteen people—for that is the secret of college week-ending. All this organization makes the week-end something you can't enjoy and she can't afford to miss. It's not as big as coming-out or getting engaged, to be sure, but it's Big—and that means Busy. She's out for maximum circulation; if you're out for a grab, you picked the wrong time and place. The idea seems to be: how much time can you block out so that you won't get to know her at all? Foolish as it may seem to you later, to be alone together on a college week-end is to be lonely and left-out together. That's just the way it is, and nothing can be done about it except super-planning.

Do the planning with at least one other classmate—five is better—and leave nothing to the girls. At this age, particularly, they *like* to be yanked from place to place. Nothing will dismay your date more than to have to speak up about what she'd like to do.

on the spot

During the course of the rat race, everyday male-female etiquette governs your conduct for the most part. But here are a few switches that make the difference between the knowing and the learning:

Don't wolf. The best you can do, if you run across something you like, is to find out how to reach her after the week-end is over. You can't cut a college-mate out then and there, and you can't leave your own date to free-lance, without bringing down the wrath of both sexes. The girls are perhaps more loyal to their dates than the men, basically—they wouldn't think of late-dating or mix-matching on the spot—but the men, too, are careful to observe the spirit if not the letter of this week-end rule. Only if your date has gone beyond the pale, and the new girl's date is passed out beyond yon sofa, can you change the order of things.

Don't deck your girl out with showy souvenirs. A first-offender may *want* a chrysanthemum for the game, but even before its petals have begun to curl she too will have realized that mums are for the subway alumni. The happiest compromise between her yen for a souvenir and your need to remain obscure is a little lapel button with football attached; you'd no more let her wave a pennant in the stands than you'd buy her a fluffy dog in a night club. Flowers for the dance (if flowers have not been ruled out by the committee) are governed by the same principle. A girl might be secretly thrilled with an orchid, at first, but when she sees that the veterans are wearing violets or camellias or other underplayed posies, she too will know that an orchid is too much of a bad thing.

Never mind about the conventional rules re chaperones. Unless you are one of the house officers (and probably even then), you can forget about the chaperones. They're largely a gag, so you needn't try to sort them out from the guests in order to present your date or do your duty-dance.

the pay-off

Except at the Service academies, all the expenses from the moment of your date's arrival to the moment of her departure are on you.

You pay for her room, usually in advance so that there is no big scene about checking out. If you have put her up with local friends, where there is no question of paying for the lodging, you give her hostess a bread-and-butter present regardless of whether or not your date also does so.

You pay for all her meals, with the possible exception of an eye-opening orange juice she may treat herself to while waiting for you to pick her up for the milk-punch breakfast party.

The only thing she pays for is her transportation. If she brings her car and turns it over to you, you might fill the tank for excursions during the week-end, but you wouldn't think of paying for her to-and-fro gas any more than you'd send her her railroad ticket.

When it's all over, the best you can hope for is a thank-you letter. But if you also get a return invitation, and are faced with the prospect of week-ending on *her* campus, see page 382.

manners for the guest

The best guest is the best guesser. He puts clue and clue together to figure out what his hosts expect of him, then does what is expected as if it were the very thing he wanted most.

As more and more rules give way to more and more ad-lib etiquette, the guest's guesses are more and more difficult. One hostess may be irritated if he does not appear on the stroke of the prescribed hour; another may be upset (and only half-dressed) if he is less than fifteen minutes "late." One host may boil if he mixes his own drinks; another may fume if he sits inert, expecting service. One couple may think their party's a failure if people leave before 4 A.M., where another will think their guests are planning to move in if they aren't out of the house by midnight.

Thus the guest's job is to read minds, assess habits and operate on a social-radar system super-sensitive to his host's hope and plans. Since the host's job is to do the same, in reverse, the guest cannot be completely flaccid: he has to have some wishes so his host can grant them, he has to have some preferences so his host can cater to them. The delicate part of the guest's role comes in adapting his wishes and preferences to the host's own wishes and preferences—and to the host's ability to provide for them.

THE EASY GUEST

To illustrate the way a good guest expresses his preferences but keeps them within the bounds set by his host, consider the usual what'll-you-have gambit where the host stands poised to serve his guest a drink:

Host: "Would you prefer a martini or a Manhattan?"

Bum Guest: "Whichever is easier" . . . or . . . "Whatever you're having." (This is so wishy-washy that it frustrates the host. Obviously he's prepared to make both, or either, so why not let him think he's making the one *you* want?)

Bum Guest #2: "How about a Daiquiri?" . . . or . . . "Have you got any Scotch?" (If he had 'em he'd have named 'em, or at least given you carte blanche. Now he's got to call the liquor store, or drink the cocktails he's made, all by himself, and get drunk on his host job. See?)

Good Guest: "Martini sounds swell." (Or, if he really can't stand either, he could say, "Gee, I'm off cocktails at the moment. Could you put the whiskey with water instead of in a Manhattan?")

One thing is sure: the guest is expected to have a good time, and by so doing to help his hosts and their other guests to have a good time too. In effect, his job is to make his host forget his worries. By act and attitude, more than by words, he constantly assures his host that his hospitable efforts are appreciated—and successful.

Most of the specific rules binding upon guests are aimed toward creating that general effect. For instance:

ANSWERING INVITATIONS

The Guest must reply immediately to all invitations. If you are asked by telephone or in person, you must accept or decline on the spot—if by mail, you must reply within twenty-four hours.

You cannot appear to take the proposition under advisement, or see if something better turns up in the meantime. The married man's position, in cases where invitations are extended to him for him and his wife, is a little touchy (see page 289), but the inviter will understand that it's the wife who runs the engagement calendar. Still, the husband must see to it that she replies to the invitation immediately.

If for any legitimate reason the unattached man cannot give an on-the-spot reply, he must explain the reason and *decline* then and there. The inviter can then say something like, "Oh, that's all right. You don't have to let me know until the day before, if it turns out you can't make it." But the guest should not say, "I'll let you know," unless he can do it within a few hours (after consulting his engagement book, say, or checking to see if his boss *is* going to take him to Montreal that week). Presumably the host will want to invite someone in his place, or otherwise firm up his arrangements. He cannot be left dangling, unless he asks for the suspense himself.

Incidentally, "Let's have lunch sometime," and "When are you coming to see us?" and "We'll have to get you out to the beach house one of these days" are *not* invitations. Let them drop, or answer them with like vagueness. Elwood P. Dowd, Harvey's friend, was given to pinning such meaningless conventions down with "When?" or "Next Saturday, say?" or "What did you have in mind?" But unfortunately this ingenuous good sense is not Etiquette.

(For forms of written replies to invitations, see page 325)

When he declines an invitation, the guest must give the reason—if not a previous engagement, then something equally unchangeable. Otherwise, it will seem that he spurns the offered hospitality willfully. The reason should be as specific as possible, without risking hurt feelings in another direction. Suppose, for example, that you can't accept the Browns' invitation to dinner on Saturday because you're going to a big party at the Smiths' that night. If the Browns and the Smiths don't know each other, you can safely tell the Browns exactly what your previous engagement is. But if the Browns might possibly be offended to learn that they have been left out of a big party at the Smiths', you should use no names: "I'm sorry, but some friends of mine have already drafted me for a party that evening; afraid they have The Girl lined up for me, too!"

If you'd really like to go and there is a loophole in your reason, make it easy for the Browns to renew the invitation. "I'm sorry, but I've already signed up a Miss Burnam for that evening." The Browns can then say, "Bring her along— we were going to suggest you bring a date, anyway," or they can mutter their "too bads" and continue their search for an extra man to match up with their visiting cousin. If you really don't want to expose Miss Burnam to the Browns, and vice versa, anticipate this possibility by saying, "—and I've promised to take her to the theatre" or something equally definite.

KEEPING YOUR WORD

Once he accepts an invitation, the guest must live up to it. Except for valid reasons which your would-be host and hostess cannot fail to understand, you just can't break dates, or change their conditions to suit your afterthoughts.

The valid reasons are few, and they do *not* include a subsequent invitation. In fact, in explaining the reason (as you must, with great regrets, as far as possible in advance of your no-show), take care to remove all suspicion that you are breaking one date to accept another which is more attractive.

In general, the valid reasons involve duty or incapacity. In line of duty, you might have to make a business trip or attend a business meeting or dispose of some crisis beyond your prior control—but if you use business as an excuse, particularly when disappointing a woman, be sure that even her feather brain can grasp that the duty is not put-offable. It's the rare hostess who will really understand that you couldn't have finished your work in time, explained to the client that you are not free that evening, postponed your trip till the next day or whatnot. In line of duty, you might also have to watch over a seriously ill member of your family, or observe a period of mourning, or spend the evening with a long-lost close relative who has just turned up for a rare and short visit, or perform some equally important task indigenous to family affairs. Most hostesses, however they may be inconvenienced by your canceling out, will understand about such things *if* it is clear that they are beyond your control. And they'd *rather* you stayed home if you were going to be wearing a long face and talking about an illness, anyway. An invitation to the White House also rates as duty: it supersedes any and all previous engagements and is its own excuse.

When it comes to incapacity as an excuse for breaking a date, you're on shifting ground. A woman may foul out simply because she feels foul, but a man has to be really sick, and really sick in bed, before he can cancel a date. A hard day at the office and a horrendous hangover are no good, and a bad cold is only as good as the hostess makes it (You are supposed to call and say that you have a cold, offering to stay home if she fears that you'll pass the germs to her other

373

guests or to her children, but if she says, "Don't be silly—come ahead," you have to be silly and go.)

Once you have canceled a date on account of illness, you are not expected to experience a miraculous recovery in time to hit the late show at Maxie's. In fact, you'd damn well better stay under the covers for a couple of days.

Okay, so you don't break the date, and you don't go hunting for medals for all the difficulties you surmounted in order to do so. There's more to it than that: you have to see the *whole* thing through. If you are going to be unavoidably late, telephone ahead with explanations and apologies. If you are going to have to leave early, say so at the outset —so no one will later think that you invented the sick child or the ten o'clock plane in order to escape a dull evening.

Punctuality is particularly important at dinner parties and at ceremonies. You should always insist that other diners go ahead without you; on your tardy arrival, you should expect to begin your dinner with whatever course is then being served and not allow your hostess to backtrack on the menu. At weddings, to be punctual is to be fifteen to thirty minutes *early;* no one will be seated after the mothers have been guided down the aisle, so the considerate guest arranges to be in his seat at least five minutes before the appointed hour.

MAKING LIKE A GUEST

Once he's in his host's hands, or on his host's property, the guest is obliged to act like a guest, not like a host. The most flagrant violations of this rule seem to be committed for dissimilar reasons. At one extreme there's the born "boss," the guy who can't help taking charge wherever he is. He snatches the reins from his helpless host, herds the other guests about, shows them where things are, introduces them to each other, organizes games, takes over as bartender, orders the servants about and generally "makes things go." Whether they "go" in the direction planned by his host, or not, is quite beside the point; the host is impressed into guesthood at his own party. The "boss" leaves nothing for the host but to pay the bills—and sometimes, as if so to excuse his hog act, he even tries to do *that*.

At the other extreme, there's Mother's Little Helper. He's a nice guy, only trying to minimize the trouble he and his fellow-guests are causing the host and hostess, but his "help" has the unintended effect of seeming to criticize the hospitality. When he passes the canapés around the room or hunts up some needed extra ashtrays or brings empty glasses to the bar, he appears to be saying "our hostess is a slouch" or "our host is a slow man with a jigger." He would be shocked to learn that his help is resented, but he, no less than the Boss, should memorize the old adage, "Never do the honors in another man's house."

In these servantless days, the adage might be appended to include, "—unless you're asked to." A hostess who is her own cook and waitress might appreciate a little help with the dishes, but if you make a move and she says, "No, please sit down; I'd rather," you are guest-bound to comply with her wishes. A host who is his own bartender at a big party may ask you (if you're a very close friend) to help him keep up with the drinks, but if he doesn't, he doesn't want you to. If you're standing nearby when he discovers the icebucket is empty, you could say "May I get some more ice?"—but if he says, "No thanks—won't take a minute," offer no more.

This doesn't mean that you should *make* work—if you break a glass you can sweep it up yourself, and you can hop to whenever your host is trying to roll up a rug or move a table. It just means that you should leave the *initiative* to your hosts, and by no means try to improve on the provisions they have made for your coming. Avoid anything which could possibly point up a deficiency in the service or an oversight on the part of your host.

In any case, *never* give orders to the servants, unless specifically instructed by your hosts to do so (see page 387). A restaurant waiter ranks as a servant, when your host is entertaining in public: like the girl guest on page 262, you order through the host, following his lead as to how much you can order.

And *never* criticize or compare. It is an indirect criticism to refuse food offered you, but if you honestly can't eat lima beans it's better to pass them than to leave them accusingly on your plate. It is an indirect comparison to talk about the terrific dinner you had last week at the Robinsons; you may think there's no connection, but your hostess of the evening will grind her teeth if you describe the Robinsons' *consommé double* while eating her one-dish dinner. If you like your steak rare and you are served it well-done, the least you can do is be quiet about it.

If you can manage to do it convincingly, you ought also to comment favorably on some part of the dinner—particularly if your hostess is her own cook. You don't have to go so far as to ask for recipes or go into raves—one guy of record dined out successfully for a whole season simply by pausing in mid-sentence to say, in parodied old-world style, "Mmmmm. My compliments to the cook." But remember your ultimate goal—to appear to be pleased with everything your hosts have provided for your pleasure (including the warm, 2 to 1 martini you can barely get past your lips).

And *never* try to pay for anything, except toll telephone calls. Those you *must* pay for, leaving at the phone or handing to your hostess, with explanatory record slip, the exact amount reported by the operator. But nothing else. If you have broken something, replace it, but don't offer money. The other expenses incurred by your hosts on your account are part and parcel of hostmanship. They are repaid when you entertain them, or sometimes by your good-guestman's presence alone, and the relationship should not be strained by money haggles.

The haggles are most apt to happen in public places, when there's a definite check to be paid. But they are unbecoming, and most unwelcome to anyone who has invited you to be his guest. There are many occasions in restaurants and night clubs and theatre parties when no one man is the host, but this is apparent at the outset. Then, one man pays the bill and the others settle with him later, or the bill is divided by the number of men present then and there and paid by "pot." But there are no arguments. It's when there is a definite host, who has made his role clear by the form of his invitation and the mode of his ordering, that the guest must restrain his impulse to get into the act. The best he can do, to "get even," is to pick up the check for an *unplanned-for* nightcap—and then only when *he* suggests it and the earlier host has gracefully relinquished his role by allowing his guest to take over for the encore.

the formal part

The seven basic standards of hostmanship have their corollaries for guests; you can read them between the lines on pages 343 to 347: the guest must shake hands with his host and hostess, in greeting and goodbye, searching them out for the purpose if necessary . . . he must acknowledge introductions (page 312), retrieve conversational balls tossed him by the host and generally get into the spirit with as little prodding as necessary . . . he must be pleasant to the other guests, knowing that an affront to a guest is an affront to his host as well . . . he should circulate, or at least be a part of the group, knowing that his host will have to come to his rescue if he appears to be stranded . . . he should spend a little time with his host and hostess . . . he should

377

go when the going's good . . . and he must not carry tales from the party, or later cast reflections upon any house where he has "broken bread."

the "going" art

Apparently the most difficult of all to live up to is: "Go when the going's good."

The guest of honor, if any, is supposed to start the exodus, with other guests following in reverse order of their close relationship to the hosts. That is, it is an affront to the guest of honor to leave before he does, an imposition on your hosts to remain till the last gasp if you are not a particularly close friend.

The guest-of-honor rule is ignored as often as not in these free-wheeling days, but the wedding reception still calls for its meticulous observance. Once the bride and groom have left, the party is over; wedding guests should move on *immediately*. Exhausted parents are slow to close the bar; sometimes they even seem to want company. But only members of the wedding party and close relatives have any right to stick around after seeing the bride and groom off.

In most situations, you can usually sense when it's time to go. And, whenever that may be, *when you're going, GO!* Stand, say you must be going, go up to your hostess and thank her, get your coat (or stand by as your host gets it for you) and *BE OFF!* Never, never stand in the doorway lingering over a last drafty story. Never, never change your mind and have one more for the road. In short, never penalize your hosts for expressing their reluctance to let you go.

THE MORNING AFTER

After the ball is over, you show your appreciation in one of two ways, or in both. You send flowers and/or you invite your hosts to be your guests. It's nice (but not strictly necessary) to send flowers to your hostess after the first time she has invited you to her house. It's nice (and almost necessary) to send them if repeated apologies are in order—if you were late or drunk or rude or clumsy, for instance. It's nice (and nearer to necessary) if you have no way to return the hospitality—if you are a bachelor without means, for example, who will not soon include your hosts in a cocktail party or take them to dinner or do them some favor to show your appreciation.

N E X T ?

Which brings up the question of reciprocity. Conventionally, the social whirl is run on an eye-for-an-eye basis; he who is host today is guest tomorrow. But the extra man is often excused from returning hospitality in kind—his serving as a pleasant guest is considered return enough by many a hostess—and the young couple should never feel that they must exactly match the entertainment given them by older, plushier hosts.

THE WEEK-ENDER

You'll find more guides for the guest in the Host section, pages 338 to 360, covering particular kinds of informal entertaining. But perhaps a little more should be said about *the week-end visit*. More friendships are strained from Friday to Sunday than at any other time on the social calendar. Try these for preventives:

TEN RULES FOR
VISITING FIREMEN

1. Be absolutely clear on the arrangements, *in advance,* so you both know what train you're taking or by what other means you'll arrive and leave, at what time. Leave nothing for debate on Sunday afternoon, and take nothing for granted. If your invitation is vague, as it shouldn't be, you may and should ask questions. If the host doesn't volunteer the information you need in order to pack your bag properly, *ask.* You don't have to say, "Are we going to any parties?", as if you were expecting a big whirl, but you can say, "Will I need anything special, like sports stuff or my polite clothes?"

Be sure you have the phone number, in case you get hopelessly lost, but don't call up simply to say you're at the station; if your host is not there to meet you he probably expects you to take a cab, and your phone call will only sound like a demand to be picked up. (Technically, the train fare is on you but the cab fare is on him. But if he hasn't alerted a cab-driver, whom he has paid in advance, don't stand on your rights or you may stand at the station for a long, long time.)

2. Arrive when you said you would, bearing a small present for your hostess or the house or the children, if you feel like if. (Antique candies and dusty toys from the newsstand at the station are not recommended.) Or if you'd rather, and if you're not sure what kind of thing might best fit the house or the kids, you may send a bread-and-butter present after the week-end is over.

3. Don't arrive with any *other* surprises. If you can't visit without your dogs or your children, and if they have not been specifically invited, don't accept the invitation in the first place. And if you have permission to bring them, *also*

bring whatever special supplies they will need. Most people, these days, have better uses for their leftovers than feeding them to dogs; that stew you spy in the icebox might very well be meant for *your* lunch, in fact, and how can the hostess possibly tell you so if you have indicated that it looks like dog food to you? And few people, even those who have children of their own, are eager to fix separate and special meals for unknown juvenile appetites. Make yourself responsible for the needs *and also the manners* of your offspring and pets, and if there's any conflict between their habits and your hosts', see to it that *your* entourage, not your hosts', gives way. This should be fairly obvious, but many's the traveling dog-owner who has blithely allowed his host's dog to be locked up to protect the visiting dog, and many's the guesting parent who has allowed his own children to do things which are forbidden the host's children.

4. Don't expect to be entertained every minute of the week-end. Fall in with your host's plans, but fall in with his lack of plan, too. Be alert to his own desire for relaxation and privacy, and maybe you'll get some yourself. (Even if you don't know what to do with either, yourself, you can be sure that your host doesn't want you standing over him, "keeping him company," while he's working, and your hostess doesn't want you getting in the way in the kitchen. If they won't let you help, or if your help would be more hindrance, go away and sit down and look as if you're *enjoying* the nothingness.)

5. Don't expect to have a drink in your hand every minute, either. You'll probably be offered a lot of "refreshments," but often as a matter of form; you don't have to say "yes" to every feeler, you know.

6. Don't make deals with other friends who live in your host's territory. You are a guest, not a social secretary, so you don't relay invitations from your other friends any more

than you invite them to your host's house or agree to meet them at the club. It's the host's role to plan your entertainment. You are at his disposal, not vice versa.

7. Don't borrow anything if you can help it—and if by mischance you *must* use your host's racket or wear his sweater, take better care of it than you would of your own. If you harm any such borrowed stuff—even if he insists it's an old racket that was bound to break sooner or later, and even if that's the truth—*replace it*. Send the replacement as soon as possible, and send it without a lot of prior conversation and promises.

8. Be neat. Even in a house full of servants, or in a servantless house where it is immediately clear that your hosts will be embarrassed if you take obvious part in the housework, keep your room and your bath tidy. Wash out the tub after you've used it, particularly if the bath is not your private territory; hang up towels; keep your stuff in drawers and closets or suitcase; *don't strew*.

9. Don't, don't, DON'T leave anything behind. If you're a chronic forgetter, try this: before you leave home, paste a little list inside your suitcase, itemizing all its contents, then check and double-check the list as you pack up to go home. And if by chance you muff it, do whatever you can to prevent your poor host's lugging your clubs in on the commuter train, or struggling to mail your glasses. Go back and pick up anything important, or send Western Union to pick it up for you, or tell 'em to throw it away.

10. As soon as you get home, or at least within a week, write a thank-you letter (see page 331).

THE COLLEGE WEEK-END

All that goes double on a college week-end, because every deviation from perfect guestiquette is a reflection not only on you but on the nervous Nellie who invited you to her campus. You can't be too proper while you're on display—which means that you have to be more clever than ever when you two are alone, to keep her from thinking you're as dull as her dean thinks you're polite!

campus variations

Only three of the foregoing guides for guests do not apply to the college week-end situation.

One: the girl will faint dead away (or think she has you in her palm) if you answer her invitation by return mail. Unless you think you can reform her age-group by dropping all pretense of casualness and popularity, you may wait a week or so before deigning to reply. But be just a little faster than that if your answer is going to be "no, thanks": give her time to line up someone else.

Two: you are not required to take a present to your hostess (unless, of course, you are staying with a private family, in which case "the lady of the house" rates a hostess present).

And three: you are a date as well as a guest, so you may sometimes be expected to take the reins. As a guest, you will take your cue from your hostess; don't impose your ideas over her firm plans. But as a date you sometimes fill voids with your own suggestions and pay checks with your own money.

This much you can be sure of: You will pay for your transportation. She will pay for tickets to the campus events which are a feature of the week-end.

This much you can be *reasonably* sure of: She will probably have reserved and paid for your room in advance (but you should ask for the bill, as you leave, just in case). She will probably buy your lunches and dinners (but be forewarned that most girls don't like the food they get in their houses, or don't think a man will like it; your date may toot you off to a public dining spot where there will be A Check. Then, if she is not really, aggressively insistent about paying the check herself, you and your wallet move in.)

And this is what makes the invitation to her campus something of a mixed blessing, if money matters: the extras are all on you. You pay for transportation to and from the scheduled parties . . . flowers for her to wear to the dance . . . Cokes, coffees, impromptu breakfasts, stadium hot-dogs and other minor munchings you do together . . . and anything which was your idea, not her plan. If she meant to feed you at her house and you suggest the hotel instead, that's your expense. If she is happy to dance all night and you suggest a breather at the nearest bar, that one's on you.

playing by the rules

Liquor is loaded with problems quite apart from finances at many women's colleges. If drinking is forbidden her, as it is in many Southern schools, it will not be encouraged for you, either. It may even be impossible, so if you really care you'd better Bring Your Own Liquor—and be subtle about its swilling. Stand six feet away from college officials if your breath is not quite like the flowers in May. Don't make your impressionable date think she has to join your tippling to rate with you, when she knows that she has to stay away from the stuff to stay in school.

So should go your attitude toward all the rules she has to live with. Your wise move is to help her to keep them. You may not be a good enough actor to pretend that you endorse her college curfew, but you don't have to embarrass her by trying to bribe the night watchman. The least you can do is to be matter-of-fact about the rules. She'll be grateful, however secretly, and, besides, it's only good guestmanship not to disparage the environment you've been invited into.

For the same reason, you don't try to talk her out of going to the glee club concert or the hockey game or whatever dull entertainment she's planned for you. Pretend that you're having a wonderful time, and maybe you will!

One more word, necessary only because your date and guest roles are sometimes ambiguous. Don't invite yourself to her campus for the sole purpose of seeing her. If you're going to be in Poughkeepsie on some other business, of course, there's nothing to prevent your letting your Vassar friend know it, and there's no rule against asking her for a Saturday night date in the usual manner. But don't move in for the week-end without her prior and specific invitation. Her life may be more complicated than you ever thought possible at a woman's college!

GUEST OF THE RICH

You might as well know the mechanics of living with a lot of servants about, just in case you are entertained by the very rich. Servants, and great specialized quantities of them, make the major difference between today's average "potluck" living and yesterday's copybook formality.

DEALING WITH SERVANTS

There remain a few hostesses who, with only the weekly cleaning lady in the kitchen, trot out the finger bowls. But, for the most part, the tipoff to an unfamiliar "form" is the chauffeur at the station, the butler at the door, the footman at the table—and never mind about the chambermaid.

When you find yourself thus surrounded, you had better

know the rules. Common sense won't get you anywhere. Basic human decency, the greatest part of good manners in the usual Twentieth Century situation, will only get in your way in this environment, because the underlying idea is a contradiction of "all men are created equal." If you shake hands with the butler you will embarrass him, his "master" and, presumably, yourself. If you do something for yourself when a servant is there to do it, your "help" will be interpreted as criticism of the service. On the other hand, if you are rude or commanding or paternal to servants, you'll be marked as a real boor.

You can't fly this one by the seat of your pants, so here are a few pieces of information:

forms of address

As a guest, you will be called "sir" or "Mr. So-and-So," and your safest course in reply is to follow Mr. Anthony's edict, "No names, please." A butler is addressed by his last name, the children's nurse is called "Nurse," the maids are known by their proper names—but unless you know them well (in which case you know what their employers call them), say simple things like "Good evening" and "Thank you" without risking the personal name. Since you never give orders, you have no need for a substitute for "hey" or "waiter!"

introductions

You will not be introduced to servants except indirectly. ("James will drive you to the station."), in which case you have only to acknowledge with thanks the service, not the "introduction." If you *are* introduced, as to an "old family retainer," you say, "How do you do" and nod, but you don't shake hands. Exceptions are those professionals who, although employed in the house, are treated almost like members of the family: the governess, the tutor, the confidential secretary, the companion. Perhaps your best clue is the uniform, or absence of one. You can't go far wrong if you treat people who are in everyday clothes as if they were everyday people, not servants.

orders

You must not give orders to your hosts' servants, not even indirectly, unless you have been specifically asked to do so in a specific situation, in which case the servant will also know of the arrangement. For example, if your week-end hostess has told you to ring for breakfast whenever you awake, the kitchen and waitress will be expecting your ring —but this does not mean you can ring from any other room in the house, or for any other purpose. If you're stranded without a drink, waiting for the golfers to return, you must just go dry unless a servant comes to *you* and asks what he may bring you.

Correctly, the only thing a guest can ask for is water or something which has already been offered, and which he at first refused. And these requests are put to his hosts, not to servants.

tips

Perhaps this is the prime example of how illogical the question of servants can be. You'd think, wouldn't you, that it would be an affront to your host to tip his servants, whom he presumably pays a living wage? You'd think your host would not want you to pay for his hospitality, that the all-powerful butler would resent your treating him like an ordinary public waiter? But NO. Tipping of household servants is a must whenever you have spent a night in the house—and, equally, a never-never for any lesser visit.

387

A Friday-to-Monday week-end in a big house can cost you more than $15 in tips: $5 to the butler or whoever is in charge of the pantry department, $5 to the valet or whoever has taken care of your clothes and packing, $2 to the chauffeur who drove you to the station or washed your car, $2 to the waitress who brought your breakfasts, $2 to the chambermaid who made up your room—and $2 each to people like the groom, the bath house attendant, the gardener who brought you all those honeysuckle slips. If your wife shared the week-end, she would have to tip separately anyone who cared for her clothes or performed a special service. If you brought your own servants, you would have to give them money to tip the servants who served *them!* In the end, you might wish you had gone to the Waldorf.

The rules are these:

Tips from a man to a man-servant should be no less than $2 and no more than $5, for one night or for a week.

Tips should go to everyone who gives you personal service, plus the one person who is in charge of the household. That is, you do not tip the cook or other general servants unless you have caused them trouble "beyond the call of duty," but you do tip the butler whether or not he has paid you personal attention. You do not tip "professionals": a present is better for the English nurse who added your children to her own charges; a "thank you" is enough for the librarian who helped you select a book.

Tips must not be given in front of host or hostess. The usual way is: in your room for the valet and maid who are helping you to get away, in the hall as you leave for the butler and waitress, at your car for the chauffeur—all at the last moment. In a private house, the public strategy of tipping in advance is considered rude.

And, as with most other tips, the graceful method is to have the money ready, folded small and hidden as much as possible in your hand, then to pass it over with a smile, a thank you, and no direct reference to the moola. For the price, you *ought* to be able to flash a roll, peel off the bills, wave them in the air and make a loud speech about how you always take care of people who take care of you. But this is a luxury you can't afford.

In a smaller and simpler household, the same scale applies. Though the maid-of-all-work has cooked, served, made up your room and pressed your flannels, $2 is still the minimum and $5 the top tip for any one person. In a large house, you are not supposed to invade the kitchen or servants' quarters to perform the tipping ceremony, but where there's only one maid she'll be so busy you'll probably have to seek her out or leave the money in an envelope in the kitchen.

THE RITUALS

Here, then, is a bow-by-bow description of the ceremonies you are apt to encounter in the "what's money?" set. (For proper dress for these occasions, see pages 206 to 229; see also the chapter on weddings, a once-in-a-lifetime ceremony not peculiar to the rich—page 278.)

the formal dinner

You arrive—no later than five minutes* after the hour for which you were invited—to find a red carpet spread from curb to door. Your host's chauffeur or footman opens your car door. The door to the house is opened by the butler or by a footman; in the latter case, the guy standing in the

---

* Dinner will not be held more than fifteen or twenty minutes, so if you are unavoidably late you have the disagreeable task of entering the dining room, making profuse (but brief and quiet) apologies to your hostess, taking your place and beginning dinner in mid-course.

389

front hall is the butler, not to be hailed as host or fellow-guest. Your coat and hat will be taken then and there by one of the door staff, or perhaps you and/or your wife will be shown to dressing rooms just off the entrance hall. In any case, wait in the front hall for your feminine half.

While you wait, a servant may offer you a silver tray filled with cards or little envelopes. This is no lottery; one of them has your name on it. Inside the envelope, or on the inside flap of the card, will be the name of the woman you are to take in to dinner.

Thus equipped for the evening, you are ready to be announced into the living room. If he doesn't know you, the butler will ask your name. You say "Mr. and Mrs. Jones," or "Miss Smith and Mr. Jones"—not "I'm Stinky Jones— what's *your* handle?" (If he asks the lady, she'll give both names if she's your wife, only her own name if she's not.) The butler will announce you in the order of your entry—ladies first, of course, unless you're the President or a king: "Mrs. Jones . . . Mr. Jones."

You go up to your hostess, who is standing just inside the living room door. You grasp her outstretched hand, match her smile of greeting with a smile of pleasure at being there and above all resist the temptation to stretch her welcoming remarks into a conversation; there are other arriving guests right behind you. The host will then come up for the usual handshake and will either wave or introduce you into a conversational group.

Everyone will be standing—the men because they cannot sit while the hostess stands, the women for reasons of their own. You won't be introduced around the room, and you are not supposed to circulate with self-introductions, but you had better make a point of being presented to your dinner partner before dinner is announced.

You may not get a drink, but if a servant does circulate with cocktails try to remember that these dinners come off

on schedule. You can't take your glass to the table and you
don't want to have to gulp your drink at the last moment, so
sip with attention to timing.

When the butler announces that dinner is served, the host
and the woman guest of honor will lead the way to the dining room. You offer your right arm to your assigned partner
and follow. The line is two by two and orderly, but there
is no order of precedence except host first, hostess last.

If your name card did not include a diagram of the table, you may find the butler at the dining room door saying
"right," "left," "right," "left." This is not a reversion to his
days as a drill sergeant. He is telling you which way to turn
as you enter, in order to find your place at the table with a
minimum of place-card peering.

When you find your dinner partner's place, unless there is
a footman waiting for the job, you hold out her chair and
seat her; you stand until all the women are seated, but your
partner sits immediately, whether or not the hostess has
come in.

Your place will be on your partner's left. If some strange
name stares out at you from the card atop that napkin,
however, don't jump to the panicky conclusion that you've
brung the wrong lassie; you are the victim of a complicated
maneuver in which the hostess has put you across the table,
on her left, so that she could come in with the man who will
be on her right.

Once you are seated, you put your place card above your
plate, put your napkin across your lap and put your wits to
making conversation with the woman you escorted to the table. You must talk to her for just as long as, and no longer
than, the hostess talks to one of the men next to her. At some
point in the ceremony, usually after the fish course, the hostess will "turn the table"—that is, she'll begin to talk to the
man on her other side. At that point, you too must change
talk-partners; if you fail to notice the turn, or if you are less

interested in "form" than in finishing the conversation with the woman on your right, you'll leave someone staring lone-somely (and noticeably) at her plate. Conversation at a for-mal dinner is never general, always in twos, and diners can't be choosers. So turn the other cheek and talk; if you don't know the name of the woman on your left, there's always her place card, and yours.

During the dinner itself, you will be served by footmen —that is, you will have to serve yourself from platters of-fered by them. Each dish will come to you with its own serving tools, usually one object that looks like a spoon and one that faintly resembles a fork. Take the spoon in your right hand, the fork in your left; slide the spoon under the food, hold food in place with the fork and lift to your plate. If it is necessary to cut, do it with the spoon, but when food has obviously been divided into portions in the kitchen, it's best not to attempt a junior grade carving exhibition from a platter held aloft. Take the *whole* squab-on-toast.

This operation goes on without conversation with the serv-ant. Presumably you go on talking with your dinner part-ner, without so much as a "thank you" in the direction of the serving hands.

As a man, you will never be served first, so you will al-ways have the advantage of watching what others do before you must tackle an unfamiliar dish. The only thing to re-member, really, is that platters from which you are to help yourself will always be offered to you at your left. Anything thrust at you from the right is meant for your neighbor, not for you.

Even with the "follow the leader" system, however, it's useful to know a few of the peculiarities of formal service. For instance, there are no cigarettes or ashtrays; you just can't smoke during dinner. There are no second servings of anything, and in some households you are apt to lose your first serving if you put your fork down before you are quite finished! There are no butter plates, and no butter; you put your bread directly on the tablecloth and wish *silently* for butter. Olives and celery are to be placed on the edge of the plate you're eating from at the time. Salt may be put on the tablecloth, but from there to be pinched onto food, not dipped into. All service is individual—the salt or nuts or condiments between you and your partner are matched in pairs around the table, so don't offer to pass them on to others. And no matter what contortions this feat requires of the staff, there will always be a clean, empty service plate before you between courses, up until the time the table is cleared for dessert. The plate is not to be used—presumably it doesn't even hide a horrible hole in the tablecloth; it's just for show. When it vanishes, time to be on guard: formal dessert service can be befuddling on first encounter.

Probably your dessert plate will come to you with spoon and fork on it; you put the silver to either side of the plate and wait for dessert. After dessert, that plate will be replaced by a fruit plate with fingerbowl, fruit knife and fruit fork upon it. You lift the fingerbowl (and the doily beneath it, if any) and put it above and to the left of your place; you put the silver beside your plate; then you are served the fruit. If the fingerbowl comes in separately, after you have had dessert and fruit, you have no problem. But if it comes in with a plate and silver you're expected to take it off the plate before whatever goes on the plate is passed. Inconsequential, to be sure, but you might be flustered if you found yourself trying to put a Baked Alaska or a perfect pear on a plate already occupied by a foolish bowl of water.

When it comes to using the fingerbowl, you use it where it sits, without moving it back into position before you. Dip, don't splash; you can wash behind your ears later.

It's not true that you should wait for the hostess to begin before you eat anything, or even that you should wait until

everyone else at the table is served; that way lies cold dinners and indigestion. Nor is it true that you must take a little
of everything offered you, and leave a little of everything
you take on your plate. If you don't want a dish, simply
say a quiet "No, thank you" to the servant and he will pass
on. If you can't eat everything you've taken, that's another
matter, but don't leave little tidbits on your plate out of a
mistaken idea of politeness.

If you don't want wine, which will be poured automatically with each course, a simple gesture will stop the flow;
don't invert your glass. If you are asked if you prefer whiskey, a simple "Scotch and water, please" or "bourbon and
soda"—not "highball," a word considered bar-roomy—will
bring it. The butler will expect you to tell him when to stop
pouring whiskey, but do it with a gesture, not a hearty
"When!"

The dinner is over when the hostess stands and moves toward the door. You stand, hold your dinner-partner's chair,
then either guide her to the living room before going to the
library for your coffee, or, if your coffee is to be served in
the dining room, remain standing at your place as the
women "retire" alone. Take your cue from your host on this
one; he's the guy who knows where you're going to be
served. Whether in dining room or library, you'll be offered
coffee, cigars or cigarettes, liqueurs and about twenty minutes of man-talk, after which the host will say, "Shall we
join the ladies?" The proper response is not a heartfelt "Let's
not"; you're now supposed to tag along to the living room.
There you infiltrate a group of women, or invite any one of
them to join you for a talk in a less congested part of the
room; the only sin is to go on talking to a man after you
have re-entered the woman's orbit.

After twenty minutes or half an hour, unless the hostess
has already indicated that there will be bridge or other
diversion, the guest of honor says a good night and a thank

you to the hostess, the host escorts her to the door of the living room, and the party is over. When one leaves, everybody leaves; the guest of honor is supposed to start the exodus, but when there is no definite guest of honor it can be any woman with a nice sense of timing. (In protocol-conditioned Washington, leave-taking is in order of rank. You can't leave until everyone who outranks you has said goodbye.)

After your farewells—to the person you were last talking to, to the hostess, to the host; not to the group at large and not lengthily to anyone—you are back in the hands of the staff. You do not tip the servants who give you your coat and see you to your car; you do not re-enter the living room for one last goodbye after you are coated; you just go. If you are a bachelor you may send flowers to your hostess the next day, with a thank you written on your cards, but this is by no means necessary (but see Formal Calls, page 400). If you are married, you and your wife will probably return the hospitality at some later date; but for tonight, your ordeal is ended when the door closes behind you. On to Tony's for a stiff drink in unstiff surroundings.

the formal luncheon

Just about the same as a dinner, in so far as the guest's role is concerned, except that you will not be given a name-card and will not be expected to take anyone in particular to the table. You just amble into the dining room with whomever you happen to be talking to when the hostess says, "Shall we go in?" If you're a lone man, or if you've been talking to another man, bring up the rear; if you're with a woman, don't offer your arm—just move along. After lunch, you will leave the table with the women and have your coffee with them in the living room. Leave-taking is the same as for dinner.

the afternoon tea

When the hostess pours, in the living room, and without waitress standing by, all gentlemen present become unofficial assistants. You rise and take the outstretched cup from her to the out-of-range woman guest; you pass the plate of cakes or whatever; and you strike a nice balance between the slug who sits inert and the eager-beaver who appears to be usurping the role of host.

If it's a big tea party, with official "pourers" at either end of the tea table, your obligation is to pass a few words with the pourers as you drink your tea—unless there is a traffic jam, in which case the best thing you can do is take your tea and get out of the way.

If it's a tea dance, your conduct is an afternoon version of that for the ball, below.

the ball

Only the very, very rich—and the old rich at that—have ballrooms in their houses these days, so the ball will probably be given at a club or hotel. The invitation will say "At Home," regardless. You will know that it is a ball only by the hour (usually ten o'clock) and by the word "Dancing" engraved in the corner of the invitation. Your acceptance may be followed up by an admission card; if so, don't fail to take it along—detectives have no manners for apparent gate-crashers.

You will be ushered in, de-coated, announced and greeted by the hostess as for a formal dinner. The host will see that you find someone you know or otherwise start your evening off right; thereafter your duty (or pleasure?) is to the feminine sex. Unless you have come with your wife or a "date," whom you must watch over lest she find herself partnerless, you are on your own, within the observance of these rules:

1. *You must do the bidding of the ushers* or members of the floor committee, young men recognizable by their white boutonnières and eagle-eyes. Their job is to prevent wall-flowering, so if they lead you to a stranded girl or signal you to cut in on a "stuck" one, you can't affect sudden blindness. (They can be useful to you, as well, for they can introduce you to anyone, whether or not they know you or the girl you want to meet. Incidentally, "the roof" is not quite enough introduction at large and formal parties. You should arrange to be introduced before talking or dancing with strangers.)

2. *Your duty-dances are:* with your hostess, with the guest of honor, with any feminine members of the hostess' family, and with the hostess and guest of honor of any party you attended before the ball. If you don't want them to *look* like the duty-dances they are, you'd better make the rounds again later in the evening.

3. *You must relinquish your partner gracefully* when you are tapped on the shoulder by a cut-in, departing with a simple "thank you" to the girl and without threatening mayhem to the man. Unfortunately, there's no way to refuse a cut-in, and you can't cut back until someone else has first cut in on the cutter-inner.

4. *You are supposed to wait for the girl* to suggest sitting out or joining the others, but if you think you're hopelessly stuck, or if you're *really* hot and tired, you may say something like "Wouldn't you like a cup of punch?" and hope for the best. The music never stops, you know, so there is no logical end to a dance if no one cuts and neither of you has the nerve to call a halt. (P.S. If the reason for stopping is *your* bad dancing, not hers, don't stand on ceremony and her toes. Say, "Sorry, but I just can't rhumba. Can't we wait this one out?")

5. *You must not leave a partner standing in mid-floor* nor sitting alone anywhere. This is not as confining as it sounds, since you have only to deposit her with a group before excusing yourself.

6. *You are supposed not to smoke in the ballroom,* and certainly not while you're dancing.

Supper will probably be a buffet, continuous from one till three. If you haven't come to the dance with anyone in particular (or if she is already taken care of by another), you may ask anyone you choose, "May I take you in to supper?" You fill her plate and take it to her, or you both help yourselves at the table, but you don't let her fetch and carry for you. You sit anywhere you like, unless there are tables marked "reserved." You can't go wrong—unless, of course, the fact that you are in a hotel leads you to tip the waiters. Don't.

When the band plays "Home Sweet Home" or "Good Night Ladies," that is *not* your cue to slip the bandleader a $10 bill for just one more samba. Say your goodbyes and your thank yous to host and hostess, get your coat (without tipping the attendant) and *go.* If you want to leave before the end, you must still seek out your host and hostess and—as unobtrusively as possible—make your excuses for leaving. If you honestly can't find your hostess (or if you want to pretend that you couldn't find her, rather than have her know you are running out on her party), it will cost you a box of flowers and a reasonably palpable excuse sent around the next day. Most hostesses realize that young stags are given to drifting from party to party on any given evening, but they like to be reminded of it only by the most indirect, most gallant methods.

the reception

Except in Washington or other official circles (for which you need a separate book and an individual tutor!), a reception is usually something else as well—a tea, a cocktail party, a wedding party—so the only special rules you need apply to the reception line. You are announced or otherwise introduced to the first in line, who introduces you to the second, who introduces you to the third, and so on. If one of them muffs the job, being caught up in a greeting of the next in line, never mind: don't introduce yourself unless asked your name—just pass along, shaking hands, saying "how do you do," and smiling pleasantly.

Once in the main room, you probably drift to someone you know. You don't usually exchange names with strangers at big shindigs.

the coming-out party

Same rules-of-the-party, be it ball or tea or whatnot, but a man who knows her is supposed to send flowers ahead to the debutante—either a bouquet for her to hold as she receives or a piece of the floral background she will stand before. And duty dances include the deb, of course. If you haven't already read it in the papers, you know it's a debutante party because the girl's name appears on the invitation, either written on her mother's card ("to meet Miss Mary Smith"—whom you've met a hundred times before) or engraved beneath her mother's name on a formal At Home invitation.

the opera

If you should ever be trapped into attending the opera with those who go for the ritual as much as for the music, there are two things you should know. *One:* a man never sits in the front row of an opera box. Usually three women sit across the front, one in a chair moved forward from a back row by one of the men in the party. But even if there's room in front, a man sits in the second row. *And two:* between acts, a man is expected to pay calls to other hostesses' boxes, or visit women friends in other boxes, but he must dash back to his own box if he sees that his own hostess is without male company. When another man enters his hostess' box, to visit her or one of the other women, the man guest sitting behind the woman in question is supposed to give up his chair to the visitor.

the formal call

As an American man who presumably has more important things to do in the afternoon, you really needn't bother about these fine and almost archaic points. Almost nobody outside official or Old Society circles observes them. Unless you're the phlegmatic type, who can picture such pointless time-killing without outrage, don't even read them. Just know that they're here, in case you find yourself in the striped-pants world or in case you run across "party call" in a cross-word puzzle.

The formal call is a kind of card game. Sometime after lunch and before cocktails, you ring the doorbell, uninvited, at the house of any woman to whom you have been properly introduced. The butler comes to the door, silver tray in hand. You ask, "Is Mrs. Jones at home?" This is etiquette for, "Is she receiving guests; does she really want to see me for the prescribed fifteen minutes of a formal call or can I get away with leaving a card on her?" More than likely, the butler says she is not at home, which means that she is upstairs clipping coupons instead of downstairs waiting to greet anyone who happens along. Thereupon, you deal a few of your visiting cards onto the silver tray—one card for each grown member of the family. (When a woman is the dealer, shuffling "Mr. and Mrs." cards and/or separate cards for her whole family, the rules are more complicated but, happily, that's a woman's complaint.) Perhaps you turn the upper right hand corner down, the folded point facing your name, to indicate that you left the card in person instead of sending your coachman to the door while you sat in the carriage. Anyway, you then say, "Good day" to the butler, turn on your heel and cross *that* call off your list. Mrs. Jones later sees your card and makes mental note that you were brung up in the old school.

If the butler crosses you up by saying that Mrs. Jones *is* at home, you put only one card on the tray. He takes your coat, takes your card to Mrs. Jones and ushers you into her presence. On the way out, which should be no less than ten minutes and no more than thirty minutes later, you leave cards for all grown members of the family whom you did not see when you were received.

Now, when are you supposed to go through this routine?

1. Within three days after your first invitation, whether or not you accepted it, from Mrs. Jones.

2. Within three days after any subsequent major or formal party to which you were invited by Mrs. Jones. Strictly speaking, your "party call" should be made the very next day.

3. Within a week after the Joneses have called on you— unless theirs was a call of condolence. (You suspect a vicious circle? Even the strict set settles for returning first calls, and an invitation can substitute for a call.)

4. Within a week of any big, lifetime event in the Jones household—when you wish to extend your sympathies, congratulations or helping hand. If you know the Joneses well enough, you should really try to see them on these occasions, but if you are not received you may write something like

"with deepest sympathy" or whatever on the card you leave.

5. As soon as possible after the Joneses have moved into your town. In this case you are introducing yourself and welcoming the newcomers; established residents must make the first call (except in Washington, as explained below).

6. As soon as possible after a new bride, to whose wedding you were invited, is "at home" after the honeymoon. Other calls required by a strict adherence to wedding rules are: on the mother of the bride and the mother of the groom, the day after the wedding, and on the fiancée of any relative of yours, after the engagement is announced.

7. In Washington, everyone is supposed to leave cards at the White House the minute he is settled in the District and even when there only on a visit. (You needn't sit home waiting for the President to return your call, of course, and you'd better wear a bulletproof vest if you try to walk up to the White House door in wartime.) A married official's wife then sets about calling on the wives of all her husband's superiors; the Washington (and European) rule is that newcomers make first calls. A bachelor making his official calls asks at the door for the superior, rather than the superior's wife, but leaves cards for both. Some Washington hostesses still have "at home" days when they actually receive, and the Embassies still expect such Continental manners, but, generally, the formal call is in its death throes even in the District of Protocol. Your best bet is to find an old hand and ask what you are supposed to do in your particular circumstances, before you start wasting your time at wholesale card-scattering.

Here's a P.S. which doubtless comes under the heading of "needless to say": unless you *know* that the people in question still subscribe to these forms and are equipped to handle them in the relatively painless "not at home" fashion, don't pay calls at all. Though you follow to the letter the old standard of good manners, your dropping in, uninvited, will seem the height of bad manners to busy, informal, butlerless people. They will feel that they must be hospitable, and in a modern, tightly-scheduled day, your unscheduled visit cannot possibly be anything but disrupting. Even if you telephone ahead, to ask if it's convenient, you are giving the other little choice in the matter of seeing you. This is still done, to be sure, for it is still considered good manners to call on a newcomer or a new mother or a convalescent—but why not *issue* an invitation instead of (in effect) asking for one, or send an appropriate note or present and wait for some indication that visitors are sought rather than suffered?

the week-end

You are met at the station by the chauffeur, with or without your host. He takes your bags; he does not take a tip (but see page 387). On the ride to the house, don't sit in the right-rear corner of the car: that's the owner's seat.

At the door, once you've run the gamut of servants, you are met by your hostess. You give her the flowers or house present or presents for her children, your advance bread-and-butter offering. When she asks you to give your keys to James, she doesn't mean your house keys—although, if you're carrying an old carpet bag, you may be tempted to pass your house keys off as luggage keys. James takes your bag up to your room. You follow him if you want to change or "freshen up," an option the hostess gives you, or you go directly to meet the other guests and have cocktails. When it's time to dress for dinner, the hostess gives you the cue and you go up to your room.

You find your suitcase empty—but just as you are about to dash down the hall, shouting, "I've been robbed!", you discover that James has not only unpacked your things but has pressed and laid out your dinner clothes. You wish you had packed your bag a little more neatly, or left out a few items not meant for James' eyes, but you have little time to brood: your valet floats in again to ask if you'd like him to draw your bath.

As he does so, you study the little messages about your room. There may be a guest card, on which you check your breakfast order and indicate whether you want breakfast in your room. (If not, your hostess will probably query you on these points after dinner, or she may tell you to ring when you awake and give your order to whoever comes.) There may be a library card, on which you write your choices of books from the library list beside it. But there will be no explanation of why you have been put in one room and your wife in a room adjoining—you'll just have to take it on faith that this is the height of delicacy on your hostess' part: for all she knows, you have separate rooms at home!

You have your own bathroom or, if you share one, it's with your wife or with another man. You will use it: if you don't bathe before dinner, a servant will ask how you want your bath in the morning.

You go down to dinner at the appointed hour, and fall in with your hostess' other plans for the evening. Unless you are very tired, and the party lasts very late, you wait for the hostess to cue in bedtime. By then, it will be clear in your mind what you're supposed to do in the morning: probably pull the servant's bell beside your bed when you awake, then blissfully prepare for a breakfast tray which will include a morning paper. When you come downstairs, dressed for whatever is up, you find your hostess and prepare to do whatever she has in mind for you. And if she suggests nothing, thus implying that you are on your own, you are free to do anything but hang about with a hang-dog look waiting for the bar to open.

When it's time to go, a predetermined time which you *must* observe, ignoring all temptation to "stay over" or take a later train, you'll find that James has packed you up again. Your only worry is your tips (see page 387). Don't pass out all your money: save three cents for a stamp, because your next responsibility is a bread-and-butter letter to your hostess. Done? Now all you have to worry about is drawing your own bath until you're invited back again.

tipping

Probably more men trip over tips than over any other single hazard marked "His." Some overtip, ostentatiously; they embarrass and annoy everyone but the waiter's stock broker. Some undertip, out of parsimony or ignorance; they save money only to lose face. Some tip just the right amount at just the right time, but in exactly the wrong way. There's a lot more to tipping than coins and computations.

Ovid said that giving calls for genius, but tipping is not as tough as all that! The preliminary steps to a socially-acceptable tipping technique are two:

1. Make up your mind that you can't beat the system. No matter what you think of the practice of tipping, tipping *is*. Rugged individualism won't get you anything (except maybe the bus boy's table in the lee of the kitchen doors). And no matter what you think of the practice of judging a man's social smoothness by his tipping, tipping *is* a criterion. So you might as well stow your principles, take the padlock off your pocket and resign yourself to your fate. The less you drag your heels, the less bother the whole business will be.

2. Once you've decided not to fight back, the rest is easy. To get classical on you with a quote from La Bruyère: "To give awkwardly is churlishness. The most difficult part is to give; then why not add a smile?" If you're in the know you're out the dough, anyway, so you might as well be nice about it. Or, as John L. Sullivan put it, "It don't cost nothin' to be a gentleman."

Admittedly, there are various techniques of tipping, but all can be handled in a reasonable manner—never as if you were giving away a house and lot, always as if a dollar were a dime. In a clip joint, there are times when you *have* to give 'em a showy flash of your wad—particularly if you don't look like that joint's idea of a big tipper—but screen the sorry act from your companions if you can.

In most places and in most circumstances, however, the nice way to tip is this: do it privately and quietly, but personally. Look at the guy when you tip him. Say "thank you" or whatever it is that the tip is saying a little more eloquently. And smile as if you meant it!

With your attitude determined by fate and your latitude determined by the going rates (see chart, page 413), you'll dodge most of the traps inherent in tipping. Still, there'll be times when there seem to be no rules, only rues. For such times, to help you make the happy move, these random notes:

FIVE CLASSES OF TIPS

There are five general classes of tips, and sometimes a single tip falls under four of the five headings:

1. *Tips that say "thanks" for a service performed for you.* If you mean "thanks *very* much"—that is, if the service was performed better than you had a right to expect—you make it a higher tip than the servant has a right to expect. But oddly enough the reverse is not true: if you mean to say "thanks for nothing; I'd have been better off without you," the least you can tip is still the minimum-norm. Never mind that women use their tips (or lack of them) as a means of discipline—after-the-fact; women have a bad reputation about tips, rightfully earned and righteously enjoyed. The only way a man can register his disapproval of the taxi-driver who doesn't lend a hand or the waiter who doesn't

407

bring the water is to hold back on the *extra* tip he'd have given if the guy had bestirred himself.

2. *Tips that say "please do right by me," sometimes translatable as "please don't make a fool of me" or "spare me the details."* In a way, the "thank you" tip you gave last time is a "please" tip the next time; insofar as your last tip was worth getting, its mate is worth cultivating again. But when you are not known by your previous tips (or sometimes when you are known only too well!) . . . when you are asking for something special or difficult . . . and particularly when you are at someone's mercy . . . it's good strategy to tip in advance.

Such tips are a form of insurance—against a strange barber's carelessness, say, or a headwaiter's snobbishness—and their handling is a little delicate. The prime rule: hesitate and ye are lost. None but the most obvious of milkmen will change his "no" to an immediate "yes" on seeing that you are going to pay up, after all. So you've got to pass the pelf the *first* time you ask for the unavailable table or the secret recipe your date wants. Presumably an honest man will decline the tip if the answer must be "no" no matter what, but that's a chance you have to take . . .

. . . unless you have enough aplomb to pull off the half-and-half technique. This is a good safety measure for one-time encounters with tippees. If you give the Pullman porter his whole tip at the beginning of your trip, you may get better service than if you waited until the end (when his regrets at having sized you up wrong can't do you much good). But then again you may not; this porter may be the one guy who thinks ten birds in the bush are better than one in hand—once he's got his money from you he just *might* concentrate on the unknown quantity to come from the other passengers. Against such a possibility, you give him half his tip at the beginning, the other half at the end of the trip.

408

The reason the maneuver calls for self-assurance, however, is that you must then *announce* your intentions; not everyone can retain his poise while saying something like, "There's another one of these for you when we get to Los Angeles, if you look out for me."

Needless to say, tipping in advance is not recommended for minimum tippers. If you're going to give the guy a quarter when he might have figured you for half a dollar, save the bad news for the *end* of the transaction. Only for the very young (always suspect in the eyes of hardened tip-extractors) is tipping-in-advance advisable for average-sized tips.

3. *Tips that are protection money, impure and simple.* They range from the quarter you give the boys who offer to "watch your car, mister?" to the big bill you give the hotel clerk when you expect him to be discreet . . . However well you understand the purpose of the tip, you don't speak of it: you give it as if it were indeed to pay the boys for fending off unknown vandals; you expect nothing but nothingness in return.

4. *Tips that are subtle extortion, given simply because it's "done."* You know that the hatcheck girl doesn't get a penny of that quarter you give her; she knows you know the money all goes to a concession; but this mutual knowledge doesn't make you look any less the hick or the tightwad if you give her a dime, or nothing. The hatcheck business is just one of the facts of night life. Face it: you have no choice about most of the tips listed on the Tipping Chart.

5. *Tips that are insulting.* These are rarer than you think. For every occasion where a tip is an insult, there are one hundred and one situations where no tip is an injury. (Okay, so maybe the waiter *does* make more money than you do . . . maybe those tips which keep him in his French accent are *not* subject to withholding. Even so, if you withhold you do him an injury—and you run a risk of getting

an unpleasant return on your non-investment, besides.)

Much less is the risk you run in trying to tip someone who is above tips. The worst that can happen is that you'll be temporarily covered with confusion and more or less permanently ahead a few bucks. The confusion can be pretty wearing, however, so here's how to avoid it in a few clearcut instances:

These people are *never* tipped:

Employees in a town club, your own or anyone else's. (But see page 123 for the country club exceptions that make the rule.) Club members give Christmas presents individually or in a fund, but they don't follow the public-room practice of tipping waiters, stewards, or locker-room attendants, etc. in their clubs.

Airline employees: stewards and stewardesses, limousine drivers, pilots, porters who wear the airline uniform. Unlike the others, the guy who loads and unloads your baggage from the plane won't fight you if you try to give him a quarter, but he doesn't count on it, and he won't hang around waiting for it. Porters who work for the airport rather than the airline are something else again: they should be tipped on the same scale as railroad station porters.

The proprietor, owner or manager of a place. You can't always tell, of course, whether the barber in the first chair owns the shop or only works there, and some restaurant owners will confuse you by working right alongside their employees. When in doubt, the best you can do is offer the tip and repocket it with as little embarrassment as possible if it is waved away. Often the guy's clothes and what he does for you will give you the steer you need. The head headwaiter, who ranks as a manager and is not to be tipped, probably does little but greet you, turn you over to a tip-hungry section headwaiter, and maybe come over to make suggestions about your order. More than likely, he'll be dressed more like you than like a waiter. If you know him well you might sometimes invite him to join you for a drink, but normally you confine your thanks to pleasant parting comments.

Not nearly so clear cut is the fourth general category of those who are not tipped. We might call them "professionals" or "craftsmen" or "people with a white-collar attitude toward jobs which happen to consist of personal service"— but whatever our heading we'd be taking in too much territory and leaving out too many individualists. Lawyers, doctors, stenographers, nurses, ships' officers, government employees, department store workers are never tipped; if you want to show appreciation beyond the fee, you give a present instead of money. Friends and "social equals" are never paid for doing you favors; the only proper payment is a favor in return. Beyond that, the problem gets cloudy: you tip the shoe-shine man but not the shoe-repair man . . . you tip the masseur but not the gym teacher . . . you might conceivably tip the caddy-master but you'd buy the pro a drink . . . and when you are face to face with a television-repair man, a crew of moving men, a Railway Express delivery man, a painter or a plumber, you don't know *what's* expected of you.

More times than not, what's expected is folding money. For a reason which is perfectly apparent on brief study of the cost of living index, folding money is never so "demeaning" as clanking change. As a frank TV-service man, who described himself as a "working stiff," told us, "The only reason anyone is ever 'insulted' by a tip is because it's not up to their standard of what a tip should be. And that's the truth!"

If you're not sure whether a tip will be expected or rejected, offer the tip as if you were asking a favor. To the garage mechanic who had just told you that you didn't have to have a new engine after all, you might say, "Gee, that's great! Let me buy you a drink to celebrate!"—meanwhile thrusting a dollar bill in his direction. You'd thus be living up to the French word for tip—"pourboire," meaning "for to drink"—and you'd be making it easy for him to accept the money.

One tip-off to tip expectations is the presence of a little silver tray. Like the saucer that the men's room attendant equips with decoy quarters, to inspire you to keep up with his idea of the Joneses, the little tray on which the bartender gives you your change tells you he doesn't want to draw it back empty. He wants to see George Washington's face in it, or at least the bald eagle's—not his own face. You've heard the story about the bellhop who brought a telegram to a hotel room? Instead of opening the door, the guest hollered, "Shove it under the door!" The bellhop answered, "I can't—it's on a tray!"

Another clue is to be found in the form of your change. The bartender who takes 95 cents out of a $5 bill by returning four singles and a nickel wants no tip; the one who gives you three singles and $1.05 in varied change expects a portion of the change in return. (Where only the amount, not the tip, is in question, you can always ask for change if you suspect that you're being high-pressured into leaving more than a fair tip.)

Even if you misjudge an ambivalent situation—even if you tip someone who is above tips—you'll probably come out all right if you're *nice* about it. A pleasant, appreciative, unassuming manner will keep an unwanted tip from being as offensive as it might have been otherwise. Sometimes, it might even make your missing tip seem naive rather than niggardly.

But only sometimes. Most times, you're expected to know the following rules, and to tip up to them.

TIPPING CHART

EATING

who	prescribed amount	rock bottom	but . . .
IN A RESTAURANT			
Waiter	15% of the food bill.	15-20¢ a person (but 50¢ a person is about par in a swanky restaurant).	When 15% exceeds $2, you may cut it down to 10% unless you've been a lot of trouble. Thus, you could tip $2 for a $20 check, but you would also tip $2 for a check of $12.50
Headwaiter	10% of the bill, or $1 to $5—if you tip at all (see col. three).	Never less than $1 and never silver in any amount. The tip must always fold.	You don't have to tip him if he does nothing but seat you or hand you the menu. A tip is a *must* only if he has helped you make advance arrangements for a dinner party. But in many spots you have to tip in order to get a decent table.
Busboys	No tips necessary —presumably the waiter tosses him a few crumbs.		
Wine Steward	10% of the wine bill.	No less than $1— and folding money always preferred.	When the waiter has doubled as wine steward or the untippable manager has carried the keys, increase the waiter's tip by the amount you'd have given a wine steward.

E A T I N G (cont'd)

who	prescribed amount	rock bottom	but . . .
Check Room	25¢, usually, but it could go down to 15¢ at lunch, or for a hat alone, or in an inexpensive restaurant.	10¢	When there's no attendant—only a coat rack—it's free.
Doorman	15-25¢ for getting a cab for you (and merely waving a waiting cab into position rates as getting a cab)—a little more if he has parked your car.	10¢ for a minimum effort.	No tip necessary if you *walk* away.
Men's Room	15-25¢ for a towel and for a vague pass with a whisk broom. More accordingly if you want something special, like a bromo or a spot-removal.	10¢ for just being there—but this can be skipped in a paper-towel, no-hustle kind of place.	

IN A NIGHTCLUB
As above with this addition:

who	prescribed amount	rock bottom	but . . .
Entertainers	No tip unless you request a particular number—then, make it folding money.	$1	Never tip a star or headliner. You may buy him a drink or send her flowers, but act as if the star were your equal, if not your superior.

AT A COUNTER

who	prescribed amount	rock bottom	but . . .
The Counterman	10% of your check.	10¢	When the signs say "No Tipping," they probably mean it— and when you're in a hat-on-head, stand - up - counter kind of place,

E A T I N G (cont'd)

who	prescribed amount	rock bottom	but . . .
			chances are no tip is expected. When the pharmacist makes the soda for you himself, or when you know for a fact that nobody tips at the campus hangout, that's something else again. But the days when you could skip the tip simply because you sat uncomfortably at a lunch counter seem to have gone forever—at least in the big cities.
AT A CAFETERIA	No tipping necessary.		The guy who cleans up after you leave would probably welcome a dime for one, a quarter for a tableful.

D R I N K I N G

AT A TABLE *Waiter*	15% of the bill (payable with each check in those places where they won't let you ride until the end).	15¢ a person	
AT A BAR *Bartender*	15% of the check	15¢ a person (or 10¢ in a sawdust-on-the-floor kind of saloon).	Watch out, though, for the bartender who is the proprietor, the artiste, the good friend, the untippable.

G R O O M I N G

who	prescribed amount	rock bottom	but . . .
Barber	25¢ for one service, 35-50¢ for two	15¢ (and that in a shop where your haircut costs about 50¢. Write for address, sent in plain wrapper).	No tip if the barber is the owner; bigger tip if you want something special (like no salestalk and no clucking over your scalp).
Manicurist	25¢	25¢—and your Don Juan line makes it cost *more*, not less.	
Porter	10-25¢, depending on how much he hustles and what he does.	10¢	
Shoeshine Boy	The difference between the cost of the shine and 25¢ —that is, 10¢ for a 15¢ shine, 15¢ for a 10¢ shine.	10¢ (leave it to the girls to hand out nickels!)	If porter & bootblack are one, 15¢ would be the minimum for shine *and* whisk broom.
Masseur (Rubber)???	?		

L I V I N G

Tips to people who serve you all year 'round are usually given in the form of Christmas "presents" but, in addition, you tip now and then during the year if you require any special service "beyond the call of duty."

who	average amount	rock bottom	but . . .
Your Own 'Staff'	Xmas: 1 to 2 week's wages. Special: Extra bills for extra-good service or extra-special occasions through the year.	Xmas: A day's pay Special: $1 an hour for extra time put in.	Xmas: Little presents, too, to an 'old retainer' or a servant with whom you have a friendly relationship.
Apt. Bldg. Employees	Xmas: 2% of your year's rent, divided equally among all service employees. (Supt. gets present of equal value—no	Xmas: money that folds for each.	Xmas: Add to the minimum base for anyone you have caused extra trouble during the year. (For this reason

L I V I N G (cont'd)

who	average amount	rock bottom	but . . .
	"tip" unless he is a janitor-super rather than a manager.)		doormen often get more than janitors —but none gets less than his share of the percentage total.)
Back-of-the-House Janitors Service-Elevator men Handy-men	Special: 25-50¢ whenever one of them does something special at your request—like changing a fuse or helping you move some furniture.		
Front-of-the-House	$1 to $5 every now and then if you often require help with guests, car-unloadings, dog-walkings, etc.		
Delivery Boys Those who come regularly, like those from grocery store, newsstand, etc.	Xmas: $1 to $5 each, depending on how well you know them.	Xmas: Folding $$s	
	Special: Usually no tip unless special service required— like running back for something you forgot to order, or returning a case of empties—then 15 to 25¢ about par.	Special: 15¢ (Dimes are déclassé!)	
Those who come irregularly, as from drug store, liquor store, etc.	Xmas: Nothing, except a bigger tip for a holiday delivery.		
	Special: 15-25¢ a trip.	Special: 15¢	
From dept. stores	No tips		
From Western Union	Officially, no tips. Practically, 15-25¢ if the delivery has		

L I V I N G (cont'd)

who	average amount	rock bottom	but . . .
	been inconvenient to make.		
Postmen	Xmas: a small present—no money.		
Hotel Employees			
Maids—Day	$3 a week, or 10% of your room-rate	25¢ a day for each room you occupy	Permanent residents usually tip weekly or monthly, at the lower rates listed here. Transients tip by the service for employees they see, leave parting tips for maids.
Night	$2 a week	$1 a week	
Bellhops & Porters	$1 a month to each, given individually or through the bellcaptain.	15-25¢ a trip	
Room Waiters	15% of each check, in cash or written in on bill	25¢ a person (40-50¢ a person in expensive hotels)	
Head Waiter for Room Service	$10 every six months	$12 a year	
Doormen	15-25¢ a service, or $1 a month if you're not much trouble.	$5 at Christmas, if you haven't been tipping regularly.	
Elevator men	$1 a month to each one who serves you—often given through the starter	Xmas: for each operator, folding money	
Room clerks, managers, etc.	Xmas: small presents, like cigarettes or liquor. No tips.		

G O I N G   P L A C E S :

who	prescribed amount	rock bottom	but . . .
IN A CAB			
Taxi Driver	15-25¢ for meter-readings up to $1, 20-25% of the fare thereafter.	Never give less than 50¢ to cover both fare and tip. And don't take your life in your hands with dime tips—a quarter is almost a minimum for a	In some towns there's no tipping —but you'll soon find *that* out!

G O I N G   P L A C E S (cont'd)

who	prescribed amount	rock bottom	but . . .
		man to tip for a short trip, 15% for a longer one.	

ON A TRAIN
Pullman Porter

who	prescribed amount	rock bottom	but . . .
Day trip	25-50¢, depending on length of trip	25¢	Can be skipped for short trip if he doesn't even lift bags off train.
Berth	50¢ to $1 a night	50¢—but make it higher if he does anything more than making up the berth.	
Roomette	$1 to $1.50 a night		}This could cover tip for two
Drawing Room	$2 a night	$5 for three-night junket	
Conductor	No tips except for unusual service requested by you—such as looking out for a child traveling solo.	Folding money.	
Dining Car Attendants	As for waiters and headwaiters in restaurants (above)	25¢ a person	
"Room Service"	As for room service in hotels, (page 418)		
Baggage handlers On the train	No tip unless you make special request (as to feed a dog in the baggage car), then 50¢ to $1 for the favor.		
Station Redcaps	Officially, 15¢ a piece (no matter how small), and this should take	15¢ a piece	It's considerate to tip in advance if you're not following right behind

who	prescribed amount	rock bottom	but . . .
	you from cab onto train. Usually you give additional tip of 5¢ to 10¢ a piece, for two or three pieces, or a plus-tip of 25¢ for assorted baggage.		the redcap—so he can be freed to hustle further. If you *have* kept him waiting, increase the tip accordingly.
Station check-rooms	The fixed fee is all that's required—an additional tip of 10 to 25¢ is optional.	The fixed fee.	Fixed fee usually paid in advance; tip given on calling for baggage.
ON A PLANE *Stewards* *Pilots* *Reservation Clerks* *Limousine driver* *Others wearing airline uniform*	No tipping—*absolutely!*		
Baggage porters	No tip required or expected—but a quarter won't be turned down, and *might* get your luggage off the cart first.		If you're going to tip, do it when he's loading the cart. He won't hang around for you later.
ON A SHIP *Purser* *Ship's officers*	No tips—a present at the end of the voyage, if you like, but never money.		
Doctor	No tip—but if he doesn't present a bill, you should send him the amount your own doctor would have charged for whatever he did for you.		
Others: To be divided	10% of the cost of your ticket, plus	10% of passage money for one can	You'd still better tip extra if you

G O I N G   P L A C E S (cont'd)

who	*prescribed amount*	*rock bottom*	*but . . .*
among all those who give regular, routine service:	whatever it takes to make this into *even* folding money for everyone.	be shaved down to about 8% of passage money for two. Thus a man alone might tip $35, but a man & wife could tip $50 instead of $70.	want (or have been given) extra service. Ship tips usually given at end of a straight voyage, at half-mark and end or weekly on a cruise.
Deck Steward	15-20% of your tipping kitty (or $5 to $7 on a $350 first class ticket to Europe). NOTE: this is in addition to the fixed fee for renting a deck chair, and covers the service of snacks, etc.		Here's a good spot for the tip-in-advance technique, if you want your deck chair in a popular place.
Cabin Steward	30% of your tipping fund. He's the guy who cleans your cabin. If he does anything more, tip proportionately more.	50¢ per person per day.	
Bath Steward	10% of your tipping fund—but if you have a private bath and it is cared for by the cabin steward, add this amount to cabin tip.	$2	Another good tip-in-advance customer—if you'd like to get at the tub when it's *fresh!*
Dining Steward (waiter)	30% of tip-kitty.	50¢ per person per day.	
Stewardess	10% of tip-kitty— unless she acts as the cabin steward, in which case she gets *that* tip, or unless she has performed more than		

who	prescribed amount	rock bottom	but . . .
	routine service, in which case follow your conscience.		
Additional tips (over & above the 10%-passage base)			
Bellhops	25¢ a service	15¢—and that out of first class	
Cabin waiters	15-20% of the check —or, if there is no charge for whatever he brings, about 15% of what it would have cost in a hotel.	25¢ per person	
Bartenders or stewards	15-20% of each bar-tab		If your bill is presented at trip's end, instead of at each barhop, you may tip at the end or each time, as you wish.
Head dining steward	$5 to $10	No tip necessary. Use same standard as for tipping head waiters in restaurant (page 413)	You may want to tip in advance, and liberally, if you have ideas about where your table should be—or if you want special foods.
Wine steward	10% of wine bill		Proffer this tip whenever you pay the wine bill.
Baggage Room attendants	25¢ to $1 each time you cause them some trouble—the amount determined by the amount of trouble.	No tip necessary if you've packed wisely and well— and don't need to get something extra from your stowed-away trunk.	
Attendants in other special rooms	A parting tip of $1 to $5 each for the swimming pool attendants, the bandleader, etc.		

VISITING

who	prescribed average	rock bottom	but . . .
IN A PRIVATE HOUSE	See manners for the guest of the rich, pages 387 to 389.		
ON SPORTS OCCASIONS	See particular sports, pages 124 to 201.		

manners *the*
for
traveler

IN THE U.S.A.

IN YOUR CAR

Ill-mannered drivers can drive *themselves* crazy. Quite apart from the havoc and hatred which rudeness arouses on the road, simple self-preservation demands that you take your best party manners with you when you slip behind the wheel of your car.

By self-preservation, we mean more than the obvious, more than prevention of accidents. No one needs an etiquette book to tell him that a good driver is a safe driver . . . that a safe driver is meticulous in his own observation of safety rules and traffic regulations but is prepared for the worst from other drivers . . . or that the highways are crowded with stupid and reckless and show-off drivers who think they are the world's best.

We're thinking, instead, of the self-preservation which prevents annoyance. You and your blood pressure will profit if you can manage to adopt this simple philosophy about the poor driving and bad manners of other drivers: You can't reform them, so for your own peace of mind you had better ignore them.

Much of the rudeness of the road seems to stem from self-righteousness. The driver who leans on the horn when the light turns green thinks he is "correcting" the car ahead for holding up traffic. The guy who leans out the window to holler at another driver thinks he is delivering a needed lecture on driving rules. The fellow who shines his bright lights at an oncoming car thinks he is administering just punishment for the other's failure to dim his lights. The man who cuts in ahead of another car, or follows too close on its tail, may think he is getting even for similar treatment a few miles back.

Perhaps, then, if *all* drivers resolved to "turn the other fender," the highway would suddenly become as pleasant as the drawing room. Cars would still break down in mid-traffic—but the drivers behind, instead of assuming a deliberate plot up ahead, would wait patiently or lend a hand instead of honking, yelling and working up ulcers. A certain amount of "pilot error" would still be in evidence, but those who were inconvenienced by it would leave its correction to the law. And even if taxi-drivers remained apart from this Utopia—blocking traffic to discharge fares, making turns from the wrong lane and continuing to set themselves up as a privileged class—drivers of private cars would not add to the general confusion (and their own annoyance) by fighting cab-fire with ire.

But whether in hopes of fostering a "brave new world" or merely in preservation of your own dignity and mental health, your best bet is to shrug off the petty annoyances you meet on the road.

If you yourself are the transgressor, your immediate move to make a courteous adjustment can save the day; if it doesn't avert a disagreeable scene, it will at least deflate the irate. Say you dent the fender of an empty parked car. If you have liability insurance, it won't cost you anything to do the right thing: leave your card, or find the owner of the other car and offer to make amends. If you haven't such insurance, and if you're a nice guy, the wear and tear on your conscience will cost you more, anyway, than the repairs for the damage you've done.

Consider, too, that others' infractions of good manners may not always be deliberate. It's just possible that the guy who slipped into your parking place while you were maneuvering into position really didn't see you. There's nothing to prevent your walking over to him and saying, "I'm afraid you didn't see me, because I had to move up to let the other car out, but I had this place staked out before you came along." Your politeness just *might* inspire him to apologize and move on, even if he knew very well that he was stealing your place. But a stream of expletives can do nothing but get his back up.

In sum, your most practical as well as your most comfortable course is to go your own polite way. Be considerate even to the inconsiderate and you'll live longer.

on long trips

On extended drives, there's no rule of etiquette to prevent your being dressed comfortably. If you are going to stop in motels, you may quite properly drive up in slacks, open-necked shirt and all the grime of the day's drive. If you expect to stop at hotels, it might be better to spruce up a little before stepping into view of the doormen, room clerks and a lobby filled with city-groomed guests. The sprucing can be as simple as a stop at an outlying gas station and the addition of a sports jacket and tie to your driving outfit. But then you should change to clean and less casual clothes before going into the dining room.

En route, of course, you'll display the same manners as in your home territory. Some people seem to think that other states take more kindly than their own to orange peels and empty bottles strewn from car windows onto countryside; some drive as if little towns were put there only to slow them down unnecessarily; some make no secret of their belief that all strange people are out to gyp them, all unfamiliar food prepared to poison them, all local regulations slightly ridiculous. Apparently they think they "should of stood in bed," and so do the "natives" they meet.

ON A TRAIN

Whenever you board a train, you should remember that you have bought only the space specified on your ticket. In a Pullman, the seat facing forward belongs to whoever has the lower berth; if yours is the upper, you should ride backwards unless you are specifically invited to share the other seat.

You have not bought the right to fill the adjoining seat or the car platform with your possessions, the entire car with your song and laughter, or your seat-mate with the story of your life. If you have too much luggage to fit into the overhead rack or into other space provided, you should check it through on the baggage car. If you mean to have a big ball en route, you should take a private room where your festivities will not be disturbing to others. If you feel sociable, you don't need an introduction to the person sitting next to you, but you should be quite certain that your seat-mate also prefers conversation to reading or just sitting. And even with a traveling companion as eager as you to pass the time in talk, you should confine your remarks to impersonal subjects.

You have not bought the personal services of train personnel; for that you must tip (see Chart, page 419). And it's no good trying to do without the porter's services in hopes of saving the tip: you can't make your own berth, you're not supposed to place or navigate the upper-berth ladder without his help, and you owe him a tip even if he does nothing special for you.

You have bought neither the right nor the duty to pay for any other passenger's drinks or meals. You're certainly free to bid for the right, if you think you've found a girl who won't be offended by your trying to transform an accident of travel into a "date." But don't think you *have* to pick up a girl's tab just because she is at your table in the dining car or in the chair next to yours in the club car—not even if it was your suggestion that you two dine at the same time.

On a long trip, your initial gallant gesture may establish an expensive precedent. A good way to keep the decks clear and the books balanced is to say, when you want to break off a conversation in order to wend your way toward food or drink, "I think I'll go up for lunch. Would you like to go now, too, or shall I look for you here later on?" (Of course, if you prefer not to have her along regardless of who pays, you simply excuse yourself, with or without looking forward to seeing her when you return to your seat again. If it is she who makes the first move, consider—before you ask if you may tag along—that she might be trying to ditch you.)

If you do walk through the train together, you go first in order to open and hold the heavy doors for her. Once the dining steward has taken the lead, she goes first to the table. Then, unless you intend to pay, let her write or speak her own order directly to the waiter. Even if you and she are both aware that this is a Dutch-treat occasion, a display of conventional "date" etiquette may confuse the waiter into giving both checks to you.

The other guides to train travel might be briefed thus:

1. Whenever you leave your seat, take your ticket along with you.

2. Whenever you want the porter, ring instead of calling out.

428

3. When you want to smoke, do it only in those places where it is permitted.

4. When you want to stay up later than the usual hour for berths to be made up and cars to be darkened, go to the club car instead of holding up proceedings in the Pullman.

5. When you want to go to bed early, make the gesture of getting your seat-mate's consent to having the berths made up early.

6. When you want to play your portable radio beyond the confines of a private room, *don't.* . . .

O N A S H I P

On a cruise ship, everybody is apt to get buddy-buddy before the voyage is over. Even on a transatlantic liner, which is a little more a vehicle and a little less a resort hotel, fellow-passengers greet each other when they meet on deck, exchange names and small talk when they are assigned to adjoining deck-chairs, and generally travel in an atmosphere of reserved friendliness rather than formality.

Even so, common sense should tell you to take it slow in striking up shipboard acquaintanceships. People are hard to shake in such close quarters, so it's better not to let them get attached until you're fairly sure they're going to wear well.

Luck will decide some of your shipboard companionship. Unless you have put in an early request to the contrary, the dining steward will assign you to a table with strangers. Table-mates are expected to hold general conversations, to share any special treat, to dine as friends, *together.* But if your table-assignment looks like bad luck, you can sometimes change it: speak to the head dining steward about moving you to another table. Unless you are trying to move away from a place of honor, such as a seat at the captain's table, you needn't make excuses.

A huddle with the deck steward may produce a similar change in your deck-chair. But you can't make either switch on your own; the stewards are in charge. If the stewards can't help you, you can always take your meals in the café instead of in the dining room, and you can take your ease at the pool instead of in your deck-chair.

The point is: you owe your ship-mates friendly courtesy when you're present, so if it's going to kill you to be pleasant to them you'll find escape only in absence.

Tipping is a regular part of traveling by ship. See the Tipping Chart, page 420, for a guide.

On most transatlantic and cruise ships, a dinner jacket is the norm after six in first class—optional in cabin class—very likely show-off in tourist class. Comfortable sports clothes are the daytime standard on deck, but jackets and ties are usually expected in the dining salon for lunch and in the public rooms during the afternoon. Your travel agent can give you the word for the particular ship you're planning to take, but in the absence of specific information it's always best to be prepared as for a fancy resort hotel.

ON A PLANE

Traveling on a plane is so simple . . . airline regulations and services are so clearly and cleverly made known to passengers . . . that the only recurring problem seems to be that faced by friends of plane-travelers: will your visitor-by-air think you impolite if you don't meet him when he arrives and drive him to the airport when he is to leave?

The answer is: he shouldn't. In fact, he should anticipate your dilemma by insisting that he *prefers* to use public transportation to and from the airport.

Airports are notoriously inconvenient to get to; airliners are sometimes late and sometimes early; air passengers are not given to carrying heavy (extra fare) luggage; the limousine service is cheap and fast. Therefore—except for the protection of small children, doddering old ladies and beautiful girls you fear to trust to crowded limousines or night-shift taxis—the whole mish-mosh of meeting planes ought to be dispensed with by both sides.

WHEN YOU GET THERE

Whenever you are about to take off to another city of the United States, somebody you know at home will tell you that you *must* look up old Joe, a guy you're sure to like, who knows his town from top to bottom, who will take you under his wing, etc., etc.

In order to avoid offending the friend who offers this long distance introduction, you should always take Joe's name and address. What you do with it is something else again.

Almost certainly, old Joe is not going to be holding his breath for your arrival. Almost certainly, if Joe lives in New York or Chicago, Los Angeles or San Francisco or New Orleans, he has long since learned that he can either live his own life or entertain friends of friends—not both. Joe is probably swooped down upon quite enough by his own friends—people he is genuinely glad to see and reasonably glad to adjust his schedule for.

There are, therefore, several very definite ways of "looking up people" away from home—and none of them begins with the phrase, "Well, here I am!", followed by the pregnant pause which says, "What are you going to do about it?"

If you really want to see Joe, whether he's a very old friend of yours or merely a distant friend of a distant friend, this is what you should do: invite him to have lunch or cocktails or dinner with you at your hotel.

To your own friend, you might write such an invitation in advance of your arrival, thus avoiding a real clash of engagements which both of you would like to avoid. But make

431

it a specific invitation, for a particular time and place. He may counter by insisting that you "come out to the house for dinner," instead, but he should feel under no obligation to entertain you.

To a friend once removed, you could merely telephone your invitation after your arrival. If he is not free at the time you suggest, he may turn you down gracefully (and/or legitimately); he may suggest another date; or he may accept your invitation. But he is under no pressure in any direction.

If you *don't* want to see Joe, the usual maneuver is to call him from the airport while you're waiting for your departing plane. You have a brief conversation, passing along whatever news your mutual friend wanted you to convey, and after conventional expressions of regret that you couldn't have telephoned sooner, you both breathe large sighs of relief.

Or, you needn't call him at all. Your benefactor back home will quite understand if you hadn't time to "look up old Joe."

P.S. But see page 335 for the formal routine when letters of introduction are involved.

FOREIGN TRAVEL

You've heard a lot about the individual American traveler's responsibilities as an "ambassador without portfolio." You've read a bit about the great difference between American and Continental customs, the wide variance in standards of conduct which you will encounter as you travel from country to country. So perhaps you're a little fearful of playing the fool abroad.

You needn't be. By now, most of the peoples of the world

know that Americans are Americans, friendly and informal. If you are not arrogant and overbearing, if you don't act as if you think everyone is after your dollars, if you are not given to invidious comparisons, they'll take you as you are— and like you. If you make allowances for the strangeness you find in them, they'll make allowances for the strangeness they find in you. Therefore, you need never apologize for being "different," nor yet flaunt your ignorance as if it were somehow superior.

In general, you need only behave like a guest. You can get away with just being yourself so long as you are reasonably friendly, courteous and dignified. You can save almost any awkward situation with an appropriate smile—a smile of frustration, a smile of embarrassment, a smile of welcome. You needn't be an expert on the local mores so long as you show a sincere respect for them and a willingness to fall in with them whenever you are able.

Still, your way will be made easier if you understand a few of the basic differences you will encounter. Here are nine things which can cause unnecessary trouble to the unknowing:

H U M O R

With the possible exception of Danes, Europeans simply do not understand American humor, based as it is on burlesque and exaggeration. To a Continental, an insult is an insult and it matters not if you "smile when you say that, podnuh." A Latin of South America and an Oriental, too, will take you quite literally if you greet him with "Hello, you fat slob." Almost no one but an American can "take a kidding"; ribbing is way beyond the limits of foreign humor. You should therefore be very, very chary of all forms of kidding, burlesque and mockery—even when you think it is beyond question that the joke is on you!

433

LANGUAGE

Americans are notoriously uni-lingual, and there is scarcely a tourist haven where you will not be able to operate quite well using English alone, but foreigners are always more flattered than amused if you make an earnest attempt to communicate in their tongue.

Never mind about the American accent you are bound to carry over to the strange language—but don't try to translate American idiom directly into foreign words which you only *think* mean the same thing. Misuse of foreign phrases can be as dangerous as a patronizing use of pidgin talk.

Remember, especially, that most languages other than English have a "familiar" as well as a "polite" form of address—and this you must never be the first to use. In French, the familiar form is "tu-toi" instead of "vous"; in German, it's "du" instead of "sie"; almost anywhere you go, you will find that the familiar form is reserved for use with intimates, "inferiors" and children, so stick to the formal pronoun and verb forms even when you think you have arrived at an informal situation.

FAMILIARITY

Your being an American will excuse and explain a lot. In fact, you would make a mistake if you were too distant, too withdrawn and too formal to jibe with the foreigner's expectation of warmth from Americans. But you should appreciate that, except for the Australians and perhaps the Canadians, Americans are the most informal people on earth. Your natural, friendly gesture may not be returned in kind; it may even be taken, at times, as a lack of the proper respect for foreign ways or individual importance.

Thus, you should not be offended if few of the people you meet abroad ever call you by your first name, invite you to their homes or inquire into your business and your opinions.

You'd better go a little slow on first names, yourself. Wait for the other fellow to shift into the more intimate form of address. Foreigners use titles much more than we do; in Sweden, for example, a man would say to an acquaintance, "Would the honorable lawyer mind closing the window?"— instead of "Would *you* mind closing the window?" Thus the use of "Mr." followed by your family name is a relatively friendly form, put into use only after a period of "Mr." followed by your "title"—Herr The American, Monsieur The Author, Mr. The Representative of the Little Widget Company, etc. Only on close, close acquaintance will you be just plain Bill.

Self-introductions are much rarer abroad than here. There is much less exchanging of names to no purpose, and much less emphasis on "getting the name" of fellow-guests in situations where "the roof is an introduction." A good practice, then, is never to be the first to introduce yourself. Smile, say "How do you do," shake hands if that's indicated— but wait for the other man to offer his name or ask yours.

The home is a good deal more of a retreat, over there, and people live in cafés more than we do. So if foreigners entertain you in public places rather than in their homes, don't think that means they don't like you.

Conversation is apt to be a bit less personal than the "rules" say it should be in polite society here—and a *lot* less personal than you are accustomed to making it. Sometimes it is almost as impolite to volunteer information about yourself as to ask personal questions of others—and almost anything beyond the weather can be branded "personal" in some areas. Americans are known to be endowed with healthy curiosity and disarming frankness, but curb both traits a little until you get the hang of the meaningless small talk which the French call "politesse." Watchful waiting is easy enough: an American abroad, in reasonably polite society, is so much the guest that he can let things come to him a little. Let the others ask the questions and set the tone of the conversation.

Personal contact is limited to handshaking, as much as possible, and even your handshake is best held in check if you are given to hard grips and energetic pumps. In the Middle East, a proper handshake is a delicate, tea-party thing; watch and see how the others do it before you demonstrate your strength. And don't ever try the hand-kissing routine. Even if a woman extends her arm, palm down, as if to await your kiss, you'll look better and feel better if you simply take her hand loosely and then drop it. And don't touch anybody, man or woman—whether by back-slapping or arm-steering—if you can possibly avoid it.

THE INNER MAN

The danger is in trying to combine American and Continental drinking habits. Either one alone is perfectly all right, but the combination is unexpectedly lethal; cocktails and wine don't mix quite as readily as you think.

If you're going to keep up with the natives in the consumption of wine during and after dinner, perhaps you'd better follow their lead before dinner and have an apéritif instead of three martinis. Drunkenness is not amusing, nor even quite credible, outside the U.S.A. If you make the mistake of attempting two-Continent drinking, the foreigners who see you will make the mistake of thinking "Americans can't drink."

The same goes for mixing American with European eating habits. If you'll notice, the Continental eats lightly at breakfast and dinner; that big lunch you are inspired to imitate is his one big meal, not one of three. But this is a matter between you and your digestion; etiquette enters in only if you try to buck the local customs—by making a big fuss in order to get a big breakfast, say, or by making loud (or faint-ing) protests against the Spanish custom of dining at ten. There is usually a parry to the situation that prevails—such as eating a sandwich *before* you go to a Spanish din-ner party—so adjust your own habits as gracefully as you can.

HAGGLING

It's true that the American fixed or marked price is more the exception than the rule, abroad, but in a reputable store, in a good section of town, the "asking" price is the real and final price. You should never haggle on the Champs-Elysées, any more than you would on Fifth Avenue.

Even where haggling is expected, and particularly where you're not quite *sure* about the firmness of the first price mentioned, there's a *nice* way to bargain. "Forty dollars," says the street vendor, the man in the little shop or kiosk. Say you, "I like it very much, but I hadn't planned to spend more than $30." That's a lot easier for him to take than a bald, "I'll give you $30." It puts the next move up to him. He can either show you something else for $30, or he can bring his $40 price down. Then if you both agree to disagree, you leave with a pleasant, "Thank you just the same"—and there are no hard feelings on either side.

You ought to be a little careful about money matters in general. The Tipping Chart on page 413 should help you with the traveler's biggest bugaboo, but even when you are tipping the proper amount take care to belie the view that Americans think they can buy anything with money. Often-times a smile, a pleasant request, an appreciative thank you will leave a better impression than a wad of bills. It's just possible that the native who was kind enough to pose for your camera would rather have a copy of his picture than a piece of your change.

POLITICS

You can't expect everyone in the world to agree with your view that "the American way" is the best way—and sometimes a bland ignorance about the country you are visiting advertises your opinion quite as tellingly as a lecture on democracy. To a Frenchman, his nation's revolving cabinet is no joke. To a Swede, your prejudices against public housing are incomprehensible. To nationals of most other countries, Communist-chasing is not the Wild West sport it has become over here. So until your foreign friends know you well enough to let you speak for yourself alone—not for the United States as a whole—you'd better remain an interested by-stander to discussions of politics.

Religion, too!

THE NICETIES

By and large, the rules are no different, abroad, but over there they are unabridged. Where there is a conflict between standard etiquette and convenience, in America, convenience usually wins out, under the label of "modern etiquette." But elsewhere in the world, the conventional forms are observed—consistently, and often with a flourish.*

Going through a door, for instance, is a real routine. The American makes a mistake if he tries to wave his host through the door first, meaning to be deferential and polite, for the rule is that the host goes last—and the rule is not to be tampered with. There is much more hopping up and down for the entrances and exits of women and older men, much more of a production made of lighting another's cigagrette, much more attention to the nice little things which are optional, here—sending flowers to your hostess after she

---

* They are observed by children, too, which means that if you are traveling with typical American kids you had better chain them up!

has entertained you at dinner, for instance, or keeping a woman companion on your right, or duty dancing, or expressing your thanks and paying pleasant compliments. And there is much more decorum in public, much less pushing and shoving everywhere. In England, for example, no one will ever cheat you out of your place in a line. In Paris, you get on the bus in the order of your arrival at the stop, as indicated by a number you tear off a nearby pad. Over there, you see, doing the right thing will not get you the wrong end of the stick.

All of which means only that you should pack your etiquette book along with your color film—and not attempt to edit it to suit your own habits. In any strange situation, you are always wise to say, "I don't want to offend anyone, and I'm not familiar with the way to do so-and-so over here. What is the right thing for me to do?" If you display an easy familiarity with everyday good manners—that is, if it doesn't appear that your education will have to begin with "Take off your hat indoors"—no foreign acquaintance will hesitate to give you a straight answer when you ask about the customs peculiar to his locale.

WOMEN, AH YES!

Except in Scandinavia, where there is even more camaraderie between men and women than in the United States, social exchanges between the sexes are on quite a different plane abroad.

On the one hand, there appears to be a kind of flirtatiousness and/or gallantry between men and married women which might be misinterpreted in this country. An American entertained by a Frenchwoman can quite properly invite her to lunch without her husband and may indeed be expected to pay a "party call" (see page 400) after he has dined in her home. In the Latin countries, extravagant personal compliments from men to married women are the norm. Yet an American is in for trouble if he takes all this public dance as an invitation to private romance!

On the other hand, unmarried women are sheltered and chaperoned to the teeth. A date in a Latin country is a platoon. A girl of the French upper or middle classes cannot be approached except through her family and her social circle. And if your experience in the cafés leads you to think otherwise, you've been fooled by the double standard: if she's out alone, and if she's friendly in the American fashion, she's no "lady."

The variations on this general theme can be confusing. In Scandinavian countries and in Switzerland, particularly at dances, what would here be considered a "pick-up" is perfectly respectable. In Yankeefied Chile, you could manage an ordinary date. In Oriental countries, everyday civility to a woman might be in the worst possible taste. In Mexico you'll see girls walking around the square together in frank expectation of being joined in their promenade by young men. In Brazil you could yell "obah" or stare long and hard at a girl—but you'd be off base if you tried to follow through.

The moral of this story, then, is: Find out precisely what your program should be before you engage in a dating campaign, and curb even your natural, "meaningless" friendliness until you know the local score. In short, be careful with women.

TIPPING

Tipping abroad is inclined to be more prevalent but often less extravagant than here. Customs and tippee expectations differ from country to country, but you will never go wrong if you follow this three-point program:

1. Before your first venture into strange territory, ask a na-

tive to brief you on the local tipping customs. If you haven't a friend-in-residence whom you can draft as a consultant, your best sources of information are the manager of your hotel or the local representative of your travel agent. Neither will expect a tip for himself, so both can afford to give you straight dope.

2. Tip in the currency of the country you are visiting. This will save you money in the long run, and it will also mean more to the tippee.

3. When in doubt, tip a little bit. Fewer foreigners than Americans consider themselves above tipping; more rely on small tips to make a living wage. An American soda jerk who was left a nickel might hurl it at his departing benefactor, but an Italian expects his 10 per cent or 15 per cent tip, even if it comes to only two cents.

The percentage system is safe almost everywhere: 10 to 15 per cent in little places or for little services; 12 to 15 per cent in good restaurants; 20 per cent in night clubs or swank spots. Where a service charge is added to the bill, a tip of 5 to 10 per cent is still expected of Americans in most places. Where you have no bill to per cent, the equivalent of an American quarter will probably be considered handsome.

You'll have no trouble with tipping in routine situations which have their American counterpart; if you simply tip there as you would here, you'll be in the clear. The confusion which besets most innocents abroad arises, instead, from unfamiliar circumstances. By the time you have learned by experience you'll have had some pretty uncomfortable experiences—unless you make a pre-departure check of current tipping scales, and unless you get some on-the-spot guidance in each country you visit.

INDEX

index

445

INDEX

454